Hiking Acadia National Park

Hiking
Acadia
National Park

A Guide to the Park's
Greatest Hiking Adventures

Third Edition

Dolores Kong and Dan Ring

FALCONGUIDES

GUILFORD, CONNECTICUT
HELENA, MONTANA

FALCONGUIDES®

An imprint of Rowman & Littlefield
Falcon and FalconGuides are registered trademarks and Make Adventure Your Story is a trademark of Rowman & Littlefield.

Distributed by NATIONAL BOOK NETWORK

All interior photographs by Dolores Kong and Dan Ring, unless otherwise noted.
Maps: Trailhead Graphics © Rowman & Littlefield

British Library Cataloguing-in-Publication Information available

ISBN 978-0-4930-1661-7 (paperback)
ISBN 978-1-4930-2525-1 (ebook)

♾™ The paper used in this publication meets the minimum requirements of American National Standard for Information Sciences—Permanence of Paper for Printed Library Materials, ANSI/NISO Z39.48-1992.

The authors and Rowman & Littlefield assume no liability for accidents happening to, or injuries sustained by, readers who engage in the activities described in this book.

Contents

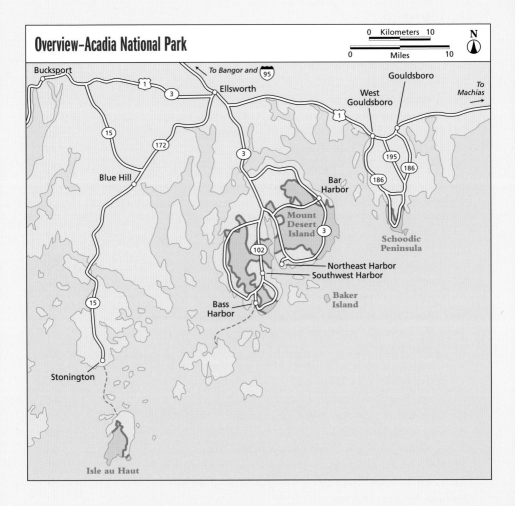

Overview–Acadia National Park

0 Kilometers 10

0 Miles 10

N

Bucksport

1

3

To Bangor and 95

Ellsworth

Gouldsboro

West Gouldsboro

1

15

172

3

195

186

Blue Hill

186

Bar Harbor

Mount Desert Island

3

Schoodic Peninsula

102

Northeast Harbor

Southwest Harbor

Baker Island

15

Bass Harbor

Stonington

Isle au Haut

To Machias

Pemetic, Triad, and Day Mountain Area

Jordan Pond, Bubbles, and Eagle Lake Area

Penobscot, Sargent, and Parkman Mountain Area

Mount Desert Island West of Somes Sound 206

Acadia Mountain Area

Beech Mountain Area

Bernard and Mansell Mountain Area

Bass Harbor Area

Isle au Haut 260

Schoodic Peninsula 281

Acknowledgments

For sharing with us their knowledge and passion for Acadia National Park, and being so generous with their time, we'd like to thank Charlie Jacobi, Gary Stellpflug, Chris Barter, David Manski, Kathy Grant, Wanda Moran, Stuart West, Karen Anderson, Anne Warner, Tony Linforth, Maureen Fournier, Alison Richardson, Nick Freedman, Angi King Johnston, and the rest of the Acadia National Park staff, past and present; Margaret Coffin Brown of the National Park Service's Olmsted Center for Landscape Preservation; Ann Marie Cummings of Eastern National; Marla S. O'Byrne; former park volunteers Jim and Jan Allen; Dianna and Ben Emory; Donald P. Lenahan; Jill Weber; and the Friends of Acadia.

And we'd like to thank family and friends who've already hiked the trails of Acadia with us, or one day will: April, Thomas, Sharon, Michelle, Stacey, Jen, Phil, Sebastian, Miranda, Laura, Mike, Jenna, and Eric, and too many others to name.

Introduction

Maine's Acadia National Park is a place like no other.

You can stroll along Ocean Path and be awestruck by the contrast of pink granite cliffs, blue skies, and white surf. From atop Cadillac, the highest mountain on the Atlantic seaboard, you can look below and see fog rolling in over Frenchman Bay, even as the sun shines brightly above.

And over on the shores of Jordan Pond, you can take part in one of the most civilized of afternoon rituals, tea and popovers, with the distinct mountains known as the Bubbles as nature's backdrop.

No wonder artists, millionaires, generations of families, and even presidents—notably Barack Obama in 2010—have been attracted to all that's preserved in Acadia.

In fact, the place has meant so much to area residents and visitors that Acadia in 1919 became the first national park created east of the Mississippi, after starting as a national monument in 1916. It is also the first national park to consist primarily of privately donated lands and the first to have trail maintenance funded by an endowment, Acadia Trails Forever, coming from $4 million in park user fees and federal appropriations and $9 million in private donations from Friends of Acadia, a private nonprofit organization based in Bar Harbor.

Over the years the scenery inspired such passion that nineteenth-century painters Thomas Cole and Frederic Church, of the Hudson River School, came here to capture the landscape; one of the wealthiest men in America, John D. Rockefeller Jr., donated millions and left miles of scenic carriage roads and uniquely designed stone bridges; and prime mover George B. Dorr dedicated his life and exhausted his family fortune to create the park.

As part of the Centennial Initiative to mark the hundredth anniversary of the National Park Service in 2016, Acadia plans to preserve and pass on the passion in a number of ways: acquiring more land, establishing more village connector trails and otherwise encouraging car-free use, and creating programs to foster young conservationists and scientists. The year 2016 also marks the hundredth anniversary for Acadia, since it was first founded as the Sieur de Monts National Monument in 1916. The motto on the Acadia Centennial logo unveiled in 2014: "Celebrate Our Past, Inspire Our Future."

Today more than two million visitors a year make Acadia one of the top-ten most visited national parks, even though it's the fifth smallest in land area. In fact, in two separate 2014 polls, viewers of ABC's *Good Morning America* as well as readers of *USA Today* voted Acadia number one. But with 155 miles of hiking trails and 45 miles of carriage roads throughout its approximately 49,500 acres (including about 12,000 acres under conservation easement), the park provides plenty of opportunities for tranquility and for experiencing nature, history, geology, and culture.

Rhodora and other flowering plants find a home on such Acadia summits as Cadillac and Sargent.

This third edition of *Hiking Acadia National Park* covers nearly all the park's trails, and comes just as the Acadia Centennial is being celebrated.

Most of the trails are located on Mount Desert Island, within a short ride—and in some cases a short walk—from Bar Harbor, the island's main town. The book also includes trails on Isle au Haut, reachable only by mail boat from Stonington, and on Schoodic Peninsula—the only part of the park on the mainland—accessible by ferry from Bar Harbor during the peak season or by car anytime.

No backpacking is allowed in the park except for a limited amount at designated campsites on Isle au Haut; the lean-to shelters require a special use permit obtained in advance. No camping is allowed on trails anywhere in the park.

Since the first FalconGuides edition of this guide in 2001, some new trails have been added, and many trail names have been changed to make them historically correct. This new edition includes those important revisions, which were made under a comprehensive multiyear, multimillion-dollar effort by the National Park Service and Acadia Trails Forever to update the historic network, and as part of the implementation of the park's 2002 Hiking Trails Management Plan. Among the historic routes recently restored: Schooner Head Path, Homans Path, Murphy Lane, and sections of the Orange & Black Path, Penobscot Mountain Trail, and Canada Cliff Trail.

A note of caution: In some cases the park service may not yet have updated trail signs—it's a multiyear process—even though the plan is to ultimately rename some of the historic trails. For that reason the old trail names are listed in this guide in parentheses for reference.

We've also added to this third edition a trail network opened in 2014. It provides connections between Blackwoods Campground, Otter Cove, Gorham Mountain, and beyond, as part of the park's Centennial efforts to reduce driving in the park. And we've highlighted rehabilitation of historic trails such as the Asticou & Jordan Pond Path, which has been funded with hundreds of thousands of dollars from the federal government, Friends of Acadia, and other sources in the years leading up to the Centennial. Also new: Trails opened in 2015 in Acadia's Schoodic Woods section.

Another addition is mention of the new Island Explorer bus stops near trailheads. If you visit during peak season, you can take advantage of this increasingly popular, fare-free, and eco-friendly way of getting around Acadia, to hikes not only on Mount Desert Island but also on Schoodic Peninsula. You can even plan a long one-way hike and take the Island Explorer back to the start, or your next destination. The bus driver may also make specially requested stops, if it's safe to do so. Be sure to buy a park pass to help support the Island Explorer and other programs offered by the park service.

Natural History

Acadia is nature's treasure trove, featuring more than three hundred species of birds, from the magnificent bald eagle to the tiny ruby-throated hummingbird; more than fifty species of mammals on land and sea, from white-tailed deer to harbor porpoises; and about nine hundred species of plants, from 100-foot white pines to the tiny mountain sandwort.

During the annual Hawk Watch atop Cadillac Mountain, from mid-August to mid-October, more than 2,500 migrating raptors are identified each year as part of a nationwide effort to monitor birds of prey. You can join park rangers and volunteers in spotting and counting such raptors as peregrine falcons and sharp-shinned hawks.

Over at the Sieur de Monts Spring area, on ME 3 south of Bar Harbor, visitors can learn about the park's flora and fauna at the Wild Gardens of Acadia and the Nature Center.

With all the different plants, the countryside of Acadia can be awash in color. Late spring and early to midsummer are probably the best times to enjoy plants in Acadia.

In parts of the park you may still see reminders of a huge fire that swept through much of Mount Desert Island over ten days in 1947. Before burning itself out at the tip of Otter Point, the blaze destroyed more than 10,000 acres within the park, about 150 average homes, and six hotels on the island, according to Jan Allen, a park volunteer who studied the fire. Sixty-three summer "cottages" in Bar Harbor's Millionaires' Row were also leveled.

When hiking in certain areas, look for tree stumps left from the lumber salvage operation the year after the fire.

You can learn more about the park's natural history and other useful information in *A Guide's Guide to Acadia National Park,* available online at www.nps.gov/acad.

Threatened, Rare, and Uncommon Species

Acadia National Park features two birds that were only recently removed from the federal endangered species list—the bald eagle and the peregrine falcon. But the park continues to protect the birds, particularly the peregrine falcon. During falcon nesting season, from spring to late summer, the park might shut down certain cliff trails for the safety of the chicks.

Possible seasonal closures include the Precipice Trail, Orange & Black Path, Jordan Cliffs Trail, Valley Cove Trail, and Beech Cliffs Trail.

Moonwort, salt marsh sedge, an arctic iris, and other vegetation uncommon in Maine grow in the park. But about two hundred other native plants, such as yellow lady's slippers, have not been documented in more than twenty years, according to *The Plants of Acadia National Park,* a project of the Garden Club of Mount Desert, Friends of Acadia, and the Maine Natural History Observatory. The book includes details on 862 plant species found in Acadia.

Geology and Climate Change

Glaciers, rivers, the ocean, the movement of tectonic plates, and volcanic activity all helped shape Acadia over the ages. The result: pink granite cliffs, the fjordlike inlet called Somes Sound, and Acadia's many mountains. At the top of the park's highest peak, you can learn more about the geology from the displays along the Cadillac Summit Loop Trail.

While today you can see eons of geologic forces written in Acadia's mountains and shorelines, yet to be understood are the potential impacts of climate change. In an attempt to raise understanding, Acadia National Park has funded research to monitor the effect of climate change on flowers and animal migration.

But the starkest warnings about the potential impact of climate change on the park come from such organizations as the Rocky Mountain Climate Organization and Natural Resources Defense Council, which released a report in 2010, "Acadia National Park in Peril: The Threats of Climate Disruption." Unless steps are taken to address climate change, the report forecasts a risk of wildfires and fiercer storms, higher sea levels and average temperatures, and damage to the economy.

Human History

Thousands of years before European explorers set eyes on Mount Desert Island, the Wabanaki Indians named this area Pemetic, meaning "range of mountains." Today Acadia's fourth-highest mountain preserves that name.

Wabanaki culture and heritage are celebrated and preserved at the seasonal Abbe Museum, located at the Sieur de Monts entrance to the park and at a separate, year-round branch in downtown Bar Harbor.

In 1604 the area was discovered by French navigator Samuel Champlain, who labeled it l'Île des Monts Déserts—or Island of Barren Mountains.

George B. Dorr, "the father of Acadia National Park" and its first superintendent, is remembered with Dorr Mountain, which towers over the land he first bought and preserved, around Sieur de Monts Spring.

John D. Rockefeller Jr., who donated millions of dollars and about 10,000 acres to Acadia, and who financed the construction of 45 miles of carriage roads and sixteen stone bridges on those roads, is memorialized with a plaque on Ocean Path, near Otter Point.

In July 2010 President Barack Obama added an important chapter to Acadia's history when he became the first-ever sitting president to visit the park. President Obama, his wife Michelle, and daughters Malia and Sasha spent three days in the park, including visits to Cadillac Mountain, Ship Harbor, and Bass Harbor Head Light.

Before Obama, William Howard Taft was the last sitting president to visit Mount Desert Island, in summer 1910, before the national park was created. A future president, Theodore Roosevelt, climbed Cadillac, then known as Green Mountain, when he visited the area as a young man.

Hiking was popular on the island long before the park was established. More than a century of trail building is documented in *Pathmakers: Cultural Landscape Report for the Historic Hiking Trail System of Mount Desert Island*, published by the National Park Service's Olmsted Center for Landscape Preservation.

The people who helped shape the park, both famous and obscure, are celebrated with numerous memorial paths and plaques dotting Acadia. In his book *The Memorials of Acadia National Park,* Donald P. Lenahan documents more than seventy sites throughout Mount Desert Island, Schoodic Peninsula, and Isle au Haut, featuring everything from faded wooden signs to elaborate stone benches.

Weather

In the space of an hour or less, the weather in Acadia can change from sunny and warm to wind-whipped rain, especially on mountaintops. Summer highs average 70 to 80 degrees Fahrenheit, although fog can be common, with lows in the 50s. In spring, highs average 50 to 60 degrees, and it can be rainy. Fall brings highs in the low 70s, but rain or snow can be expected. Winter temperatures range from below zero to 30 degrees, and snowfall averages about 60 inches a year. Be prepared no matter what season you are hiking.

Rules and Regulations

Pets must be kept on a leash no longer than 6 feet and are not allowed on ladder trails or in public water supplies. They are also prohibited from Sand Beach and Echo Lake from May 15 to September 15, public buildings, ranger-led programs, and the Wild Gardens of Acadia. (Service animals are an exception to these rules.) The park service is continually reevaluating the pet policy. Be sure to follow the rules to avoid ruining the visit for other hikers and pet owners or risking harm to your pet and wildlife.

Parking, camping, and fires are only allowed in designated spots. No camping is allowed in the backcountry. Firearms are prohibited in the park unless they are packed away or unless exceptions under federal and Maine law apply.

A view north toward Great Head and the Beehive from Ocean Path.

Visitor Information

Park information may be obtained by contacting Acadia National Park, 20 McFarland Hill Rd., PO Box 177, Bar Harbor, ME 04609-0177; (207) 288-3338; www.nps.gov/acad.

The Hulls Cove Visitor Center is located on ME 3, northwest of Bar Harbor. It is open from 8:30 a.m. to 4:30 p.m. daily from April 15 through May, plus June, September and October. It is open from 8 a.m. to 6 p.m. daily in July and August. There is a well-stocked bookstore run by Eastern National here.

The Village Green Information Center across from the Island Explorer bus hub in Bar Harbor is open from 8 a.m. to 5 p.m. daily from late June through Columbus Day.

The winter visitor center is located at Acadia National Park Headquarters on ME 233, west of Bar Harbor. It is open year-round 8 a.m. to 4:30 p.m. Monday through Friday, closed on off-peak federal holidays, and at 2 p.m. the days before Thanksgiving, Christmas, and New Year's. It's also open weekends in November and December, and March 1 through April 14.

Some hiking trails and parts of the 27-mile Park Loop Road are seasonally closed or may be closed for safety reasons or to protect nesting peregrine falcons. Check for trail and road closures with National Park Service officials.

Park entrance fees apply between May 1 and October 31, with a 7-day pass available for one vehicle; a 7-day pass for one individual on foot, motorcycle, or bicycle; and an annual pass for one vehicle. Passes may be purchased at the visitor center, park headquarters, the Acadia Park Loop Road Entrance Station just north of Sand Beach, park campgrounds and other local sites

The Bates-style cairn that marks the trail appears to tower over the Porcupine Islands on the Dorr North Ridge Trail.

Acadia offers two campgrounds on Mount Desert Island, Blackwoods and Seawall, where pets are permitted.

Blackwoods Campground, 5 miles south of Bar Harbor on ME 3, is open year-round, with reservations recommended from May 1 through October 31. Seawall Campground, open late May through September 30, is off ME 102A, 4 miles south of Southwest Harbor. About half the sites are first-come, first-served; the rest can be reserved. For reservations as early as 6 months in advance for Blackwoods or Seawall, call (877) 444-6777 or go to www.recreation.gov.

The only backpacking allowed in Acadia is on Isle au Haut between May 15 and October 15, and it's limited to getting you to and from the mail boat landing to designated campsites at lean-to shelters at Duck Harbor Campground. You need a special use permit, available at www.nps.gov/acad or by calling (207) 288-3338. No camping is allowed along the trails, and no phone reservations are accepted.

Newly opened in 2015 is park-run Schoodic Woods Campground, 3 miles southeast of Winter Harbor on Schoodic Peninsula. Open from late May until Columbus Day. Reservations through www.recreation.gov, or by calling (877) 444-6777, are highly recommended. Hiking trails and bike paths connect the campground to the park. As this guide went to press, discussions about accepting Schoodic Woods from the private landowner and incorparating it into the park, were ongoing.

From late June to Columbus Day, the fare-free Island Explorer bus operates between points on Mount Desert Island and the park, as well as on Schoodic Peninsula. For schedules, routes, stops, and other information, go to www.exploreacadia.com.

From late June to late August, you can take a ferry between Bar Harbor and Winter Harbor, where you can then catch the fare-free Island Explorer bus to hike some of Acadia's trails on Schoodic Peninsula. You can even take your bicycle on the ferry and the bus to ride Schoodic's paved one-way loop road. Check www.exploreacadia.com for the Schoodic bus and ferry schedule.

Hikers might find the detailed United States Geological Survey (USGS) map of the park helpful. The park's visitor center sells the USGS Acadia National Park and Vicinity map, along with other maps and literature.

For information on conservation and historic preservation projects in the park, as well as membership and volunteer opportunities, contact the nonprofit Friends of Acadia at (800) 625-0321 or go to www.friendsofacadia.org.

Leave No Trace

Many of the trails in Acadia National Park are heavily used, particularly in the peak summer months into September. We, as trail users and advocates, must be especially vigilant to make sure our passage leaves no lasting mark.

Follow these Leave No Trace principles:

- Leave with everything you brought.
- Leave no sign of your visit.
- Leave the landscape as you found it.

Here are some additional guidelines for preserving trails in the park:

- Pack out all your own trash, including biodegradable items like orange peels.
- Don't approach or feed any wild creatures. It's prohibited in the park.
- Don't pick wildflowers or gather rocks, shells, and other natural or historic features along the trail. It's prohibited in the park.
- Don't alter cairns, piles of rocks that serve as trail markers. Leave rocks where they lie.
- Stay on the established route to avoid damaging trailside soils and plants.
- Walk single file in the center of the trail.
- Don't cut switchbacks, which can promote erosion.
- Be courteous by not making loud noises or casual cell phone calls while hiking.
- Use facilities at trailheads where available. In areas without toilets bury human waste at least 6 inches deep and 200 feet from water or trails; pack out toilet paper.
- Pick up after pets.

For more information on Leave No Trace, visit www.LNT.org.

How to Use This Guide

This guide is designed to be simple and easy to use.

It's divided into four sections: Mount Desert Island East of Somes Sound, Mount Desert Island West of Somes Sound, Isle au Haut, and Schoodic Peninsula. Hikes in the same geographic area are grouped together, allowing easy comparison.

The "Trail Finder" section lists hikes by characteristic, such as "Best Hikes for Children" or "Best Hikes for Great Views."

Each hike is described with a map and a trail's vital statistics including length, difficulty, and canine compatibility.

Directions to the trailhead are provided, along with a general description of what you'll see along the way. A detailed route finder ("Miles and Directions") sets forth mileage between significant landmarks along the trail. The trailhead is listed as the first key point at mileage 0.0. When part of another trail must be hiked before reaching the trailhead for the described hike, 0.0 represents the initial trailhead.

Trailhead GPS coordinates listed in the "Finding the trailhead" section of each hike description are based on data collected by us, provided by Acadia National Park, or gathered from other reliable sources, such as the US Board of Geographic Names (http://geonames.usgs.gov). If your GPS uses a different notation than the one used here, you can convert data here: http://transition.fcc.gov/mb/audio/bickel/DDDMMSS-decimal.html.

But as with any GPS data provided for recreational use, there are no warranties, expressed or implied, about data accuracy, completeness, reliability, or suitability. The data should not be used for primary navigation. Readers of this guide assume the entire risk as to the quality and use of the data.

Note: For hikes requiring traversing another trail to access the featured trail, the trailhead GPS coordinates provided are for the start point and the start of the featured trail.

Acadia National Park officials advise that visitors obey posted signs and park regulations, use common sense, and avoid accidentally traveling on private lands while using a GPS unit.

Difficulty Ratings

To aid in the selection of a hike that suits particular needs and abilities, each is rated easy, moderate, strenuous, or expert only. Bear in mind that even the most challenging routes can be made easier by hiking within your limits and taking rests when needed.

Looking north along the Pemetic North Ridge Trail.

Easy hikes are generally short and flat, taking no longer than one to two hours to complete.

Moderate hikes involve relatively mild changes in elevation and will take one to two and a half hours to complete.

Strenuous hikes feature some steep stretches, greater distances, and generally take longer than two and a half hours to complete.

Expert only hikes are nontechnical climbing routes with near-vertical ascents or iron rungs, although taking it slow and being well prepared and comfortable with heights can make the trail more manageable.

These are completely subjective ratings—consider that what you think is easy is entirely dependent on your level of fitness and the adequacy of your gear. If you are hiking with a group, you should select a hike with a rating that's appropriate for the least fit and prepared in your party.

Hiking times are based on the assumption that on flat ground, most walkers average 2 miles per hour. Adjust that rate by the steepness and difficulty of the terrain and your level of fitness.

Trail Finder

Best Hikes for Great Views

4   Champlain North and South Ridge Trails
8   Sand Beach and Great Head Trail
9   Ocean Path
19 Dorr Mountain Loop via Ladder and Dorr South Ridge Trails
25 Cadillac Summit Loop Trail
30 Pemetic North and South Ridge Trails
43 Penobscot Mountain Trail via Asticou & Jordan Pond Path
48 Sargent South Ridge Trail via Carriage Road
54 Acadia Mountain Trail
56 Flying Mountain, Valley Cove, and Valley Peak Loop

Best Hikes for Children

1   Bar Island Trail
8   Sand Beach and Great Head Trail
9   Ocean Path
25 Cadillac Summit Loop Trail
66 Wonderland
67 Ship Harbor Trail
68 Bass Harbor Head Light Trail

Best Hikes for Dogs

1   Bar Island Trail
2   Compass Harbor Trail
7   Schooner Head Overlook and Path
66 Wonderland
67 Ship Harbor Trail

Best Loop Hikes

41 Jordan Pond Carry to Eagle Lake and Bubbles Trails Loop
47 Sargent Mountain Loop via Giant Slide and Grandgent Trails
51 Parkman Mountain and Bald Peak Loop via Hadlock Brook Trail
52 Norumbega Mountain and Hadlock Ponds Loop
57 Beech Cliffs and Canada Cliff Trails
58 Beech Cliff Loop Trail
59 Beech Mountain Loop Trail

Best Hikes for Cliffs and Scrambles

6   Precipice Trail
11   The Beehive Trail
28   Cadillac West Face Trail
44   Jordan Cliffs Trail via Spring Trail
57   Beech Cliffs and Canada Cliff Trails
70   Duck Harbor Mountain and Goat Trails (on Isle au Haut)

Best Hikes for History and Geology Buffs

2   Compass Harbor Trail
5   Orange & Black Path
12   Gorham Mountain and Cadillac Cliffs Trails
15   Homans Path
25   Cadillac Summit Loop Trail
33   Hunters Beach Trail
35   Day Mountain Trail

Best Hikes for Peak Baggers

4   Champlain North and South Ridge Trails
14   Kebo Mountain and Dorr North Ridge Trails
27   Cadillac South Ridge Trail and Eagles Crag Loop
30   Pemetic North and South Ridge Trails
43   Penobscot Mountain Trail via Asticou & Jordan Pond Path
47   Sargent Mountain Loop via Giant Slide and Grandgent Trails
48   Sargent South Ridge Trail via Carriage Road
51   Parkman Mountain and Bald Peak Loop via Hadlock Brook Trail
65   Bernard Mountain Loop

Best Hikes for Lake and Ocean Lovers

1   Bar Island Trail
8   Sand Beach and Great Head Trail
9   Ocean Path
10   The Bowl Trail
18   Kane Path
37   Jordan Pond Path
76   Sundew Trail (on Schoodic Peninsula)

Map Legend

Transportation

═(102)═	State Highway
════	Paved Road
═ ═ ═ ═	Unpaved Road
▪▪▪▪▪▪	Featured Trail
- - - - - -	Trail
- - - - -	Ferry Route

Water Features

⬭	Body of Water
	Marsh/Swamp
∿	River/Creek
	Intermittent Streams
⚲	Springs
≋	Waterfall

Land Management

▭	National Park Boundary

Symbols

①	Trailhead
🏠	Ranger Station
❓	Visitor Center
🅿	Parking
🚻	Restroom
▲	Campground
🔭	Viewpoint/Overlook
⛟	Picnic Area
▪	Point of Interest/Structure
⌣	Bridge
🕯	Lighthouse
▯	Fire Tower
⛵	Boat Ramp
○	Town
▲	Peak/Summit
→	Direction Arrow

Mount Desert Island
East of Somes Sound

Most of Acadia National Park's trails, the main Park Loop Road, and many of the best views are here on the eastern half of Mount Desert Island.

The hikes in this section are grouped into seven geographic divisions: the Bar Harbor and Champlain Mountain area; the Gorham Mountain area; the Dorr Mountain and Sieur de Monts Spring area; the Cadillac Mountain area; the Pemetic, Triad, and Day Mountain area; the Jordan Pond, Bubbles, and Eagle Lake area; and the Penobscot, Sargent, and Parkman Mountain area.

From the summit of Cadillac Mountain, the highest point on the Atlantic coast, you can see Bar Harbor, Frenchman Bay, and the Porcupine Islands, one of Acadia's best-known vistas. A summit road takes you to the top, or you can hike up one of the mountain's several trails.

You can get even closer-up views of the ocean from such lower peaks as Champlain and Gorham Mountains, such easy to moderate trails as Ocean Path and Sand Beach and Great Head Trail, and strenuous cliff climbs like the Beehive and Precipice Trails.

This part of the park also features the Jordan Pond House, famous for its afternoon tea and popovers and its view of the distinctive mountains called the Bubbles. The Jordan Pond House, the only dining facility in the park, is open late May to late October, and serves lunch, tea, and dinner. A series of trails leaves from the Jordan Pond House, ranging from a pond loop to long routes up Penobscot and Sargent Mountains.

Another major jumping-off point for trails in this part of the park is at the Sieur de Monts entrance on ME 3, south of Bar Harbor. The Wild Gardens of Acadia, the Nature Center, and the Abbe Museum are also located here, and you can spend hours learning about the Native American and natural history of the area.

As part of efforts to emphasize car-free use of Acadia, a growing network of connector trails in this area allows visitors to walk from Bar Harbor to the heart of the park, including Great Meadow Loop and Schooner Head Path. New in 2014 are the

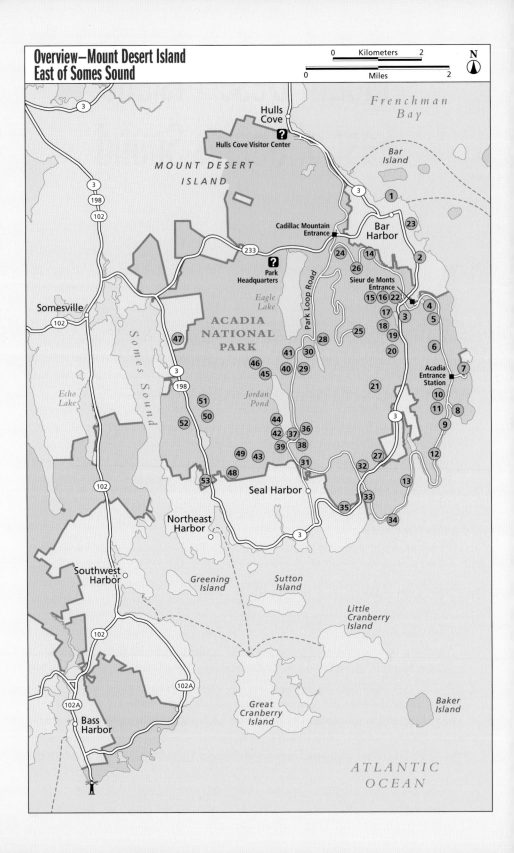

Overview—Mount Desert Island East of Somes Sound

0 Kilometers 2
0 Miles 2

N

Frenchman Bay

Hulls Cove

Hulls Cove Visitor Center

MOUNT DESERT ISLAND

Bar Island

1

Cadillac Mountain Entrance

Bar Harbor

23

2

Park Headquarters

233

24

14

26

Sieur de Monts Entrance

15 16 22

17

3

4

5

6

Eagle Lake

Somesville

ACADIA NATIONAL PARK

102

47

Park Loop Road

18

19

20

25

7

Acadia Entrance Station

Echo Lake

3

198

28

41 30

46 40 29

45

Jordan Pond

10

11

8

9

51

50

52

44

42 37 36

39 38

21

3

12

49 43

31

27

32

13

48

53

Seal Harbor

35

33

34

Northeast Harbor

3

Greening Island

Sutton Island

Southwest Harbor

102

Little Cranberry Island

102A

102A

Bass Harbor

Great Cranberry Island

Baker Island

ATLANTIC OCEAN

Champlain North Ridge Trail provides views of the Porcupine Islands.

Quarry and Otter Cove Trails, which allow campers at Blackwoods to hike outside their tent to Gorham Mountain and beyond.

The westernmost peaks in this section of the park include Norumbega, Parkman, Sargent, and Penobscot Mountains. The views from these open summits range from Somes Sound to the west, the Cranberry Isles to the south, and Cadillac Mountain to the east.

Bar Harbor and Champlain Mountain Area

1 Bar Island Trail

A low-tide walk leads to a rocky island off Bar Harbor, providing a unique perspective back toward town and its mountain backdrop. The trail can also offer a close-up view of seagulls feeding, as they drop mussels from midair to crack open the shells, or starfish exposed by the tide.

Distance: 2.0 miles out and back
Hiking time: About 1 to 1.5 hours
Difficulty: Easy
Trail surface: Low-tide gravel bar, gravel road, forest floor, rock ledges
Best season: Spring through fall
Other trail users: Joggers, motorists on gravel bar
Canine compatibility: Leashed dogs permitted

Map: USGS Acadia National Park and Vicinity
Special considerations: Accessible only 1.5 hours on either side of low tide. Check the tide chart on Bar Island, in local newspapers, or at http://me.usharbors.com/monthly-tides/Maine-Downeast/Bar%20Harbor. There is a public restroom at the intersection of West and Main Streets.

Finding the trailhead: From the park's visitor center, head south on ME 3 for about 2.5 miles toward downtown Bar Harbor. Turn left (east) onto West Street at the first intersection after the College of the Atlantic. The trail, visible only at low tide, leaves from Bridge Street, the first left off West Street on the edge of downtown. There is limited on-street parking on West Street. The closest Island Explorer stop is Bar Harbor Village Green, which is available on the Campgrounds, Eden Street, Sand Beach/Blackwoods, Jordan Pond, Brown Mountain, and Southwest Harbor lines. GPS: N44 23.30' / W68 12.35'

The Hike

The Bar Island Trail is a short, easy jaunt within shouting distance of Bar Harbor, but you feel transported to another world. That is the beauty of being on an island, even a small one, so close to a busy summer resort town.

It's easy enough for the least-seasoned hiker, with Dolores's mother, April, a first-time visitor to Acadia at 71, effortlessly strolling across. But the Bar Island Trail also provides a bit of risk to satisfy the thrill-seeking adventurer—it can only be traveled at low tide, when a gravel bar connecting Bar Harbor and the island is exposed. "Time your hike carefully," a sign warns hikers once they reach the island's rocky shores. "The tide changes quickly. Plan to be off the bar no later than 1.5 hours after low tide." For your convenience, a tide chart is posted.

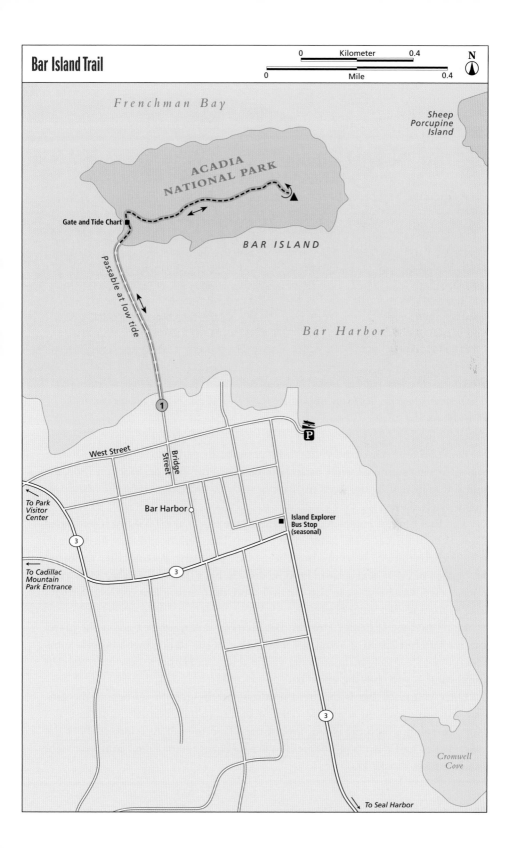

0   Kilometer   0.4

0   Mile   0.4

N

Frenchman Bay

Sheep
Porcupine
Island

ACADIA
NATIONAL PARK

Gate and Tide Chart

passable at low tide

BAR ISLAND

Bar Harbor

1

West Street

Bridge
Street

To Park
Visitor
Center

3

Bar Harbor

Island Explorer
Bus Stop
(seasonal)

To Cadillac
Mountain
Park Entrance

3

P

3

Cromwell
Cove

To Seal Harbor

The summit view from Bar Island includes the resort town of Bar Harbor and the mountains of Acadia.

Don't become one of the visitors who periodically gets stranded on the island, or whose cars get swamped while parked on the gravel bar. First described in 1867, the trail was reopened by the National Park Service in the 1990s when the island was still privately owned.

The Park Service completed ownership of the island in 2003 when it purchased 12 acres from former *NBC News* correspondent Jack Perkins and his wife, Mary Jo, who lived for thirteen years in a small home they built here. Perkins called the island his "garden of Eden" and detailed his time there in his 2013 book, *Finding Moosewood, Finding God.* Maybe you can also discover God, or at least a sign of God, during a hike to the half-mile-long island.

From the foot of Bridge Street in Bar Harbor, walk northwest across the gravel bar, reaching the island at about 0.4 mile. Some of the resort town's historic summer "cottages"—really mansions—are visible along Bar Harbor's shoreline to the left (southwest) as you cross the gravel bar.

Once you reach Bar Island, head northeast up the gravel road behind the gate. The trail soon levels off at a grassy field. At about 0.6 mile bear left (northeast) at a trail sign pointing into the woods toward Bar Island summit. At a fork at about 0.8 mile, marked by a cairn (a pile of rocks to mark a change in trail direction), bear right (southeast) up a rocky knob.

At about 1.0 mile you reach the summit, with its views toward Bar Harbor. From here you can hear the town's church bells, see the fishing and recreational boats along the harbor, and take in the smells of the sea and the views of the mountains.

Return the way you came.

Miles and Directions

0.0 Start at the Bar Island trailhead, at the foot of Bridge Street.

0.4 Reach the shore of Bar Island. Check the posted tide chart to time your return, otherwise you'll have to wait more than twelve hours for the next low tide. Head northeast up the gravel road behind the gate.

0.6 Cross a grassy field and come to a junction; bear left (northeast) into the woods at the trail sign.

0.8 Reach another junction marked by a cairn; bear right (southeast) up to the island's summit.

1.0 Reach the island's summit, with views back toward Bar Harbor and the mountains.

2.0 Arrive back at the trailhead.

2 Compass Harbor Trail

Situated just outside Bar Harbor, this easy trail offers both important history—it's the former site of park pioneer George B. Dorr's estate—and sweeping ocean views—its point is right on Frenchman Bay. The trail features some remnants of Dorr's family home, older growth trees, Dorr Point, and sights along the bay. Take a recently developed ranger-led "Missing Mansion" program in season to learn more about the history.

Distance: 0.8 mile out and back
Hiking time: About 30 minutes
Difficulty: Easy
Trail surface: Gravel road, forest floor, sandy trail at end
Best season: Spring through fall, particularly off-peak times

Other trail users: Dog walkers, joggers, area residents
Canine compatibility: Leashed dogs permitted
Map: USGS Acadia National Park and Vicinity
Special considerations: No facilities

Finding the trailhead: From downtown Bar Harbor head south on ME 3 for 1 mile. A small parking lot is located on the left (east) just after Nannau Wood, a private road, and just before Old Farm Road, also private. The trail begins off the parking lot. If the parking lot is full, often the case during peak times, you can park at the town ball fields and walk south just over 0.5 mile along ME 3 to the trailhead. The Island Explorer bus does not have a stop here, although the Sand Beach line goes by, and you may be able to ask the bus driver to let you off if it is safe to do so. GPS: N44 22.25' / W68 11.51'

The Hike

Standing out over Compass Harbor, you can imagine park trailblazer George B. Dorr taking his daily swim in the cold waters of Frenchman Bay or tending to the gardens that once surrounded his home here.

The trail begins as a wide gravel road off the parking lot and soon comes to a sign pointing to Compass Harbor. The trail goes left and narrows as it approaches the harbor and the crashing surf in the distance.

Head out on a sandy trail on a peninsula toward Dorr Point, but stop before an eroded section of the trail. Compass Harbor and Ogden Point are located to the left (north and northwest), and Sols Cliff is to the right (southeast). Frenchman Bay is straight ahead. You may hear the cry of the pileated woodpecker, or even get an extended close-up view of one pecking, as we did one time here.

Just before reaching the point, an unofficial trail leads to the ruins of the Dorr estate, Old Farm, which was built on land purchased by Dorr's father in 1868 and accepted by the federal government as part of the park in 1942, according to an article in *Chebacco*, the magazine of the Mount Desert Island Historical Society.

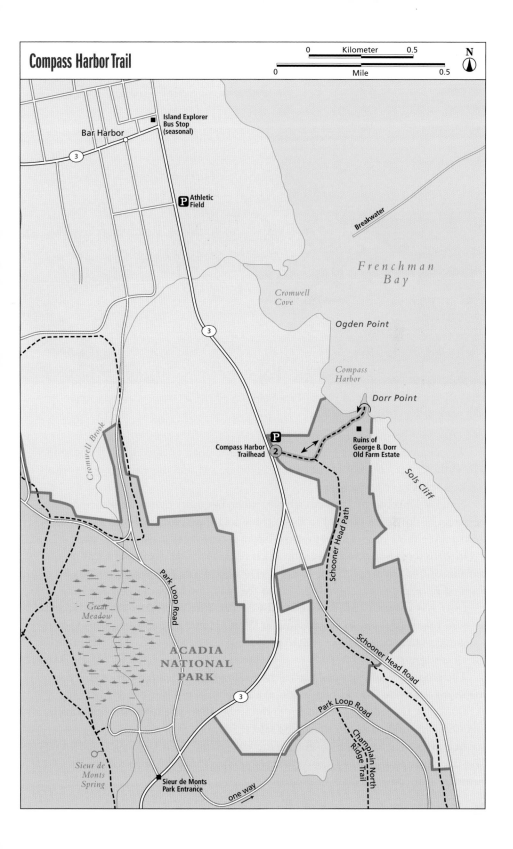

From Compass Harbor, you can see Bald Porcupine Island and, on occasion, a passing cruise ship nearly as big as Bald.

We counted forty-three granite steps and came upon an aged brick foundation. The Park Service does not maintain the old home site, and there were no historical markers at the time of our visit.

None of Dorr's formal gardens remain, either, but many nonnative plants can still be found at the home site and in the surrounding forest, some of which may have been among those originally transplanted from the family's Massachusetts estate.

In 2010 former park volunteer Jim Allen researched and developed a tour of the remains of Old Farm and "The Missing Mansion." A ranger-led program has been featured since, providing clues to the estate, the man, and his passion for Acadia.

Dorr was adamant that his cherished Old Farm become part of the park, and he even offered the property as a summer White House to both Presidents Calvin Coolidge and Franklin D. Roosevelt to garner support, according to the 2004 historical society article.

The property finally became part of the park two years before Dorr died, according to the article by Ronald Epp, writer of a biography on Dorr. But after the end of World War II, the federal government found it too expensive to preserve and maintain Old Farm and razed the estate, Epp said.

At that time in the nation's history, in the wake of the Great Depression and World War II, one can imagine the federal government didn't have the funds to keep up Old Farm, or many other facilities or programs.

Today the National Park Service calls Dorr the father of the park and credits him for his indefatigable work in leading the effort to create Acadia.

There's no better spot to ponder that than Compass Harbor.

Return the way you came.

Miles and Directions

0.0 Start at the Compass Harbor trailhead, which leaves from the parking lot on the left (east) side of ME 3, just south of Nannau Wood, a private road.

0.1 Turn left at the junction toward Compass Harbor.

0.4 Approach Dorr Point and the remains of George B. Dorr's Old Farm estate.

0.8 Arrive back at the trailhead.

3 Beachcroft Path

Intricately laid stone steps lead much of the way to open views along Huguenot Head, on the shoulder of Champlain Mountain. In line with its more than century-old history, this route's name is reverting to the original description as a path, rather than a trail, to better characterize its highly constructed nature. It's a mostly moderate ascent to Huguenot Head; more strenuous to reach Champlain and its ocean views.

Distance: 2.4 miles out and back
Hiking time: About 2 to 3 hours
Difficulty: Moderate to strenuous
Trail surface: Granite steps, rock ledges, forest floor
Best season: Spring through fall
Other trail users: None

Canine compatibility: Leashed dogs permitted but not recommended on upper Beachcroft
Map: USGS Acadia National Park and Vicinity
Special considerations: There are no facilities at the trailhead. Seasonal restrooms are available at the nearby Sieur de Monts park entrance.

Finding the trailhead: From downtown Bar Harbor head south on ME 3 for about 2.2 miles, just past the park's Sieur de Monts entrance, to the parking lot on the right (west) just before the glacially carved lake known as the Tarn. The trailhead is on the left (east) side of ME 3, across the road diagonally (southeast) from the parking lot. The closest Island Explorer stop is Sieur de Monts on the Sand Beach and Loop Road lines. GPS: N44 21.30' / W68 12.19'

The Hike

The Beachcroft Path climbs first to the shoulder of Huguenot Head, with an average elevation gain of 100 feet each 0.1 mile, but at times it feels remarkably like a walk along a garden path. The gradual switchbacks and neatly laid stepping stones turn what would otherwise be a vertical scramble into a gentler ascent.

Adding to the wonder are the constant open views north toward Frenchman Bay, west toward Dorr Mountain, south toward the Cranberry Isles, east toward Champlain Mountain, and down to the Tarn.

The dome-shaped Huguenot Head, visible from Bar Harbor, has been a popular destination for more than a century. The Beachcroft Path, built and rebuilt in the late 1800s and early 1900s, was named for the estate of the Bar Harbor summer resident who financed its construction. It consists of hundreds of hand-hewn stepping stones and countless switchbacks.

When it was originally constructed by George B. Dorr and the Bar Harbor Village Improvement Association, the path began at Sieur de Monts Spring, but the path's start later had to be moved because of road construction.

From the trailhead across from the Tarn parking area, ascend via the switchbacks and stone steps, catching your breath on the plentiful level sections. But be careful, as

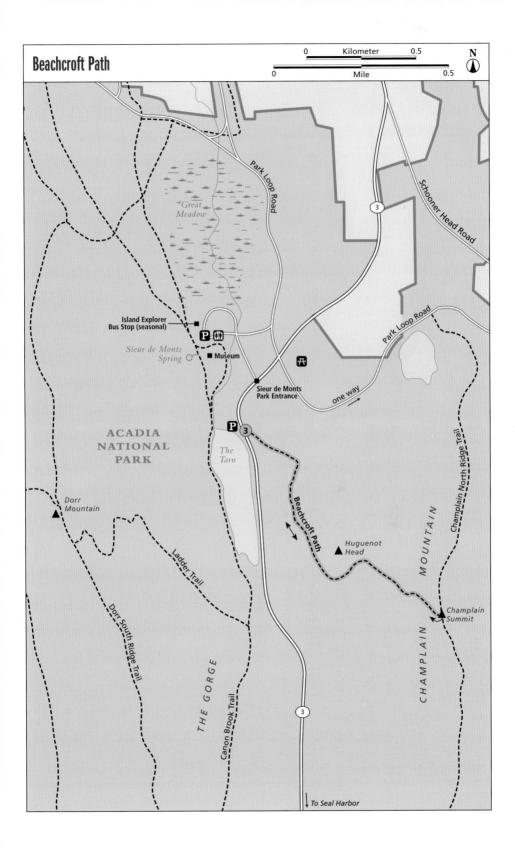

Beachcroft Path

Kilometer
0 0.5

Mile
0 0.5

N

Park Loop Road

Great Meadow

Schooner Head Road

3

Park Loop Road

Island Explorer Bus Stop (seasonal)

P

Sieur de Monts Spring

Museum

Sieur de Monts Park Entrance

one way

ACADIA NATIONAL PARK

P 3

The Tarn

Dorr Mountain

Ladder Trail

Dorr South Ridge Trail

THE GORGE

Canon Brook Trail

Beachcroft Path

Huguenot Head

CHAMPLAIN MOUNTAIN

Champlain North Ridge Trail

Champlain Summit

3

To Seal Harbor

The garden-like stepping stones of the Beachcroft Path take you up Huguenot Head.

even the flattest-looking rock along the path can be loose, and watch your step as you travel on open rock ledges.

Near the shoulder of Huguenot Head, the path widens and levels off. It circles to the northeast as you reach the open ledge just below the head's summit at 0.7 mile, with views south toward the Cranberry Isles. To the east (left) is Champlain Mountain; to the west (right) is Dorr Mountain. Down below are the Tarn and ME 3. Some people turn around here, to keep it a moderate hike.

The trail then dips into a gully before it begins the strenuous ascent up the sheer west face of Champlain Mountain. Carefully pick your steps and follow the cairns up the rock slabs. You reach the open summit at 1.2 miles.

Return the way you came.

Miles and Directions

0.0 Start at the Beachcroft Path trailhead, diagonally (southeast) across ME 3 from the parking lot that's just south of the Sieur de Monts park entrance.

0.7 Reach the open ledge on the shoulder of Huguenot Head and enjoy the views.

1.2 Summit Champlain.

2.4 Arrive back at the trailhead.

4 Champlain North and South Ridge Trails (Bear Brook Trail)

Enjoy expansive views from the summit of Champlain Mountain and all along the open ridge, the closest to the ocean of all of Acadia's ridges. At the southern end of the ridge, you may get glimpses of a great blue heron or turkey vulture soaring over a mountain pond known as the Bowl.

Distance: 5.2 miles out and back
Hiking time: About 3 to 4 hours
Difficulty: Moderate to strenuous
Trail surface: Rock ledges, forest floor
Best season: Spring through fall
Other trail users: None

Canine compatibility: Leashed dogs permitted
Map: USGS Acadia National Park and Vicinity
Special considerations: No facilities at the trailhead; seasonal restrooms at nearby Bear Brook picnic area

Finding the trailhead: Enter the park at the Sieur de Monts entrance, about 2 miles south of downtown Bar Harbor on ME 3. Turn right (south) onto the one-way Park Loop Road. The trailhead is 0.8 mile from the entrance, on the right (south) after the Bear Brook picnic area. There is a small parking area on the left (north), across the road just beyond the trailhead. The closest Island Explorer stop is Sieur de Monts on the Loop Road and Sand Beach lines, but it's a bit of a walk; ask if the bus driver can let you off at the trailhead. GPS: N44 21.46' / W68 11.39'

The Hike

On the Champlain ridge early one morning, a blanket of fog rolled in and enveloped the Porcupine Islands in the space of a few minutes. Amazingly, the ridgetop trail continued to be bathed in sunshine as the foghorns sounded their warnings below.

Another time, we started a late-afternoon walk under sunny skies, but by the time we got to the summit a mile away, strong rain forced us to put on full storm gear from head to toe. It was sunny once again as we returned to the trailhead.

Contrasts like these are part of the very nature of Acadia, where the mountains meet the sea and the weather can vary from moment to moment.

The Champlain North Ridge and South Ridge Trails, recently renamed as part of a multiyear effort to update some of the park's historic routes, offer spectacular views from Frenchman Bay to the Cranberry Isles as you ascend the northern ridge of 1,058-foot Champlain Mountain and head down south to the mountain pond known as the Bowl.

These two trails, formerly known as the Bear Brook Trail, make up one of the oldest marked paths on Mount Desert Island, showing up on 1890s maps, when Champlain was known as Newport Mountain.

Champlain is on Acadia's mountain ridge that is closest to Frenchman Bay, providing spectacular views of the Porcupine Islands.

From the trailhead for the North Ridge Trail, the climb to the peak is close to a 1,000-foot ascent. That's a steep hike in a mile, but the sweeping views are worth the effort.

Start the hike by ascending through a birch grove. The trail levels off a bit at about 0.2 mile and then ascends more steeply up some stone steps.

The junction with the Orange & Black Path (formerly known as the East Face Trail) is at 0.4 mile. Continue straight (south), and climb a steep pink granite face. Follow blue blazes and Bates-style cairns (artfully placed groups of four to six rocks that point the way), as you near the summit.

As part of staying true to the history of Acadia's trails, the Bates cairns, pioneered by Waldron Bates, chair of the Roads and Paths Committee of the Bar Harbor Village Improvement Association from 1900 to 1909, have replaced conical piles of rocks and supplement blue blazes as trail markers, particularly on ridgelines on the east side of Mount Desert Island. Don't be tempted to move, add, or take away rocks from the seemingly Zen-like Bates cairns, cautions Charlie Jacobi, Acadia natural resource specialist. The cairns are designed with a purpose, with the gap in the base and the top stone pointing in the right direction. Any alteration can wreak havoc for other hikers, never mind for those maintaining the trails. "It's part of the leave-no-trace principle," says Jacobi. "If it is a native rock, leave it where it is. Don't move it around." It's also part of respecting history, with some Bates cairns dating back a century.

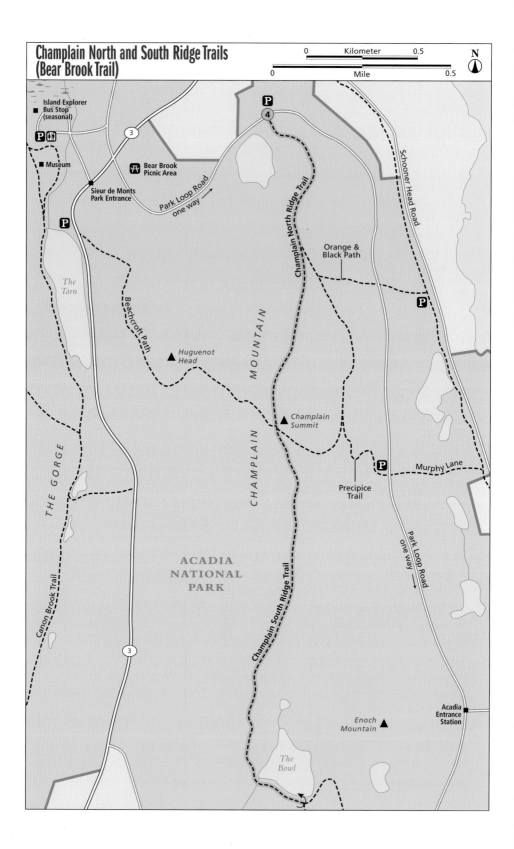

At 1.0 mile reach the Champlain summit, with the closest mountaintop views of Frenchman Bay and the Porcupine Islands in all of Acadia. During summer and fall, you might even see a giant cruise ship passing through the bay on its way out to the Atlantic. Also at or near the summit are the junctions with the Precipice and Champlain South Ridge Trails and the upper Beachcroft Path.

Many people turn around at the summit, for a round-trip hike of 2.0 miles. However, for the hardy hiker looking for more mileage and views, the Champlain South Ridge Trail descends about 700 feet in elevation in about 1.6 miles to the Bowl.

Along the South Ridge Trail, there are some special views to the west of the more wild side of Cadillac Mountain. There is no auto road in sight, only the vast, wooded southern portion of Cadillac and 1,270-foot Dorr Mountain.

As you descend farther along the South Ridge, you get another breathtaking view of the Bowl, framed by the Beehive to the southeast, with the Cranberry Isles in the distance.

Carefully follow the blue blazes and Bates cairns. The trail ends at the Bowl at 2.6 miles. Return the way you came, for a round-trip of 5.2 miles.

Miles and Directions

0.0   Start at the Champlain North Ridge trailhead, on the right (south) side of the one-way Park Loop Road, after the Bear Brook picnic area.

0.4   Reach the junction with a spur to the Orange & Black Path. Bear right and continue on the main trail.

1.0   Arrive at the Champlain Mountain summit and the junction with the Champlain South Ridge Trail. (***Option:*** Turn around here for a 2.0-mile round-trip hike.)

2.6   Reach the southern shore of the mountain pond known as the Bowl and a junction with the Bowl and Beehive Trails.

5.2   Arrive back at the trailhead.

5 Orange & Black Path (East Face Trail)

See evidence of a 2006 earthquake that closed the trail for three years and the craftsmanship that rebuilt it, and get breathtaking views of Frenchman Bay below and Champlain's precipitous east face above. A recently reopened historic section of the path gives you the chance to imagine yourself retracing the steps of visitors of yore.

Distance: 2.0 miles out and back
Hiking time: About 1.5 to 2 hours
Difficulty: Moderate to strenuous
Trail surface: Granite steps, rock ledges, forest floor
Best season: Spring through fall
Other trail users: Hikers climbing Champlain
Canine compatibility: Leashed dogs permitted
Map: USGS Acadia National Park and Vicinity
Special considerations: No facilities or special parking area at the trailhead. Park 1.2 miles away at the Schooner Head Overlook parking area and walk north along Schooner Head Path to the junction with the Orange & Black Path, or park just over 2 miles away at the town ball fields and walk south along ME 3 and then along Schooner Head Road and Path to the junction with Orange & Black. If you loop up the Precipice Trail, be aware that dogs are not permitted on that cliff climb. The upper mountain section of the path may be closed during peregrine falcon nesting season, from mid-May to mid-August.

Finding the trailhead: From downtown Bar Harbor head south on ME 3 for about 1.3 miles, and bear left on Schooner Head Road. Travel 1.2 miles on the road and look for the Schooner Head Path and Orange & Black Path trailheads on the right (west) side of the road. The Island Explorer does not go down Schooner Head Road, but drivers on the Sand Beach and Loop Road lines may let you off at the Acadia Park Loop Road Entrance Station if it is safe to do so. From there you can walk east toward the Schooner Head Overlook parking area and then head north 1.2 miles on Schooner Head Path to the Orange & Black Path trailhead. GPS: N44 21.20' / W68 11.07'

The Hike

Nowhere is the force and grandeur of nature, and the handiwork of past and present-day trailblazers, more visible than along the Orange & Black Path.

Remnants of a massive rockslide and other damage from a 3.8-magnitude earthquake that struck in October 2006 can still be found along what was formerly known as the East Face Trail. The earthquake caused enough damage to close the trail for three years. The path reopened in the fall of 2009 after it was cleared and rebuilt with dozens of new stairs.

First described in the early 1900s, the Orange & Black Path allows access to Champlain via the Precipice Trail (if it's not closed for peregrine falcon nesting season) or the more gradual Champlain North Ridge Trail, or it can be hiked as a destination unto itself.

The coastline of Acadia stretches below the Orange & Black Path.

The trail was originally cut by Rudolph E. Brunnow, a professor at Princeton University, and is named for the school's colors. Brunnow, who led the path committee of the Bar Harbor improvement association from 1912 to 1917, is one of the storied early trail builders on Mount Desert Island, having also designed the Precipice and the Beehive Trails, two of the more daring and intricate trails in the park.

From the trailhead off Schooner Head Path and Schooner Head Road, head northwesterly and gradually uphill along the recently reopened historic section, crossing the one-way Park Loop Road at 0.3 mile. (For a shorter hike, you can start the Orange & Black Path here if you're riding the Island Explorer bus and it's safe for the bus driver to let you off at the trail's junction with the Park Loop Road.)

The Orange & Black Path now starts climbing more steeply along some giant pink granite slabs, and at 0.5 mile a series of about fifty granite steps brings you to a terraced area and junction with a spur to the Champlain North Ridge Trail.

A separate 1990s rock slide—not the earthquake—wiped out a stone bench that was in this area. A replacement bench was built and this intersection remains a good place for a rest and chatting with other hikers.

As long as peregrine falcon nesting season hasn't closed the southerly section of the path, bear left (southeast) at the junction and head along the rocky east face of Champlain. Climb a steep stretch of twenty stone stairs to get a bird's-eye view of Frenchman Bay, Schoodic Head, and Egg Rock to the left (east) and of cliffs soaring above you to the right (west). After some more strenuous climbing, you reach a wide open swath created by a rockslide during the earthquake.

The Orange & Black Path ends at a junction with the Precipice Trail at 1.0 mile. (If the Precipice Trail is open and you decide to clamber up the cliff face to the top of Champlain, be aware that it is safer to loop back down to the Orange & Black Path via the Champlain North Ridge Trail.)

Return the way you came.

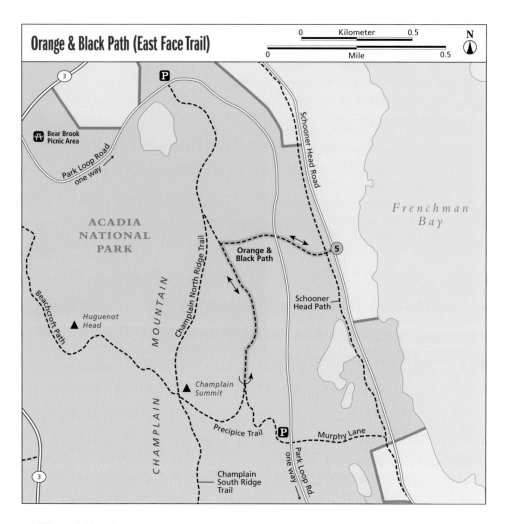

Orange & Black Path (East Face Trail)

Bear Brook Picnic Area

Park Loop Road one way

ACADIA NATIONAL PARK

Champlain North Ridge Trail

Orange & Black Path

Schooner Head Path

Beachcroft Path

Huguenot Head

MOUNTAIN

Champlain Summit

CHAMPLAIN

Precipice Trail

Murphy Lane

Park Loop Rd. one way

Champlain South Ridge Trail

Schooner Head Road

Frenchman Bay

Miles and Directions

0.0 Start at the Orange & Black Path trailhead, on the right (west) side of Schooner Head Road, off Schooner Head Path.

0.3 Cross the one-way Park Loop Road and start ascending more steeply. Look right to watch for traffic.

0.5 At the top of a series of granite steps, reach a terraced area and junction with a 0.1-mile spur to the right (north) to the Champlain North Ridge Trail. Bear left (south) to continue along the path, as long as this section hasn't been closed for peregrine falcon nesting season.

1.0 Reach the end of the path at a junction with the Precipice Trail.

2.0 Arrive back at the trailhead.

6 Precipice Trail

A dramatic and strenuous cliff climb to the top of Champlain Mountain, this is arguably the most difficult trail—and one of the most spectacular—in all Acadia. Signs caution that the unprepared have been seriously injured or died on this trail; heed the warning. The trail may be closed during peregrine falcon nesting season, spring through late summer, but you may be able to participate in a peregrine watch instead.

Distance: 2.5-mile lollipop
Hiking time: About 3 to 4 hours
Difficulty: Strenuous to expert only
Trail surface: Iron ladders and rungs, wooden bridges, forest floor, rock ledges
Best season: Late summer to fall
Other trail users: None
Canine compatibility: Dogs prohibited

Map: USGS Acadia National Park and Vicinity
Special considerations: No facilities. If the trail is closed for peregrine falcon nesting season, you can join in a peregrine watch at the parking area. A park official or volunteer will be set up with a viewing scope from 9 a.m. to noon on most days, mid-May to mid-August, weather permitting.

Finding the trailhead: Enter the park at the Sieur de Monts entrance, about 2 miles south of downtown Bar Harbor on ME 3. Turn right (south) onto the one-way Park Loop Road. The trailhead is 2 miles from the entrance, on the right (west), at the Precipice parking area. The closest Island Explorer stop is Sieur de Monts on the Loop Road and Sand Beach lines; ask if the bus driver can let you off at the Precipice parking area. GPS: N44 20.58'/ W68 11.17'

The Hike

The Precipice Trail ascends more than 900 feet in less than a mile, taking you by cliffs where peregrine falcons nest and providing an aerial view of the coast.

At the start of the trail, a sign warns: "This trail follows a nearly vertical route with exposed cliffs that requires climbing on iron rungs. Falls on this mountain have resulted in serious injury and death. Small children and people with a fear of heights should not use this trail." And the sign goes on to warn that dogs are prohibited, and that hikers should wear sturdy hiking shoes, avoid hiking in dark or wet conditions, and come down an alternate route.

As if to drive home the warning and test your fitness and nerve, the trail soon brings you to the first rock face requiring a climb up iron rungs and then ascends a rockslide shortly thereafter. We've seen hikers who ignored the trailhead signs have to turn around when faced with these early, relatively mild obstacles, including those who disregarded the ban on dogs on this trail.

At 0.4 mile the trail reaches a junction with the Orange & Black Path (East Face Trail), which leads north to an intersection with the Champlain ridge trail, and which you'll be returning on when you loop back to the trailhead.

Hold on dearly to the iron railings as you climb the Precipice, and don't be distracted by the views.

Bear left (southwest) at this junction to continue climbing the Precipice Trail via switchbacks.

The trail soon levels off slightly, but don't let that mislead you into thinking you're near the top. Next begins the really precipitous climb up scores of metal rungs and even a multirung ladder bolted into the rock face.

Strategically placed wooden bridges help you across otherwise impassable crevices in the narrow, exposed rock ledge. Nearing the end of the steep pitch, a sign warns that it's easier to go up the Precipice Trail than down it and recommends an alternative descent via the Champlain North Ridge Trail (Bear Brook Trail) ten minutes ahead.

The rest of the trail is a more gradual hike up a ledge of Champlain Mountain, with a final set of iron rungs sunk into one last rock face. At 0.9 mile reach the 1,058-foot summit of Champlain Mountain and the junction with the Champlain North and South Ridge Trails (Bear Brook Trail).

The peak is the closest mountain in Acadia to Frenchman Bay. You almost feel as though you're right on top of the Porcupine Islands here. To the west are Dorr and Cadillac Mountains, while across the bay to the east is Schoodic Peninsula, the only section of Acadia that's on the mainland. To the south is the Gulf of Maine.

To descend as recommended by the trail warning sign, turn right (north) on the Champlain North Ridge Trail.

At 0.6 mile north of the summit, bear right (southeast) off the Champlain North Ridge Trail and onto a 0.1-mile spur to the Orange & Black Path. Then bear right (south) at a terraced area along the Orange & Black Path to circle back another 0.5 mile to the intersection with the Precipice Trail. Bear left (south) on the Precipice Trail and return to the parking area in another 0.4 mile, for a total hike of 2.5 miles.

Precipice Trail

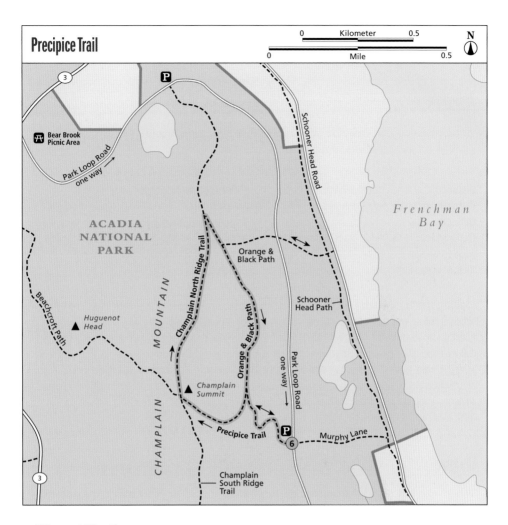

Miles and Directions

0.0 Start at the Precipice trailhead, on the right (west) side of the Park Loop Road.

0.4 Reach a junction with the Orange & Black Path. Bear left (southwest) to continue up the Precipice.

0.9 Attain the summit of Champlain, and reach a junction with the Champlain North Ridge and Champlain South Ridge Trails. Turn right (north) onto the Champlain North Ridge Trail.

1.5 Bear right (southeast) at a spur to the Orange & Black Path; descend a series of eighty-five stone steps.

1.6 Reach a terraced area and fork in the Orange & Black Path. Bear right (south).

2.1 Bear left (southeast) at the junction with the Precipice Trail.

2.5 Arrive back at the trailhead.

7 Schooner Head Overlook and Path

Sample a unique Acadia experience by walking along recently reopened historic trails from a spectacular shore overlook to the base of Champlain's cliffs, with options for longer treks. Along the way you'll pass through deciduous forest and by grand cliff views, and you can imagine what it was like when nineteenth-century rusticators traveled these same footpaths.

Distance: 2.0 miles out and back
Hiking time: About 1 to 1.5 hours
Difficulty: Easy
Trail surface: Forest floor, graded gravel path, wooden bridge
Best season: Spring through fall

Other trail users: Joggers, dog walkers, area residents
Canine compatibility: Leashed dogs permitted
Map: USGS Acadia National Park and Vicinity
Special considerations: No facilities at trailhead

Finding the trailhead: From the park's visitor center, drive south on the Park Loop Road for about 3 miles and turn left (east) at the sign for Sand Beach. Follow the one-way Park Loop Road for about 5 miles. Turn left (east) just before the park entrance station and head straight 0.2 mile, across Schooner Head Road, to the Schooner Head Overlook parking lot. The trailhead is at the northwest corner of the parking lot, before the exit to Schooner Head Road. There is no nearby Island Explorer stop, but the Sand Beach and Loop Road lines pass through the nearby park entrance station, and you may ask the bus driver to let you off there if it is safe to do so. GPS: N44 20.22' / W68 10.44'

The Hike

Where else but in Acadia can you go from shore to cliff in just a mile? And also step through time?

Start off by taking in the oceanfront views at Schooner Head Overlook, at the easternmost end of the parking lot. To the north (left) is the rocky peninsula known as Schooner Head, and out in Frenchman Bay is Egg Rock, with its lighthouse.

The view here was restored in September 2014 as part of a grand plan to rehabilitate thirty historic vistas along the Park Loop Road, pull-outs and parking areas that have grown in over the decades.

Head to the northwest corner of the parking lot and pick up Schooner Head Path, a recently reopened historic route. While the hike described here is along only a portion of Schooner Head Path, you can still imagine yourself a modern-day rusticator, seeing some of the same views that Hudson River School artists like Thomas Cole and Frederic Church saw, or that George B. Dorr, regarded as the father of

Acadia, fought so hard to protect. The path, first built in 1901, recently reopened with funds from the Acadia Trails Forever initiative and the private Fore River Foundation, and is a cooperative effort of the Park Service, Friends of Acadia, area residents, the town of Bar Harbor, and nearby Jackson Laboratory.

Follow the well-graded and slightly hilly path through the woods for 0.1 mile, then cross Schooner Head Road and pick up the trail as it continues on the other side. The path eventually levels off and parallels Schooner Head Road, taking you over a wooden bridge built over the outlet of a pond at 0.2 mile. Take in the grand views of the Champlain cliffs, your destination on this hike.

At 0.7 mile turn left (west) onto Murphy Lane, another recently reopened historic trail that was once open to horses and known as the Blue Path, showing up on maps dating back to the 1890s. Follow Murphy Lane straight (west) through the woods, and don't be confused by old trails that may crisscross in spots.

At 1.0 mile cross the one-way Park Loop Road (look right for traffic) and arrive at the base of Champlain's cliffs, at the Precipice parking area. The Precipice Trail begins here, but it is one of the most difficult cliff climbs in Acadia and not suitable for novices

Schooner Head Path connects to Murphy Lane, bringing you to the Precipice of Champlain.

or people afraid of heights. If the trail is closed for peregrine falcon nesting season, you can participate in a peregrine watch with park rangers and volunteers who set up spotting scopes in the Precipice parking area.

Return the way you came.

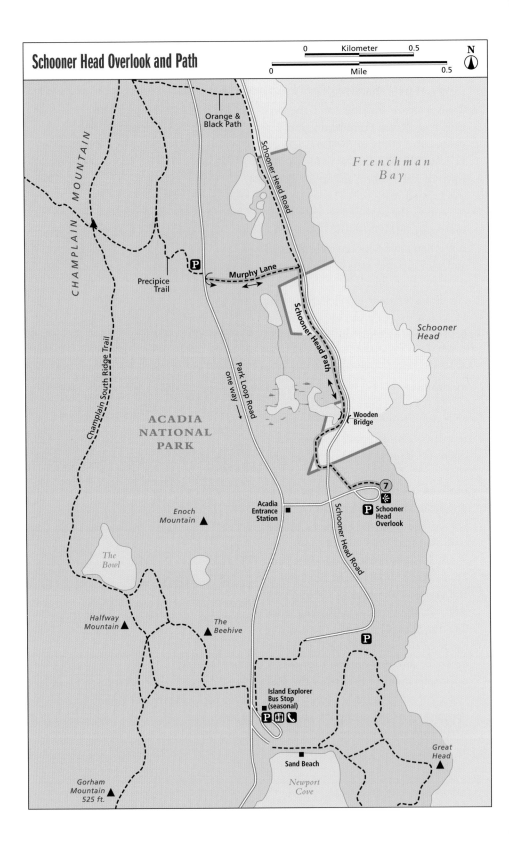

Schooner Head Overlook and Path

Orange &
Black Path

*Frenchman
Bay*

Schooner Head Road

CHAMPLAIN MOUNTAIN

Murphy Lane

Precipice
Trail

Schooner Head Path

*Schooner
Head*

Champlain South Ridge Trail

one way

Park Loop Road

ACADIA
NATIONAL
PARK

Wooden
Bridge

*Enoch
Mountain* ▲

Acadia
Entrance
Station ■

7
⛷

P Schooner
Head
Overlook

*The
Bowl*

Schooner Head Road

*Halfway
Mountain* ▲

*The
Beehive*

P

Island Explorer
Bus Stop
■ (seasonal)

P ⚧ ☎

Sand Beach ■

*Newport
Cove*

*Great
Head* ▲

*Gorham
Mountain* ▲
525 ft.

0   Kilometer   0.5

0   Mile   0.5

N

Miles and Directions

0.0 Start at the Schooner Head Path trailhead, in the northwest corner of the Schooner Head Overlook parking lot, before the exit to Schooner Head Road.

0.1 Cross Schooner Head Road and continue on the path on the other (west) side of the road.

0.2 Cross a wooden bridge over the outlet of a pond, with views toward the Champlain cliffs.

0.7 Reach a junction with Murphy Lane. Turn left (west) and stay straight on the woods trail.

1.0 Cross the one-way Park Loop Road (look right for traffic) to reach the base of the Champlain cliffs at the Precipice parking area. Participate in a peregrine watch if it's peregrine falcon nesting season.

2.0 Arrive back at the trailhead.

Options

To explore more of Schooner Head Path, instead of turning left on Murphy Lane, continue straight (north) on the well-graded path as it parallels Schooner Head Road. In another 0.5 mile you reach a junction with the Orange & Black Path on the left (west), a more difficult trail that leads up Champlain's east face and connects to the Champlain North Ridge and Precipice Trails. Beyond that junction, Schooner Head Path continues another 1.6 miles northwest and then north by northeast all the way to Compass Harbor on the outskirts of Bar Harbor. Some parts of the northern section of Schooner Head Path cross private property, so be respectful of property owners' rights and stay on the established route.

Gorham Mountain Area

8 Sand Beach and Great Head Trail

Enjoy Acadia's only ocean beach, made of sand, tiny shell fragments, quartz, and pink feldspar. Then take a hike along the Great Head Trail for its expansive views of the Beehive, Champlain Mountain, Otter Cliff, Egg Rock, and the Cranberry Isles. Also visible just off the tip of Great Head peninsula is an unusual rock formation called Old Soaker.

Distance: 1.7-mile lollipop
Hiking time: About 1 to 1.5 hours
Difficulty: Moderate
Trail surface: Beach, rock ledges, forest floor
Best season: Spring through fall, particularly early morning or late afternoon in summer to avoid the beach crowds
Other trail users: Sunbathers on Sand Beach in summertime

Canine compatibility: Dogs prohibited on Sand Beach from May 15 through Sept 15; leashed dogs permitted other times of year
Map: USGS Acadia National Park and Vicinity
Special considerations: Seasonal restrooms, a changing area, and a pay phone are available at the Sand Beach parking lot. Bring extra socks or a towel in case your feet get wet when you cross a small channel to get from the beach to the trailhead.

Finding the trailhead: From the park's visitor center, drive south on the Park Loop Road for about 3 miles and turn left (east) at the sign for Sand Beach. Follow the one-way Park Loop Road for about 5.5 miles past the Park Loop Road Entrance Station, to the beach parking lot on the left (east) side of the road. The Island Explorer's Loop Road and Sand Beach lines stop at the beach parking lot. Walk down the stairs at the eastern end of the parking lot and head across Sand Beach to the Great Head trailhead. GPS for parking area: N44 19.45' / W68 11.01'

The Hike

A hike on the Great Head peninsula is a perfect way to break up a lazy summer afternoon lounging on Sand Beach. Because it is so quintessentially Acadia, it's also a perfect place to bring first-time visitors, as we have with our nieces Sharon, Michelle, and Stacey.

A relatively modest scramble up the rocky slope of Great Head leads to dramatic views of the beach you just left behind, as well as vistas of such other notable park features as the Beehive, Champlain Mountain, and Otter Cliff.

Once, when we hiked Great Head with Sharon and Michelle, the views were made even more dramatic by the fog that first enveloped Sand Beach and the Beehive behind us, and then receded like the outgoing tide.

"I feel like I'm living in a postcard," said Sharon, fifteen at the time.

The Beehive looms in the distance beyond Sand Beach.

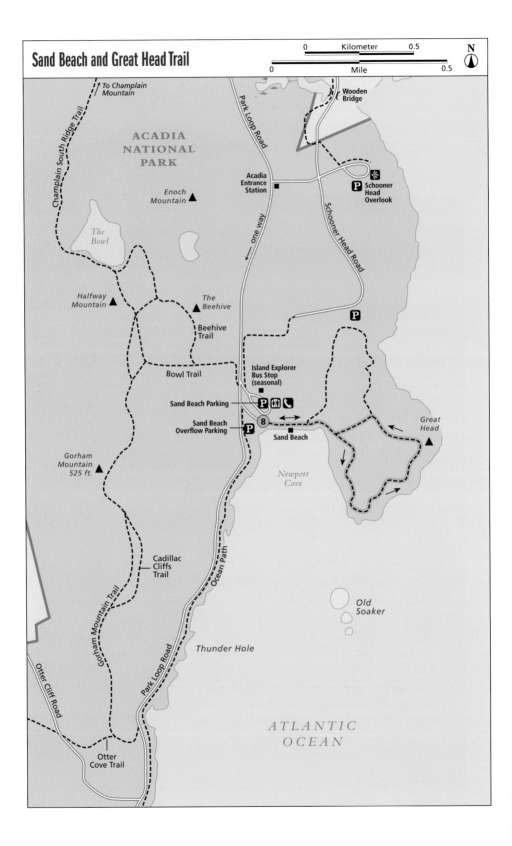

Sand Beach and Great Head Trail

N

0   Kilometer   0.5
0   Mile   0.5

To Champlain Mountain

Champlain South Ridge Trail

ACADIA NATIONAL PARK

Park Loop Road

Wooden Bridge

Enoch Mountain

The Bowl

Acadia Entrance Station

Schooner Head Overlook

Schooner Head Road

one way

Halfway Mountain

The Beehive

Beehive Trail

Bowl Trail

Island Explorer Bus Stop (seasonal)

Sand Beach Parking

Sand Beach Overflow Parking

8

Sand Beach

Great Head

Newport Cove

Gorham Mountain 525 ft.

Cadillac Cliffs Trail

Gotham Mountain Trail

Ocean Path

Old Soaker

Park Loop Road

Thunder Hole

Otter Cliff Road

ATLANTIC OCEAN

Otter Cove Trail

"This is really fun," said Michelle, twelve at the time, as opposed to the "kind of fun" rating she'd given to a hike with less dramatic views that we'd done the day before.

Since the 1840s and 1850s, Great Head has been a popular destination for artists and tourists. A stone teahouse, known as Satterlee's tower, once stood on the summit, and the ruins of it are still visible.

Once, as we stood by the ruins with Stacey, the ringing of a nearby buoy almost sounded like a clock tower, chiming that it's time for tea. It was one of Stacey's first hikes in Acadia, and she was struck by the contrast of sandy beach and rocky summit. "That's very rare," said Stacey.

From the parking lot, head down the stairs to the beach and walk 0.1 mile to the farthest (easternmost) end. Cross a channel—best at low tide to keep your feet dry—to the Great Head trailhead.

Go up a series of granite steps bordered by a split-rail fence. At the top of the steps, at 0.2 mile, turn right (southeast) and follow the blue blazes up the rocky ledges. Views of Sand Beach, the Beehive, and Champlain Mountain are immediately visible.

At the next trail junction, at about 0.3 mile, bear right (south) to head toward the tip of the peninsula, with views of Old Soaker, a nearby outcropping that appears rectangular at low tide, and of Otter Cliff and the Cranberry Isles in the distance.

At 0.6 mile the trail rounds the peninsula. At 0.9 mile it reaches the summit of Great Head, where there are views of Frenchman Bay and Egg Rock.

At about 1.2 miles, along a level section of the trail, you reach a junction in a birch grove. Turn left (southwest) and ascend gradually up Great Head ridge, with views of Champlain Mountain, the Beehive, and Gorham Mountain. If you go straight (northwest) at this junction to a parking lot near Schooner Head Road, and then circle back, you can add another 0.8 mile to the loop.

At the last junction, at 1.4 miles, bear right (northwest) to return to the trailhead and Sand Beach. Head back to the parking lot for a loop hike of 1.7 miles.

Miles and Directions

0.0 Begin at the edge of the parking lot, heading down the stairs and walk east along Sand Beach.

0.1 Cross a small channel at the east end of the beach to reach the Great Head trailhead.

0.2 Bear right (southeast) at the top of the stairs.

0.3 At the junction with the spur trail inland, go right (south) along the shore.

0.6 Reach the south end of the Great Head peninsula and follow the trail as it curves northeast along the shore.

0.9 Arrive on the Great Head summit, where the remnants of a stone teahouse can be found.

1.2 At the junction in the birch grove with the spur trail to Great Head ridge, bear left (southwest). (**Option:** Keep straight and continue northwest to a parking lot near Schooner Head Road, then circle back to add 0.8 mile to the loop.)

1.4 Bear right (northwest) at the junction.

1.6 Arrive back at the Great Head trailhead.

1.7 Walk west along the beach back to the parking lot, completing the loop.

9 Ocean Path

This easy hike takes you along Acadia's distinct pink-granite coastline, bringing you to Thunder Hole, where you may hear a reverberating boom as the surf crashes against the shore; Otter Cliff, where you may see rock climbers on the 60-foot precipice; and Otter Point, where you may catch a colorful sunset.

Distance: 4.0 miles out and back
Hiking time: About 2 to 2.5 hours
Difficulty: Easy
Trail surface: Graded gravel path, forest floor
Best season: Spring through fall, particularly early morning or late afternoon in summer to avoid the crowds

Other trail users: Motorists stopping along the Park Loop Road to view Thunder Hole or Otter Point, rock climbers accessing Otter Cliff
Canine compatibility: Leashed dogs permitted
Map: USGS Acadia National Park and Vicinity
Special considerations: Seasonal restrooms and a pay phone available at Sand Beach parking lot; restrooms at Thunder Hole (seasonal) and Fabbri (year-round) parking areas

Finding the trailhead: From the park's visitor center, drive south on the Park Loop Road for about 3 miles, and turn left (east) at the sign for Sand Beach. Follow the one-way Park Loop Road for about 5.5 miles, past the Park Loop Road Entrance Station, to the beach parking lot on the left (east) side of the road. The trailhead is on the right (east), just before the stairs to the beach. The Island Explorer's Loop Road and Sand Beach lines stop at the beach parking lot. GPS for parking area: N44 19.45' / W68 11.01'

The Hike

The sounds of the ocean and the views of rocky cliffs and pink-granite shoreline are never far from Ocean Path. When the conditions are just right at Thunder Hole, halfway along the path, the surf crashes through rocky chasms with a thunderous roar. At Otter Point, at trail's end, the sound of a buoy ringing fills the air. Rock climbers can be seen scaling Otter Cliff, one of the premier rock climbing areas in the eastern United States, while picnickers, birders, and sun worshippers can be found enjoying themselves on the flat pink-granite slabs that dot the shore here.

First used as a buckboard road in the 1870s, Ocean Path and Ocean Drive were incorporated into John D. Rockefeller Jr.'s vision of scenic roads, bringing visitors to many of Mount Desert Island's unique features. He began motor-road construction in the park in 1927 and hired landscape architect Frederick Law Olmsted Jr. to lay out many of the routes, including the Otter Cliff section of Ocean Drive. The Civilian Conservation Corps rebuilt Ocean Path during the Great Depression of the 1930s with funding assistance from Rockefeller.

Because of its ease and accessibility, Ocean Path can be crowded during the height of the tourist season. The best time to walk it is either very early or very late on a

A view southwest toward Baker Island and Little Cranberry Isle.

summer's day or, as we have, in spring or fall. If you explore the shore along Ocean Path, park officials ask that you please stay on designated routes to and from the path.

The Ocean Path trailhead is on the right just before the stairs to Sand Beach. Follow the gravel path past the changing rooms and restrooms, up a series of stairs, and then left (south), away from a secondary parking area. The easy trail takes you southwest along the shore, paralleling the Ocean Drive section of the Park Loop Road.

Thunder Hole, a popular destination, is at 1.0 mile. Many visitors driving through the park on calm summer days stop here and cause a traffic jam but go away disappointed because their timing was off. The best times to experience the power of Thunder Hole are after a storm and as high tide approaches, when the surf crashes violently through the chasms, pushing trapped air against the rock and creating a sound like the clap of thunder.

Even when you know the best time to visit Thunder Hole, it can still take a number of times before you hit it right. On one trip to Acadia, we went with our nieces Sharon and Michelle to this spot three times, once late at night with stormy seas, but didn't hear the thundering boom we expected.

If you visit Thunder Hole during stormy conditions, be careful. Visitors have been swept out to sea here and at Schoodic Peninsula, a reminder of how powerful nature can be along Acadia's coast. Watch out for large waves, stay a safe distance away, and don't turn your back on the ocean.

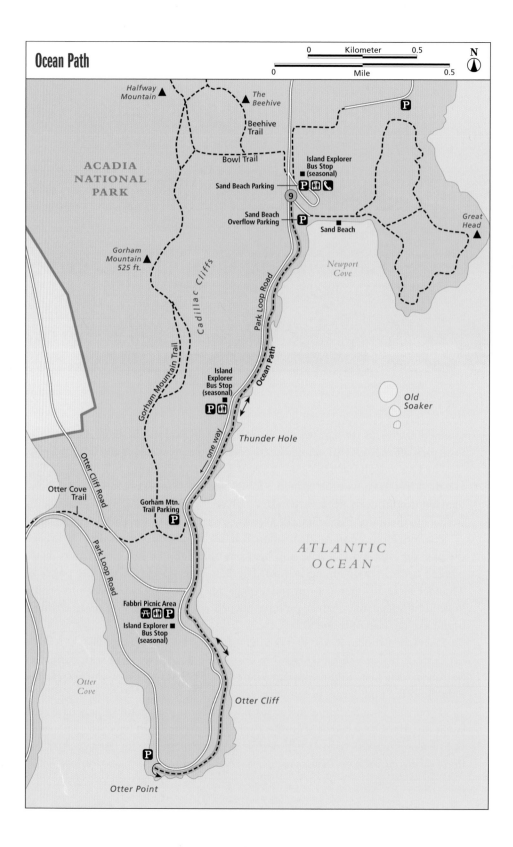

At 1.3 miles on Ocean Path, you pass a short series of stairs on the right (west), which lead across the Park Loop Road to the Gorham Mountain trailhead.

The path's only noticeable elevation gain comes as it rises through the woods toward Otter Cliff, reached at 1.8 miles. On the approach, you can see rock climbers scaling the rock face or waiting at the top of the cliff for their turn. A staircase leads down on the left (east) to the rock climbers' registration board.

Ocean Path ends at 2.0 miles at Otter Point, where you can watch the sun set over Acadia and find a nearby commemorative plaque dedicated to Rockefeller.

Return the way you came.

Miles and Directions

0.0 Start at the Ocean Path trailhead, on the right just before the stairs to Sand Beach. Follow the gravel path up a series of stairs and then left (south), away from a secondary parking area.

1.0 Reach Thunder Hole (a viewing platform may be closed during stormy seas).

1.3 Pass the Gorham Mountain trailhead, which is across the Park Loop Road.

1.8 Reach Otter Cliff, where you can see rock climbers scaling the precipice.

2.0 Arrive at Otter Point, where you can watch the sun set.

4.0 Arrive back at the trailhead.

10 The Bowl Trail

This hike leads to a mountain pond called the Bowl, where you may encounter wildlife. You can connect to the Gorham Mountain and Champlain South Ridge Trails and find more moderate ascents up the back side of the nearby Beehive—a nice alternative to climbing the iron ladder rungs up that peak's cliff.

Distance: 1.6 miles out and back
Hiking time: Approximately 1.5 to 2 hours
Difficulty: Moderate
Trail surface: Forest floor, rock ledges
Best season: Spring through fall, particularly early morning or late afternoon in summer to avoid the crowds

Other trail users: Hikers climbing the Beehive
Canine compatibility: Leashed dogs permitted on Bowl Trail but prohibited on the ladder climb up the Beehive
Map: USGS Acadia National Park and Vicinity
Special considerations: Seasonal restrooms and a pay phone at Sand Beach parking lot

Finding the trailhead: From the park's visitor center, drive south on the Park Loop Road for about 3 miles, and turn left (east) at the sign for Sand Beach. Follow the one-way Park Loop Road for about 5.5 miles, past the Park Loop Road Entrance Station, to the beach parking lot on the left (east) side of the road. The Island Explorer's Loop Road and Sand Beach lines stop at the beach parking lot. The trailhead is diagonally (northwest) across the Park Loop Road from the beach parking lot. GPS: N44 19.54' / W68 11.07'

The Hike

Views of a great blue heron taking off low across the water's surface or of a turkey vulture soaring high on the thermals are among the possible rewards when you hike to the Bowl, a mountain pond at more than 400 feet in elevation. We got lucky and got both views in the same day as we walked along the shoreline.

Another time, during a hike down from the Bowl, we heard a loud snorting in the woods. A couple of white-tailed deer darted through the trees, the snorting apparently an alarm call. And yet another time, on the way off an early Beehive climb, we were surprised by a large barred owl, staring silently down at us from a tree.

Hike in the early morning or late afternoon to improve your chances of such wildlife encounters.

The Bowl Trail begins by climbing gradually through a lowland birch forest, passing a junction with the very steep Beehive Trail, which features iron ladder rungs, at 0.2 mile. Recent rerouting of the next portion of the Bowl Trail has eased the gradient a bit and lengthened the distance by 0.1 mile so that a spur to the Gorham Mountain Trail is now at 0.5 mile, and another spur to the Beehive, a more gradual alternative to the ladder approach, is at 0.6, at the same place where the Gorham Mountain Trail comes in.

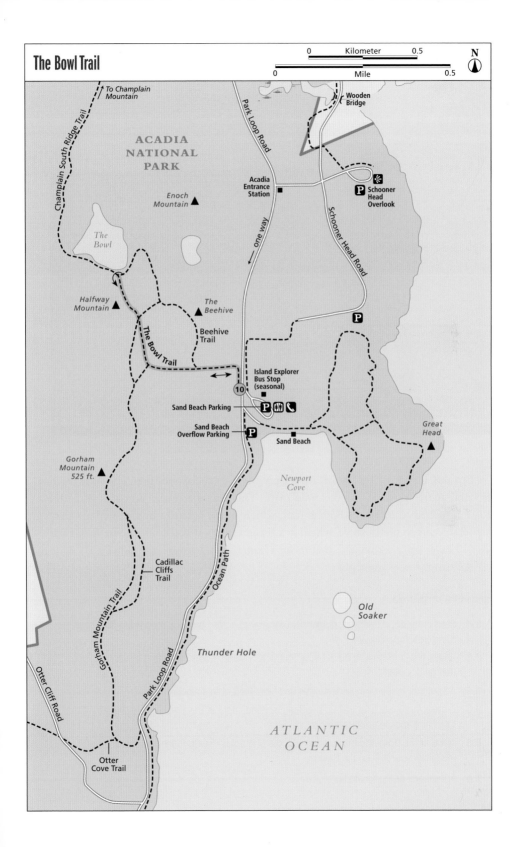

The Bowl Trail

0 Kilometer 0.5
0 Mile 0.5

N

To Champlain Mountain

Champlain South Ridge Trail

ACADIA
NATIONAL
PARK

Park Loop Road

Wooden Bridge

Acadia Entrance Station

P Schooner Head Overlook

Enoch Mountain

The Bowl

one way

Schooner Head Road

Halfway Mountain

The Beehive

Beehive Trail

The Bowl Trail

P

Island Explorer Bus Stop (seasonal)

10

Sand Beach Parking P

Sand Beach Overflow Parking P

Sand Beach

Great Head

Gorham Mountain 525 ft.

Newport Cove

Cadillac Cliffs Trail

Ocean Path

Gorham Mountain Trail

Old Soaker

Otter Cliff Road

Park Loop Road

Thunder Hole

Otter Cove Trail

ATLANTIC OCEAN

The evening sky glows pink above the Bowl, a mountain pond northwest of the Beehive.

Beyond, the Bowl Trail heads up steeply through the woods then goes downhill, arriving at the Bowl at the 0.8-mile mark. This also marks the junction with the 1.6-mile Champlain South Ridge Trail, which heads left (northwest), and another moderate spur to the Beehive, which heads right (east). If you're lucky, you may even spot a beaver or other wildlife that make a home in and around the Bowl.

Return the way you came.

Miles and Directions

0.0 Start at the Bowl trailhead, diagonally (northwest) across the Park Loop Road from the Sand Beach parking lot.

0.2 Reach the junction with the Beehive Trail, a very steep ladder climb that heads right, up that peak's cliff.

0.5 A spur trail to the Gorham Mountain Trail heads left at this junction.

0.6 A more moderate spur trail up the Beehive heads right at this junction. The Gorham Mountain Trail heads left at this junction.

0.8 Arrive at the Bowl and the junction with the Champlain South Ridge Trail and another moderate spur trail up the Beehive.

1.4 Arrive back at the trailhead.

11 The Beehive Trail

A nearly vertical climb up the 520-foot Beehive using iron rungs rewards you with spectacular close-up views of Sand Beach, Great Head, and the ocean beyond. If you hike this trail in summer, plan to start early or late to avoid crowds. You may then find solitude and even encounter wildlife, like the barred owl we saw early one morning on the way down from the Beehive.

Distance: 1.8-mile lollipop
Hiking time: About 2 to 3 hours
Difficulty: Strenuous to expert only
Trail surface: Iron ladders and rungs, wooden bridges, forest floor, rock ledges
Best season: Spring through fall, particularly early morning or late afternoon in summer to avoid the crowds

Other trail users: Hikers climbing to the Bowl
Canine compatibility: Dogs prohibited
Map: USGS Acadia National Park and Vicinity
Special considerations: Seasonal restrooms and a pay phone at Sand Beach parking lot

Finding the trailhead: From the park's visitor center, drive south on the Park Loop Road for about 3 miles, and turn left (east) at the sign for Sand Beach. Follow the one-way Park Loop Road for about 5.5 miles, past the Park Loop Road Entrance Station, to the beach parking lot on the left (east) side of the road. The Island Explorer's Loop Road and Sand Beach lines stop at the beach parking lot. The hike begins at the Bowl trailhead, diagonally (northwest) across the Park Loop Road from the beach parking lot. GPS: N44 19.54' / W68 11.07'

The Hike

The Beehive Trail is not for the faint of heart or weak of limb, nor for anyone afraid of heights or crowds. It features an almost perpendicular climb up iron rungs at its steepest and a Grand Central Station–like atmosphere at its busiest. So crowded is the narrow trail during the peak summer season that, from a distance, people climbing up and down it look like bees swarming around a hive.

The Beehive, a 520-foot-high granite dome overlooking Sand Beach, was named by nineteenth-century artist Frederic Church of the Hudson River School for its jagged, glacially carved face. The trail up it was built in the early 1900s by the Bar Harbor Village Improvement Association and was historically referred to as the Short Precipice Trail.

From the Bowl trailhead across from the Sand Beach parking lot, hike gradually up, reaching the junction with the Beehive Trail in 0.2 mile. You know you're there when you see this sign: "Warning! This trail follows a nearly vertical route with exposed cliffs that requires climbing on iron rungs. Falls on this mountain have resulted in serious injury and death. Small children and people with a fear of heights

Sand Beach, Great Head, and the rocky formation known as Old Soaker as seen from the Beehive Trail.

should not use this trail." Turn right (north) onto the Beehive Trail, swiftly climbing above the trees. Iron hand and foot rungs take you over the most difficult parts of the cliff face. Only one hiker can pass at a time in many spots, so there is often a trail jam as people wait their turns.

If you're not too afraid of heights to look as you hike this precarious stretch, you can get magnificent bird's-eye views of Sand Beach and Great Head. You may also be able to wave down at people below, as our nieces Sharon and Michelle did when we hiked this one late summer afternoon.

At 0.5 mile you reach the top of the Beehive, where you can take in the panorama without having to worry about falling off the edge. The trail starts descending with a view of Otter Cliff to the south, and at 0.6 mile it reaches a junction with a spur back down to the Bowl Trail. Continue straight on the Beehive Trail, and at 1.0 mile reach the mountain pond known as the Bowl.

As with many of Acadia's precipitous trails with iron rungs, it's easier to go up the Beehive than to go down. So rather than turning around to return the same precarious way, bear left (southwest) at the mountain pond and travel 0.1 mile, then turn left (southeast) onto the Bowl Trail, looping back less steeply for a total distance of 1.9 miles.

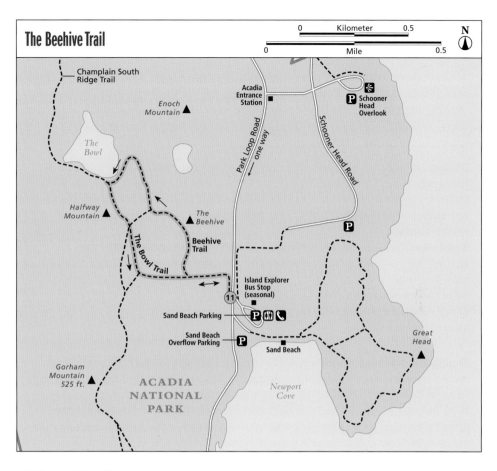

The Beehive Trail

Miles and Directions

0.0 Start at the Bowl trailhead, diagonally (northwest) across the Park Loop Road from the Sand Beach parking lot.

0.2 Arrive at the junction with the Beehive Trail. Turn right (northwest) toward the very steep ladder climb up that peak's cliff.

0.5 Reach the summit of the Beehive. Continue northwest down the back side of the Beehive.

0.6 At the junction with a spur to the Bowl Trail, continue straight (northwest) on the Beehive Trail.

1.0 Reach the Bowl and bear left (southwest) along the mountain pond's shoreline.

1.1 At the junction with the Bowl and Champlain South Ridge Trails, turn left (southeast) onto the Bowl Trail.

1.9 Arrive back at the trailhead.

12 Gorham Mountain and Cadillac Cliffs Trails

This is a classic Acadia hike to a 525-foot peak with sweeping views of Great Head, Sand Beach, Otter Cliff, Champlain Mountain, and the Beehive. The trail, among the most traveled in the park, is also one of the most historic, dating back to the early 1900s. The hike includes a spur trail to Cadillac Cliffs and an ancient sea cave.

Distance: 1.8 miles out and back with a loop

Hiking time: About 1.5 to 2 hours

Difficulty: Moderate

Trail surface: Forest floor, rock ledges, wooden boardwalk

Best season: Spring through fall, particularly early morning or late afternoon in summer to avoid the crowds

Other trail users: Campers at Blackwoods Campground hiking up Gorham via the new Quarry and Otter Cove Trails

Canine compatibility: Leashed dogs permitted but not recommended on the spur to the Cadillac Cliffs Trail, which features a couple of iron rungs

Map: USGS Acadia National Park and Vicinity

Special considerations: No facilities at the trailhead; restrooms nearby at Thunder Hole (seasonal) and Fabbri (year-round) parking areas

Finding the trailhead: From the park's visitor center, drive south on the Park Loop Road for about 3 miles, and turn left (east) at the sign for Sand Beach. Follow the one-way Park Loop Road for about 7 miles, passing the Park Loop Road Entrance Station, Sand Beach, and Thunder Hole, to the Gorham Mountain sign and parking lot on the right (west) side of the road. The closest Island Explorer stop is the Fabbri picnic area on the Sand Beach line; ask if the bus driver can let you off at the Gorham Mountain parking area. GPS: N44 19.00' / W68 11.28'

The Hike

The Gorham Mountain Trail, marked by blue blazes and historic Bates-style cairns, takes hikers to some of the most rewarding views in Acadia, with nearly uninterrupted ridgetop panoramas of everything from Great Head and Sand Beach to the Beehive, and from Cadillac Mountain to Dorr Mountain. The trail follows the great ridge that runs north all the way to Champlain Mountain and is the closest to the ocean of all of Acadia's mountain ridges.

An additional bonus is the spur trail to the once-submerged Cadillac Cliffs and an ancient sea cave, which illustrate the powerful geologic forces that helped shape Mount Desert Island. There is also a new Otter Cove Trail that connects to Blackwoods Campground, coming in on the left (southwest) near the Gorham Mountain trailhead.

From the parking lot, bypass the Otter Cove Trail and bear right on the Gorham Mountain Trail to climb gradually through an evergreen forest and up open ledges, heading north. Though the trail is often shaded by conifers, the sounds of the ocean

Late afternoon sun brings into sharp relief Gorham's pink granite. In the distance are Baker Island and Little Cranberry Island.

and the bells of a buoy signal that the shore is nearby. Bunchberry was blooming during our hike one late spring day.

At 0.2 mile the Cadillac Cliffs Trail leads right (northeast), paralleling and then rejoining the Gorham Mountain Trail at 0.5 mile. Don't miss a plaque at this intersection honoring Waldron Bates, chair of the Roads and Paths Committee of the Bar Harbor Village Improvement Association from 1900 to 1909, who developed a historic style of cairn now used to mark many Acadia trails.

The Cadillac Cliffs Trail, built in the early 1900s and eligible for the National Register of Historic Places, got a major facelift in 2015, to fix erosion and collapsing stone stairs and retaining walls. The trail work was part of the larger Acadia Trails Forever program, a joint effort with the nonprofit Friends of Acadia to maintain the trails.

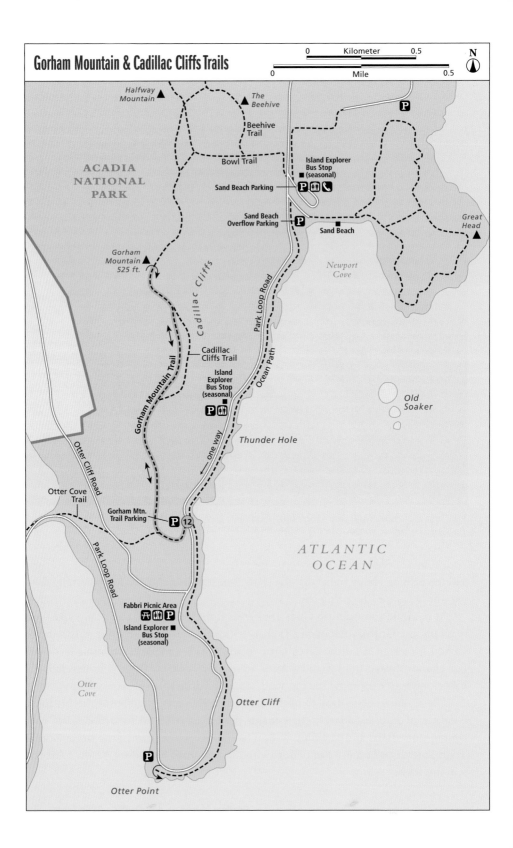

Gorham Mountain & Cadillac Cliffs Trails

Kilometer
0   0.5

Mile
0   0.5

N

Halfway
Mountain ▲

▲ The
Beehive

Beehive
Trail

Bowl Trail

**ACADIA
NATIONAL
PARK**

Island Explorer
Bus Stop
(seasonal)

Sand Beach Parking — P 🚻 ☎

Sand Beach
Overflow Parking — P

Sand Beach ■

Great
Head ▲

Gorham
Mountain ▲
525 ft.

Cadillac Cliffs

*Newport
Cove*

Cadillac
Cliffs Trail

Park Loop Road

Island
Explorer
Bus Stop
(seasonal)

P 🚻

Ocean Path

one way

Thunder Hole

*Old
Soaker*

Gorham Mountain Trail

Otter Cliff Road

Otter Cove
Trail

Gorham Mtn.
Trail Parking — P 12

**ATLANTIC
OCEAN**

Park Loop Road

Fabbri Picnic Area
⛱ 🚻 P

Island Explorer ■
Bus Stop
(seasonal)

*Otter
Cove*

Otter Cliff

P

Otter Point

Bear right onto the spur to include the Cadillac Cliffs on the way up, since it is best to do it on the ascent rather than the descent because of the iron rungs and steep rock face along the way. Start ascending along difficult granite rock and soon come alongside some high cliffs.

You'll go under two rock slabs perched against each other. The towering cliffs, about 75 to 100 feet high, and ancient sea cave soon loom on the left. A path has been worn through the woods at the base of the cliffs, but the official trail takes you along one of the pinkish rock ledges right along the mouth of the sea cave. Cross the short wooden boardwalk to get off the ledge. Look back to see the cliffs at their most impressive. The layers of smooth pink granite look like giant blocks stacked neatly atop one another.

The sea now washes against the shore hundreds of feet below the pink Cadillac Cliffs, but the waves once crashed along here. As the glacier that covered the area melted, the sea level rose and the earth's surface rebounded as it was freed from the weight of the ice. (Visit www.nps.gov/acad for more information on Acadia's geology.)

Next the spur brings you up a series of iron rungs and mostly stone stairs to rejoin the Gorham Mountain Trail at 0.5 mile. Bear right (northwest) on the ridge trail, and ascend moderately. All along this portion of the route you will enjoy views south to Otter Cliff, northeast to Great Head and Sand Beach, and north to the Beehive and Champlain Mountain. Frenchman Bay and Egg Rock can be seen in the distance.

You will find Bates-style cairns along here, with their four or six stones placed just so, the opening at the base and the top pointer stone guiding the way. Remember the rules of the trail, and do not add to, take away from, or otherwise alter the cairns that help guide hikers. Two signs, near the beginning of the trail and at the summit, serve as reminders to leave the cairns untouched. Reach the 525-foot summit of Gorham Mountain at 0.9 mile. From here you can barely see Huguenot Head, but it's easy to spot Dorr Mountain between Champlain and Cadillac Mountains.

Return the way you came, but bypass the Cadillac Cliffs Trail and stay straight on the Gorham Mountain Trail.

Miles and Directions

0.0   Start at the Gorham Mountain trailhead, which leaves from a parking lot on the right (west) side of the one-way Park Loop Road.

0.2   Reach the junction with the southern end of the Cadillac Cliffs Trail. Bear right (northeast) to take the spur to the ancient sea cave. (**Option:** Stay straight to continue on the Gorham Mountain Trail.)

0.5   Reach the junction of the northern end of the Cadillac Cliffs and Gorham Mountain Trails. Bear right to continue northwest to Gorham.

0.9   Arrive on the Gorham summit. Return to the trailhead, bypassing the Cadillac Cliffs Trail and staying straight on the Gorham Mountain Trail.

1.8   Arrive back at the trailhead.

13 Quarry and Otter Cove Trails

This two-section trail is for people staying at the Blackwoods Campground or for hikers eager to explore a new trail in the park. The trail, inaugurated on National Trails Day in 2014, is excellent for campers seeking a hike to Gorham Mountain, Sand Beach, or Thunder Hole or just a short walk to Otter Cove. An endowment from the Friends of Acadia helped finance construction of the trails. Volunteers from the Friends and the Acadia Youth Conservation Corps helped the Park Service construct the trails.

Distance: 1.8 miles out and back
Approximate hiking time: 1 to 1.5 hours
Difficulty: Easy
Trail surface: Graded gravel path, forest floor, grassy strip along the Park Loop Road
Best season: Spring through fall, particularly early morning or late afternoon in the summer to avoid the crowds

Other trail users: Motorists or bicyclists exploring Otter Cove along the Park Loop Road, other hikers coming from the Gorham Mountain Trail
Canine compatibility: Leashed dogs permitted
Map: USGS Acadia National Park and Vicinity
Special considerations: Full facilities available seasonally at Blackwoods Campground

Finding the trailhead: For campers and guests at the Blackwoods Campground, walk to the entrance station and across the road to the trailhead, east of the entrance station. For day hikers in season, take the Island Explorer Sand Beach line to Blackwoods Campground. GPS: N44 18.37' / W68 12.13'

The Hike

Amid the sounds of buoy bells from the nearby Atlantic Ocean, the Quarry Trail starts along fresh, packed gravel just outside the entrance station of the Blackwoods Campground.

Named for a quarry that used to operate in the area, the trail follows an overhead electric power line and then bears right along a graded path. Soon the cove comes into view through pine trees on the right; intermittent stone steps and wooden cribbing, or interlocked logs, help guide a sometimes steep descent to the cove.

The hike reaches a triple-arch stone bridge along a causeway of the one-way Park Loop Road over the cove, at 0.4 mile. The trail offers great views north over intertidal mudflats toward Dorr and Cadillac Mountains and south to Otter Cove.

Turn left (northeast) to pick up the Otter Cove Trail as it starts on a grassy route along the loop road and eventually takes you through a large grove of ash trees. The trail quickly ascends to a wooden footbridge and then a second, tiny footbridge. It crosses over Otter Cliff Road at 0.7 mile, goes over a third wooden bridge, and ends at the Gorham Mountain Trail at 0.9 mile.

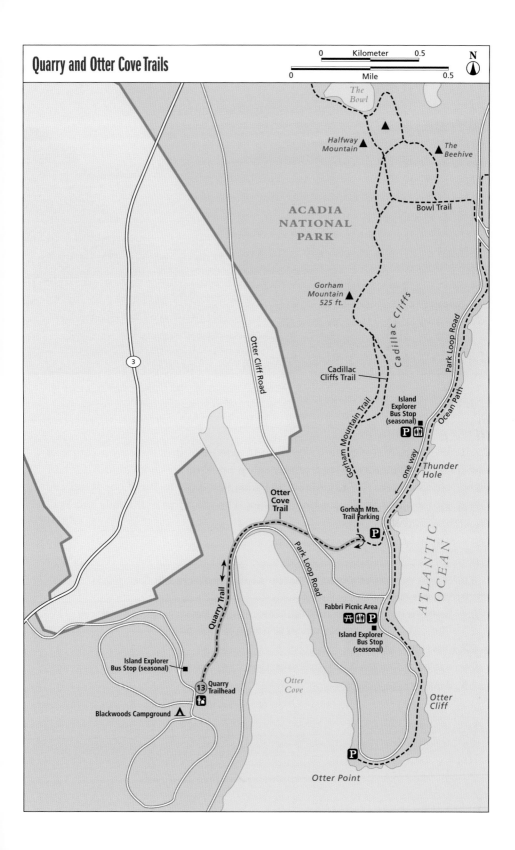

Quarry and Otter Cove Trails

0   Kilometer   0.5

0   Mile   0.5

N

The Bowl

▲

Halfway
Mountain ▲

▲ *The Beehive*

ACADIA
NATIONAL
PARK

Bowl Trail

Gorham
Mountain ▲
525 ft.

Cadillac Cliffs

Otter Cliff Road

3

Park Loop Road

Cadillac
Cliffs Trail

Gorham Mountain Trail

Island
Explorer
Bus Stop
(seasonal)

P 👫

Ocean Path

one way

*Thunder
Hole*

Otter
Cove
Trail

Gorham Mtn.
Trail Parking

P

ATLANTIC
OCEAN

Park Loop Road

Quarry Trail

Fabbri Picnic Area

🏕 👫 P

Island Explorer
Bus Stop
(seasonal)

Island Explorer
Bus Stop (seasonal) ▪

13 Quarry
Trailhead

👫

*Otter
Cove*

Blackwoods Campground ⛺

*Otter
Cliff*

P

Otter Point

The Quarry and Otter Cove Trails join up along the Park Loop Road, where there is a view of Otter Cove.

Return the way you came. If you want to explore further, there are a couple of options: Turn left (northwest) to ascend less than a mile to 525-foot Gorham. Or bear right (east) toward the Gorham Mountain parking lot, cross the Park Loop Road, and take a left (north) along Ocean Path, reaching Thunder Hole in 0.3 mile and Sand Beach in 1.3 miles.

Miles and Directions

0.0 Start at the Quarry trailhead, to the left (east) of the Blackwoods Campground entrance station.

0.4 Reach the Park Loop Road at the Otter Cove causeway. Turn left (northeast) to pick up Otter Cove Trail as it starts on a grassy strip along the loop road.

0.7 Cross Otter Cliff Road.

0.9 Reach the junction with Gorham Mountain Trail.

1.8 Arrive back at the trailhead.

Dorr Mountain and Sieur de Monts Spring Area

14 Kebo Mountain and Dorr North Ridge Trails

The short climb up and views atop the 407-foot Kebo Mountain are just a preview of the hike and vistas to come if you continue on to 1,270-foot Dorr Mountain along the north ridge. From Kebo you'll get intimate, closer-up views of the Porcupine Islands and Egg Rock with its lighthouse. From the higher Dorr, you'll get a panorama of Frenchman Bay and Champlain and Cadillac Mountains.

Distance: 3.6 miles out and back
Hiking time: About 3 to 4 hours
Difficulty: Moderate to strenuous
Trail surface: Forest floor, rock ledges
Best season: Spring through fall

Other trail users: None
Canine compatibility: Leashed dogs permitted
Map: USGS Acadia National Park and Vicinity
Special considerations: No facilities or special parking area at the trailhead

Finding the trailhead: From the park's visitor center, drive south on the Park Loop Road for about 3 miles. Turn left (east) at the sign for Sand Beach, and follow the one-way Park Loop Road for 1.4 miles. The trailhead is on the right (south) side of the road, across from a series of huge boulders lining the road and just before a rock outcropping as the road starts to curve to the right. Park at a pullout area at the Stratheden trailhead, 0.1 mile farther down the one-way Park Loop Road, and walk back on the new easy Kebo Brook Trail on the north side of the Park Loop Road. Better yet, if you're hiking when the Island Explorer is running, take the Loop Road line to the Cadillac North Ridge stop and walk east on the well-graded Kebo Brook Trail for 0.7 mile to the trailhead. GPS: N44 22.36' / W68 13.08'

The Hike

Previously combined under one name, these trails are now known as Kebo Mountain Trail and Dorr North Ridge Trail to be more historically accurate. This hike gives you the option of doing the shorter, easier climb to Kebo or adding the steep clamber up the north ridge of Dorr Mountain. The Kebo summit section dates to the late 1800s and originally started at the Kebo Valley Golf Club on the outskirts of Bar Harbor.

From the current trailhead along the Park Loop Road, the Kebo Mountain Trail begins with a series of seven small stone steps. The path then climbs steeply up rocky knobs and more stone steps, providing views beginning at 0.1 mile all the way to the Kebo summit at 0.3 mile.

From the partially wooded summit, you can see Frenchman Bay and the Porcupine Islands to the northeast, with Cadillac Mountain's north ridge to the west and Dorr Mountain to the south. Hikers content with Kebo Mountain's views can turn around here, for a 0.6-mile round-trip.

Rhodora flashes pink along the Dorr North Ridge Trail.

Those who want more open and grander views from atop Dorr, and are willing to work for them, can continue straight (south). Kebo Mountain Trail goes up and down more rocky knobs lined with lowbush blueberries and offers more tantalizing views through pitch pines until it descends and ends at an intersection with the Hemlock Trail. (Hikers wanting a short 1.8-mile loop can turn left on the Hemlock Trail and then left again to circle back to the Park Loop Road on Stratheden Path.)

Pick up the start of the Dorr North Ridge Trail here, at 0.9 mile, and continue straight (south) along a brief level section. The trail then starts a short steep climb through rock-strewn woods. Birches and striped maple (also known as moosewood because its shoots are a favorite food of moose) dominate here.

The North Ridge Trail then ascends to pitch pine territory and above the tree line, going occasionally up smooth rock slabs. The views that were first hinted at atop low Kebo Mountain open up dramatically here, high on Dorr Mountain's rocky north ridge.

At 1.7 miles reach a junction with the Cadillac-Dorr Trail, which heads down precipitously to the right (west) 0.2 mile to the gorge between Cadillac and Dorr, and with Schiff Path, which heads left (east) toward Sieur de Monts Spring. This is also where the Dorr South Ridge Trail officially meets the Dorr North Ridge Trail.

Continuing straight (south) along the ridge, reach 1,270-foot Dorr Mountain at 1.8 miles. The magnificent vistas of mountains and sea here are a fitting tribute to George B. Dorr, who loved the area so much that he helped found Acadia, and for whom this mountain is named.

Return the way you came.

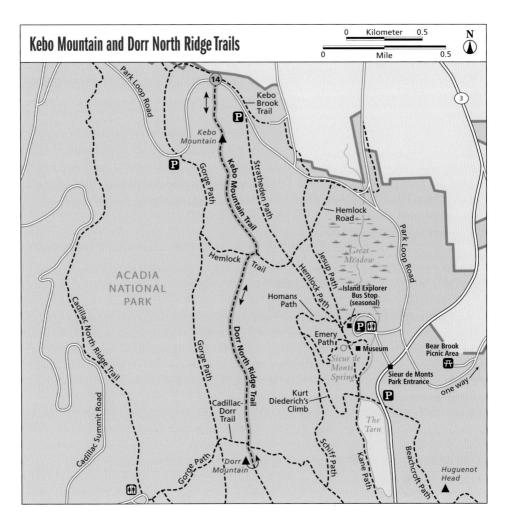

Kebo Mountain and Dorr North Ridge Trails

0   Kilometer   0.5

N

0   Mile   0.5

Miles and Directions

0.0 Start at the Kebo Mountain trailhead, on the right (south) side of the one-way Park Loop Road.

0.3 Reach the 407-foot summit of Kebo Mountain. Continue straight (south). (*Option:* Turn around here and return to the trailhead for a 0.6-mile round-trip.)

0.9 Cross an intersection with the Hemlock Trail. Pick up the start of the Dorr North Ridge Trail here and head straight (south) toward Dorr Mountain.

1.7 Reach a junction with the Cadillac-Dorr Trail coming in from the right (west) and Schiff Path coming in from the left (east). Continue straight (south) on what is now officially the Dorr South Ridge Trail.

1.8 Attain the peak of 1,270-foot Dorr Mountain.

3.6 Arrive back at the trailhead.

15 Homans Path

Originally built by park founder George B. Dorr himself, Homans Path offers terrific views of the Porcupine Islands and Great Meadow, as well as the opportunity to climb some amazing winding stone steps.

Distance: 0.6 mile out and back
Hiking time: About 1 hour
Difficulty: Moderate to strenuous
Trail surface: Granite steps, forest floor, rock ledges
Best season: Spring through fall

Other trail users: Hikers climbing Dorr Mountain
Canine compatibility: Leashed dogs permitted
Special considerations: Seasonal restrooms at the Sieur de Monts parking area

Finding the trailhead: From downtown Bar Harbor head south on ME 3 for about 2 miles, and turn right (northwest) into the park's Sieur de Monts entrance, then a quick left (west) into the Sieur de Monts parking area. From the parking area walk behind the Nature Center and follow the wooden sign pointing right (west) toward trails, over a small wooden bridge, and past a stone inscribed with the words "Sweet Waters of Acadia," and past the Sieur de Monts Spring House. Follow the Emery Path for a short distance to the base of the stone steps that go up Dorr Mountain. Turn right (north) onto Jesup Path for 0.1 mile then left at the gravel Hemlock Path. Homans Path is near the junction of Jesup and Hemlock, on the left (southwest) side of Hemlock Path. The Island Explorer's Sand Beach and Loop Road lines stop at Sieur de Monts. GPS for parking area: N44 21.47' / W68 12.33'

The Hike

Take a series of spiraling stone stairs and ascend along bigger blocks, then walk through a cavelike structure created by a massive rock slab hoisted and placed across a narrow chasm. That architectural feature is just one reason the Homans Path work is special.

Stepping over scores of stone stairs, hikers soon realize they are lucky that Homans Path is a survivor—even withstanding an earthquake that recently shook the area.

The trail is named for Eliza L. Lothrop Homans, who in the early 1900s donated land that later helped create the park.

Despite being created by park pioneer George B. Dorr, Homans was not included in a 1928 path guide and disappeared from park maps during the 1940s. It was restored to fine historical detail and reopened in 2003 as part of Acadia Trails Forever, an effort by Friends of Acadia and Acadia National Park to upgrade trails and implement the park's Hiking Trails Management Plan.

In fall 2006 rockslides caused by an earthquake and its aftershocks damaged some of the stairs and dislodged boulders and slabs, again prompting the closure of Homans.

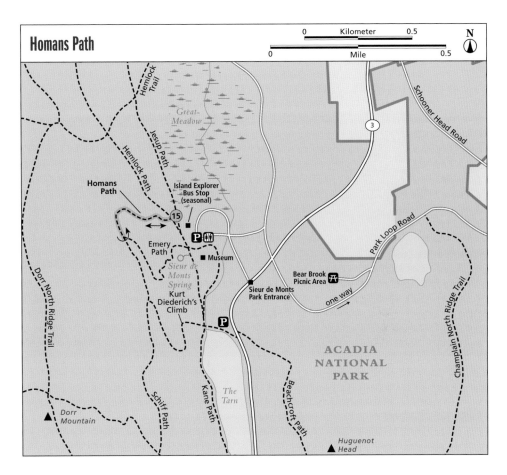

Homans Path

0 Kilometer 0.5

0 Mile 0.5

N

Great-Meadow

Hemlock Trail

Jesup Path

Hemlock Path

Homans Path

Island Explorer Bus Stop (seasonal)

15

P ℹ

Emery Path

Dorr North Ridge Trail

Sieur de Monts Spring

Kurt Diederich's Climb

Museum

Bear Brook Picnic Area

Sieur de Monts Park Entrance

one way

Schooner Head Road

3

Park Loop Road

Champlain North Ridge Trail

P

Schiff Path

Kane Path

The Tarn

Beachcroft Path

ACADIA NATIONAL PARK

Dorr Mountain

Huguenot Head

Acadia ranger Chris Barter estimated the earthquake left a couple of slides, each 20 to 30 feet long and 12 feet wide, on Homans Path. Granite weighs about 180 pounds per cubic foot, so a blasting operation was required to clear at least one huge boulder from the path, Barter says.

Proving its resilience, Homans was repaired and cleared by park trail crews and reopened in August 2007.

Switchback up stone steps flanked by birch and pine and soon enjoy some good views of Frenchman Bay. Then climb another twenty-five stairs and squeeze through a crevice with a single slab forming another cavelike structure.

Hike about one hundred finely laid stone steps, rising steadily, and then reach a level area along a stone face just before the path ends at the intersection with Emery Path. Turn around to catch some great views of the Porcupine Islands, Schoodic Peninsula, and the Great Meadow. If you're up for the challenge, you can take Emery and Schiff Paths steeply up to Dorr Mountain in another 1.3 miles.

Return the way you came.

Spring colors tinge Great Meadow.

Miles and Directions

0.0 Start at the Homans Path trailhead, near the junction of Jesup Path and the gravel Hem-lock Path, about 0.1 mile from the Sieur de Monts parking area and on the left (south-west) side of Hemlock.

0.3 Reach the junction with Emery Path (Dorr Mountain East Face Trail).

0.6 Arrive back at the trailhead.

16 Emery and Schiff Paths (Dorr Mountain East Face Trail)

Emery and Schiff Paths offer spectacular panoramas of Great Meadow, Champlain Mountain, and Frenchman Bay and lessons in Acadia trail history and craftsmanship. Named after two late-nineteenth and early-twentieth-century residents of Bar Harbor, the routes are part of a nearly century-old network of memorial paths emanating from Sieur de Monts Spring, the original heart of the park.

Distance: 3.2 miles out and back
Hiking time: About 2 to 3 hours
Difficulty: Moderate to strenuous
Trail surface: Granite steps, forest floor, rock ledges
Best season: Spring through fall

Other trail users: Hikers climbing Dorr via Homans Path, Kurt Diederich's Climb, or the Ladder Trail
Canine compatibility: Leashed dogs permitted
Map: USGS Acadia National Park and Vicinity
Special considerations: Seasonal restrooms at the Sieur de Monts parking area

Finding the trailhead: From downtown Bar Harbor, head south on ME 3 for about 2 miles, and turn right (northwest) into the park's Sieur de Monts entrance, then a quick left (west) into the Sieur de Monts parking area. From the parking area walk behind the Nature Center and follow the wooden sign pointing right (west) toward trails, over a small wooden bridge, and past a stone inscribed with the words "Sweet Waters of Acadia," and past the Sieur de Monts Spring House, to the Emery Path trailhead. The Island Explorer's Sand Beach and Loop Road lines stop at Sieur de Monts. GPS: N44 21.41' / W68 12.30'

The Hike

Like a stairway to heaven, this route's hundreds of granite steps take you along switchbacks and the base of sheer rock walls to the grand views atop Dorr Mountain. In addition to the mountaintop vistas, you have to admire the handiwork that went into constructing the stairs.

The route begins behind the spring named for French explorer Pierre Dugua, Sieur de Mons, whose navigator, Samuel Champlain, gave the name l'Île des Monts Déserts—Island of Barren Mountains—to this area. The hike takes you up Dorr Mountain via Emery and Schiff Paths and along a short spur of the Dorr South Ridge Trail.

George B. Dorr, a founder of Acadia National Park, bought the spring in 1909 from the owners of a failed commercial springwater business and donated it and the surrounding land as a foundation for the park. As part of returning to the historic roots of the park, the park service recently restored the original trail names to what had been called Dorr Mountain East Face Trail.

Sun filtering through the trees casts a soft light on the stone steps of Emery Path.

Emery Path memorializes John Josiah Emery, whose "cottage," a stone mansion called The Turrets, is now owned by the College of the Atlantic. Schiff Path is named in remembrance of Jacob Schiff, an internationally known banker and philanthropist who founded the Jewish Theological Seminary in New York. Schiff Path was named by Dorr and was the last memorial path added to the Sieur de Monts trail network.

From beyond the Sieur de Monts Spring House and the stone inscribed with the words "Sweet Waters of Acadia," take Emery Path up the rugged east side of Dorr Mountain.

The stone steps begin right away. The trail soon brings you to a view of Huguenot Head, the domelike shoulder of Champlain Mountain, southeast across the valley.

As you climb higher, you will see the Porcupine Islands and Bar Harbor to the northeast and a fuller view of Huguenot Head and the taller Champlain Mountain behind it to the southeast. In one of the most amazing architectural feats on Emery Path, the stone steps wind around like a spiral staircase through a huge rock crevice.

At 0.3 mile you'll reach a junction with the recently reopened Homans Path, coming in from the right (north). Continue along Emery as it turns left (south) and levels off, passing a shady area with a stone bench.

Climb about thirty stone steps to a sandy clearing and then continue along nicely carved steps, about one hundred in all. Soon reach a section of thick pitch pine and

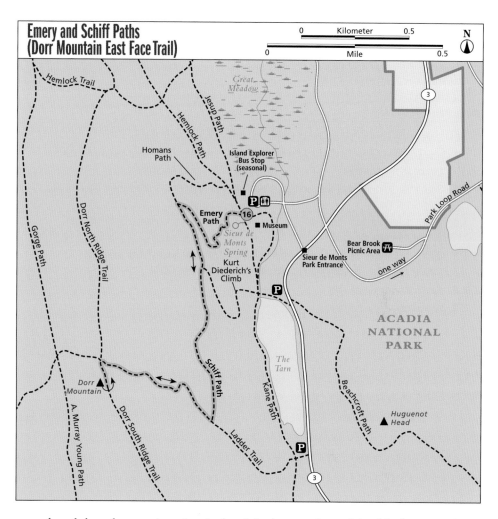

oak and then the next junction. In late July there are lots of ripe blueberries off this section of Emery.

At 0.5 mile Emery ends at an intersection with Schiff Path and Kurt Diederich's Climb. Bear right (south) onto Schiff Path, continuing up Dorr via switchbacks. Reach a junction with the Ladder Trail at 1.0 mile. Turn right (northwest) and climb steadily up Schiff, following blue blazes and historic Bates-style cairns along the way. You can get views of Huguenot Head and Champlain Mountain off Schiff, along with other sights.

One day in early July, a snake close to 3 feet long, apparently a milk snake, slithered off a rock on Schiff. It was the largest snake we've ever seen in Acadia.

At 1.5 miles attain Dorr's ridge at an intersection with the Dorr South and North Ridge Trails and the Cadillac-Dorr Trail. Turn left (south) onto Dorr South Ridge Trail for a brief spell, reaching the 1,270-foot summit at 1.6 miles. Among the views here are the Porcupine Islands and Bar Harbor to the northeast, Champlain Mountain and Huguenot Head to the east, the Cranberry Isles and Gulf of Maine to the south, and Cadillac Mountain to the west.

Return the way you came.

Miles and Directions

0.0 Start at the Emery Path trailhead, beyond Sieur de Monts Spring House.

0.3 Homans Path comes in on the right (north). Turn left (south) to continue on Emery Path toward Dorr Mountain.

0.5 Reach the start of Schiff Path and a junction with Kurt Diederich's Climb. Bear right (south) onto Schiff Path.

1.0 Reach a junction with the Ladder Trail. Turn right (northwest) to continue on Schiff Path toward Dorr Mountain.

1.5 Reach Dorr's ridge and the intersection with North Dorr and South Ridge Trails and Cadillac-Dorr Trail. Turn left (south) onto the Dorr South Ridge Trail.

1.6 Reach the summit of Dorr.

3.2 Arrive back at the trailhead.

17 Kurt Diederich's Climb

This steep-stepped trail is one of four ways up the rugged east face of Dorr Mountain, providing a connection to the history of memorial-path building of the area, as well as to the ever-spectacular views atop the third-highest peak in Acadia. Starting near sea level at the outlet of the Tarn, a mountain pond, the path ascends nearly vertically.

Distance: 3.2 miles out and back
Hiking time: About 2 to 3 hours
Difficulty: Moderate to strenuous
Trail surface: Granite steps, forest floor, rock ledges
Best season: Spring through fall
Other trail users: Hikers climbing up Dorr via the Ladder Trail or Homans or Emery Paths

Canine compatibility: Leashed dogs permitted
Map: USGS Acadia National Park and Vicinity
Special considerations: No facilities at the trailhead; seasonal restrooms at the Sieur de Monts parking area, 0.3 mile north on the Jesup or Wild Gardens Path

Finding the trailhead: Drive south of downtown Bar Harbor on ME 3 a little more than 2 miles, just past the Sieur de Monts park entrance, to the Tarn parking lot on the right (west). Follow a dirt path at the south end of the parking area. Turn right at the end of a split-rail fence, following another dirt path to a junction. Cross over the outlet of the Tarn on a series of well-placed level rocks. Do not follow the signs that point right to Sieur de Monts Spring. Reach the trailhead in 0.1 mile, at a four-way intersection. Go straight (northwest) up stone steps. The Island Explorer's Sand Beach and Loop Road lines stop at Sieur de Monts, requiring a 0.3-mile hike to the trailhead on either the Wild Gardens Path or the southern spur of Jesup Path. GPS: N44 21.30' / W68 12.25'

The Hike

Arguably the most difficult way to access the summit of Dorr Mountain, Kurt Diederich's Climb takes you up 450 feet in only 0.5 mile, averaging nearly 100 feet of elevation gain for each 0.1 mile, to a junction with Schiff and Emery Paths (Dorr Mountain East Face Trail). By contrast, the rest of the way up the summit, 1.0 mile on Schiff Path and 0.1 mile on Dorr South Ridge Trail, averages only about 70 feet of elevation gain for each 0.1 mile.

The hike starts across the outlet of the Tarn, a mountain pond nestled in the gorge between Dorr and Champlain Mountains, at the junction of two other memorial paths, Jesup and Kane (Tarn Trail). The granite step engraved with the words "Kurt Diederich's Climb" is the sixth one up from the start.

Like so many of the historic trails in Acadia, this trail was built in remembrance of someone who loved the mountains here even before they became part of a national park. Diederich died in his late twenties in 1913 from complications of surgery and is buried in Milton, Massachusetts, along with his wife, Sybil, and his aunt, Enid Hunt Slater, who funded the trail in her nephew's memory.

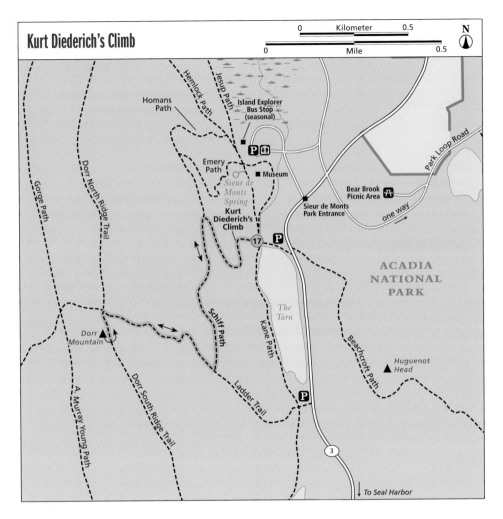

Constructed by George B. Dorr around 1915, the climb contains some historic-style stone steps and some great views of Champlain Mountain, at 1,058 feet the seventh-highest peak in the park. In one section, Kurt Diederich's Climb goes up 230 continuous steps.

The trail technically ends at 0.5 mile at the junction with Schiff and Emery Paths. Turn left (south) onto Schiff Path.

At 1.0 mile reach a junction with the Ladder Trail. Turn right (northwest) to continue on Schiff Path, reaching the ridge of Dorr at 1.5 miles. Turn left (south) onto the Dorr South Ridge Trail, and at 1.6 miles reach the 1,270-foot Dorr summit with its spectacular views of mountains and the sea.

Return the way you came.

A view of Huguenot Head across from Kurt Diederich's Climb.

Miles and Directions

0.0 Start at the Kurt Diederich's Climb trailhead, 0.1 mile from the Tarn parking lot, across the outlet of the Tarn. Go west up the granite steps.

0.5 Reach a junction with the Schiff and Emery Paths (Dorr Mountain East Face Trail); turn left (south) onto Schiff Path.

1.0 Turn right (northwest) at a junction with the Ladder Trail and continue up Dorr Mountain on Schiff Path.

1.5 Attain the ridge of Dorr at a four-way intersection. Turn left (south) onto the Dorr South Ridge Trail.

1.6 Reach the summit of Dorr.

3.2 Arrive back at the trailhead.

18 Kane Path (Tarn Trail)

Huge stepping-stones placed just so along the Tarn, a mountain pond at the base of Dorr Mountain, turn what would otherwise be a tough clamber into practically a garden stroll. Along the way you get views of Huguenot Head on the shoulder of Champlain Mountain, across the glacier-carved valley. If you're lucky you might catch glimpses of otters, bats, and other wildlife that find a home at the Tarn.

Distance: 1.8 miles out and back
Hiking time: About 2 to 2.5 hours
Difficulty: Easy to moderate
Trail surface: Granite steps, wooden bridges, forest floor, rock ledges
Best season: Spring through fall
Other trail users: Hikers climbing Dorr Mountain

Canine compatibility: Leashed dogs permitted
Map: USGS Acadia National Park and Vicinity
Special considerations: No facilities at the trailhead; seasonal restrooms at the Sieur de Monts parking area, 0.3 mile north on the Jesup or Wild Gardens Path

Finding the trailhead: Drive south from downtown Bar Harbor on ME 3 a little more than 2 miles, just past the Sieur de Monts park entrance, to the Tarn parking lot on the right (west). Follow a dirt path at the south end of the parking area. Turn right at the end of a split-rail fence, following another dirt path to a junction. Cross over the outlet of the Tarn on a series of well-placed level rocks. Do not follow the signs that point right to Sieur de Monts Spring. Reach the trailhead in 0.1 mile at a four-way intersection. Go left (south) along the western shore of the Tarn. The Island Explorer's Sand Beach and Loop Road lines stop at Sieur de Monts, requiring a 0.3-mile hike to the trailhead on either the Wild Gardens Path or the southern spur of Jesup Path. GPS: N44 21.30' / W68 12.25'

The Hike

Rather than just driving by the Tarn on ME 3, take this path to get a better appreciation of the mountain pond in the gorge between Dorr and Champlain Mountains and of Acadia's ever-changing, ever-surprising nature. We've seen artists painting along the pond and have heard that photographers come here at sunrise to capture the Tarn's reflection-pool effect. Our nieces Sharon and Michelle, who joined us on a hike here one unusually hot July, even found tiny fish swimming in a brook that empties into the Tarn. Fish like pumpkinseed sunfish and ninespine stickleback are native to the pond. Otters, herons, bats, and a variety of pond plants also find a home here. One time, while we were descending Kurt Diederich's Climb to the pond near dusk, we saw bats flitting around.

Kane Path begins on the north end of the pond, across the outlet, at an intersection with Jesup Path coming in on the right and Kurt Diederich's Climb coming down from Dorr. At the northwest corner of the intersection, there's a 1913 plaque

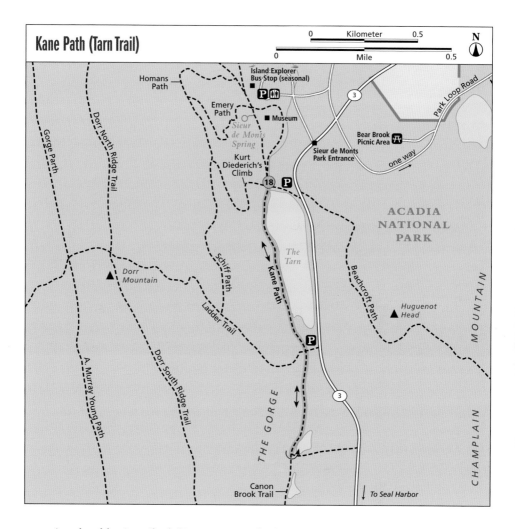

set in a boulder inscribed: "In Memory of John Innes Kane, a man of kindness who found his happiness in giving others pleasure."

Turn left (south) at the intersection to follow Kane Path along the west shore of the pond. Huguenot Head to the left (east) and Dorr Mountain to the right (west) soon come into view. You may also hear the traffic whizzing by on ME 3 across the pond.

Much of this part of the trail is on the flat surfaces of huge granite slabs along the base of a Dorr Mountain rockslide. Some of the granite is pink, mirroring the pink of the rockslide on Huguenot Head across the gorge. Although the trail is fairly level, there is some rock hopping involved. The best views are along the Tarn, so don't make the mistake of failing to notice them along the way.

After passing the south end of the Tarn at 0.5 mile, the trail reaches a junction with the Ladder Trail, which heads steeply right (west) up Dorr Mountain. This is

Step across these stones over the mouth of the Tarn to reach Kane Path.

where our nieces rested in the shade one hot July afternoon and spotted tiny fish in the brook.

Continue straight (south) on what has now become an easy wood path, reaching trail's end at 0.9 mile at a junction with the Canon Brook Trail.

Return the way you came.

Miles and Directions

0.0 Start at the Kane Path trailhead, 0.1 mile from the Tarn parking lot, across the outlet of the Tarn. Turn left (south) along the western shore of the mountain pond.

0.5 Reach a junction with the Ladder Trail. Continue straight (south) on Kane Path.

0.9 Trail ends at the junction with the Canon Brook Trail.

1.8 Arrive back at the trailhead.

19 Dorr Mountain Loop via Ladder and Dorr South Ridge Trails

Variety abounds on this circuit: Go up Dorr via iron ladders and rungs, come down the mountain's open south ridge, and circle around via a relatively easy section of the Canon Brook Trail that may have been part of a pre–Revolutionary War route. This is one of a couple dozen hikes featured in the park service handout "Paths into the Past: Acadia's Historic Trails."

Distance: 3.3-mile loop
Hiking time: About 3 to 4 hours
Difficulty: Strenuous to expert only
Trail surface: Iron rungs and ladders, granite steps, forest floor, rock ledges
Best season: Spring through fall

Other trail users: Hikers climbing to and from the Featherbed and Cadillac Mountain
Canine compatibility: Dogs prohibited on the Ladder Trail
Map: USGS Acadia National Park and Vicinity
Special considerations: No facilities

Finding the trailhead: Drive about 2.6 miles south of downtown Bar Harbor on ME 3, past the Sieur de Monts park entrance and the Tarn parking lot, to the first gravel pullout south of the mountain pond, on the right (west) side of ME 3. The trailhead is on the right (west) side of ME 3. The Island Explorer's Sand Beach and Loop Road lines stop at Sieur de Monts, requiring a 0.8-mile hike to the trailhead via the Kane and Jesup Paths. GPS: N44 21.06' / W68 12.18'

The Hike

This challenging circuit offers nontechnical climbing up iron ladders and rungs, panoramic views from Dorr's open south ridge, and an opportunity to walk along historic routes, part of which may have been a Native American carry trail to Otter Creek.

Beginning at the Ladder Trail, one of the most challenging ways up Dorr Mountain with its alternating iron ladders, rungs, and hundreds of stone steps, you immediately rise above the gorge between Dorr and Champlain Mountains, getting views of the Porcupine Islands to the northeast.

Quite a feat for its day, this trail was originally constructed under the leadership of architect Herbert Jaques, one of the big early trail builders in the 1890s on the island, along with George B. Dorr and Waldron Bates. The Civilian Conservation Corps showed a great care for detail in a massive reconstruction of this trail in 1934 and 1935, during the Great Depression. Some of the granite steps are fitted into narrow rock crevices or built to bring you up rock faces that would otherwise be impassable without full climbing gear.

Soon you'll squeeze through a crevice and see an iron bar at the end, placed to keep you from falling off a cliff. Look sharp left and you'll see the first iron ladder bolted into sheer rock, with its ten rungs and hinged sections. Be careful climbing this

Near the top of the Ladder Trail is this boulder that rivals Bubble Rock in stature.

ladder. It's safer to use the iron handholds to the left rather than grabbing the ladder rungs to pull yourself up and risk getting your fingers caught between the rock and the rungs.

Next comes a series of five metal rungs set into rock with more handrails, then another multistep ladder. At times the trail snakes between cavelike structures formed by a jumble of huge boulders or under rock overhangs that take on shapes limited only by your imagination.

The trail continues on scores of granite steps. You can still hear ME 3 below. You know you're nearing the top of the Ladder Trail when it starts to level off beyond a series of granite steps and iron rungs.

At 0.4 mile reach the junction with Schiff Path. Bear left (northwest) to continue up Dorr on Schiff. You'll begin to get views of the Tarn below, as well as of Champlain Mountain, Frenchman Bay, and the Porcupines farther to the east and northeast. The trail alternates between open ridge and scrub oak and pitch pine, then climbs steeply to the ridge. Follow the historic Bates-style cairns and blue blazes to the top.

At 0.9 mile, at the intersection with Cadillac-Dorr and Dorr South and Dorr North Ridge Trails, turn left (south) onto Dorr South Ridge Trail.

At 1.0 mile reach the 1,270-foot summit of Dorr. To the east are Champlain and Frenchman Bay. To the northeast are the Porcupine Islands, with Cadillac Mountain to the west. To the south are Otter Cove, the Cranberry Isles, and the Gulf of Maine.

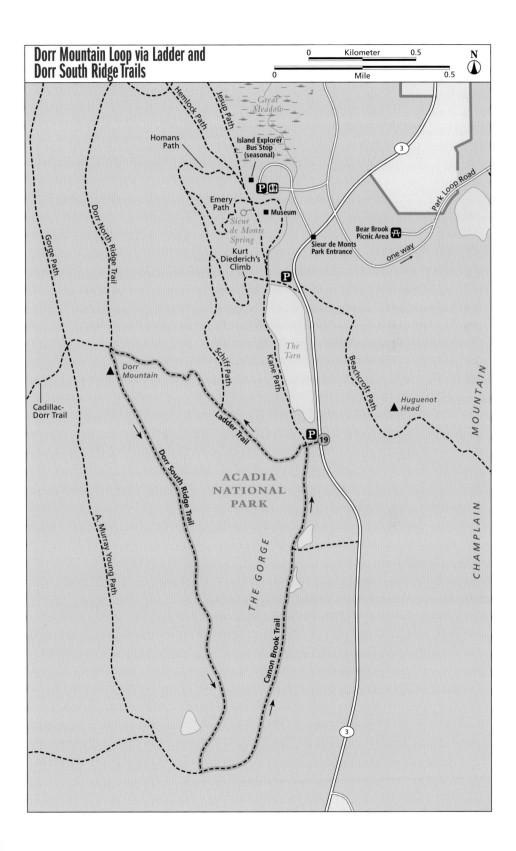

Dorr Mountain Loop via Ladder and Dorr South Ridge Trails

0 Kilometer 0.5

0 Mile 0.5

N

Hemlock Path

Jesup Path

Great Meadow

Homans Path

Island Explorer Bus Stop (seasonal)

Emery Path

Museum

Sieur de Monts Spring

Park Loop Road

3

Bear Brook Picnic Area

Sieur de Monts Park Entrance

Kurt Diederich's Climb

one way

Gorge Path

Dorr North Ridge Trail

The Tarn

Kane Path

Beachcroft Path

Schiff Path

▲ Dorr Mountain

Huguenot Head ▲

MOUNTAIN

Cadillac-Dorr Trail

Ladder Trail

P 19

ACADIA NATIONAL PARK

Dorr South Ridge Trail

A. Murray Young Path

THE GORGE

CHAMPLAIN

Canon Brook Trail

3

Go straight (south) on the Dorr South Ridge Trail, getting ever-closer views of Otter Cove and the Cranberry Isles as you head down the classic Acadia pink granite, dotted with historic Bates-style cairns and blue blazes to point the way.

At 2.3 miles, as Dorr South Ridge ends, turn left (east) at the junction with the Canon Brook Trail to loop around the base of Dorr Mountain.

At 3.0 miles reach the junction with Kane Path. Stay straight (north) on Kane to continue the loop rather than bearing right, as the Canon Brook Trail heads east toward ME 3.

At 3.3 miles return to the Ladder trailhead, closing the loop. The pullout parking on ME 3 is to the right (east).

Miles and Directions

0.0 Start at the Ladder trailhead, on the right (west) side of ME 3 south of the Tarn. You'll be looping back on the return on the section of Kane Path that comes in from the left (south).

0.4 Reach the junction with Schiff Path. Bear left (northwest) on Schiff to continue the climb.

0.9 Attain the ridge of Dorr at an intersection with Cadillac-Dorr and Dorr South and North Ridge Trails. Turn left (south) onto Dorr South Ridge Trail.

1.0 Summit Dorr Mountain. Continue straight (south) on Dorr South Ridge Trail.

2.3 The Dorr South Ridge Trail dead-ends at the Canon Brook Trail. Turn left (east) onto the Canon Brook Trail to loop back.

3.0 Head straight (north) onto Kane Path rather than following the Canon Brook Trail to the right (east).

3.3 Arrive back at the Ladder trailhead, closing the loop. The pullout parking area on ME 3 is to the right (east).

20 Canon Brook Trail

Starting at the base of the steep east face of Dorr Mountain, this trail skirts south and west around the ridge and up the eastern flank of Cadillac, bringing you to a peaceful mountain pond called the Featherbed. Some of the best views come as you climb the sheer open ledges on the way up to Cadillac's ridge. You may even see a pileated woodpecker and other bird life, especially as you near the pond.

Distance: 4.0 miles out and back
Hiking time: About 3 to 4 hours
Difficulty: Moderate to strenuous
Trail surface: Granite steps, forest floor, rock ledges
Best season: Spring through fall
Other trail users: Hikers climbing to and from Dorr or Cadillac Mountain

Canine compatibility: Leashed dogs permitted but not recommended if you continue on the Canon Brook Trail west beyond the Featherbed, along what was formerly known as the Pond Trail
Map: USGS Acadia National Park and Vicinity
Special considerations: No facilities

Finding the trailhead: Drive about 2.6 miles south of downtown Bar Harbor on ME 3, past the Sieur de Monts park entrance and the Tarn parking lot, to the second gravel pullout south of the mountain pond, on the right (west) side of ME 3. There is also a paved pullout on the east side of ME 3 here. The trailhead is on the right (west) side of ME 3. The Island Explorer's Sand Beach and Loop Road lines stop at Sieur de Monts, requiring a 1.1-mile hike to the trailhead via the Kane and Jesup Paths. GPS: N44 20.53' / W68 12.07'

The Hike

The trail begins with an easy jaunt through the woods. At 0.3 mile reach a junction with the Kane Path at the base of the sheer east face of Dorr Mountain. Turn left to head south on the relatively level part of the Canon Brook Trail.

Soon the trail veers right (west) and starts ascending as it rounds the base of Dorr. The trail levels off as it nears the junction at 1.0 mile with Dorr South Ridge Trail, which comes in on the right (north).

At 1.1 miles the A. Murray Young Path comes in on the right (north) from the gorge between Cadillac and Dorr Mountains. A series of rock ledges here along Canon Brook make for a pleasant resting place. Cross the brook and start climbing steeply to the left up stone stairs. Then go up along a cascade, crossing from one side of it to the other. As you go up the sheer rock slabs, which can have water coming down them depending on the season, you get views of Champlain, the Beehive, and Otter Cliff behind you to the east.

The trail next heads into the woods, leveling off as you skirt a marsh. More than one hundred stone steps take you up one more time. We saw a pileated woodpecker once along this stretch, pecking at a tree.

The rock face on the Canon Brook Trail gets slippery when wet.

At 2.0 miles reach the Featherbed, where you can sit on log benches and take in the views around the mountain pond or see a turkey vulture soar on the thermals, as we did one beautiful morning. This is also where the Cadillac South Ridge Trail intersects. You can continue west along the Canon Brook Trail another 0.1 mile beyond the Featherbed to a ledge providing open views toward the Cranberry Isles.

Return the way you came.

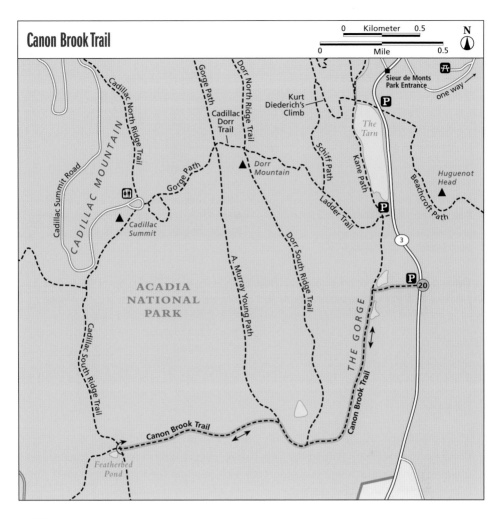

Canon Brook Trail

0 Kilometer 0.5

0 Mile 0.5

N

Cadillac North Ridge Trail

Cadillac Summit Road

CADILLAC MOUNTAIN

Cadillac Summit

Gorge Path

Gorge Path

Dorr North Ridge Trail

Cadillac Dorr Trail

Kurt Diederich's Climb

Dorr Mountain

Schiff Path

Ladder Trail

Kane Path

The Tarn

Sieur de Monts Park Entrance

one way

P

P

Huguenot Head

Beachcroft Path

ACADIA NATIONAL PARK

A. Murray Young Path

Dorr South Ridge Trail

THE GORGE

Canon Brook Trail

3

P

20

Cadillac South Ridge Trail

Canon Brook Trail

Featherbed Pond

Miles and Directions

0.0 Start at the Canon Brook trailhead, on the right (west) side of ME 3 south of the Tarn. Head west toward the base of Dorr.

0.3 Reach a junction with the Kane Path. Turn left (south) and continue following Canon Brook Trail around the ridge of Dorr.

1.0 Reach a junction with Dorr South Ridge Trail coming in on the right (north). Stay straight (west).

1.1 Pass the A. Murray Young Path coming in on the right (north), and continue straight (west) up Cadillac's southern ridge.

2.0 Reach the Featherbed with its wooden benches and the intersection with the Cadillac South Ridge Trail.

4.0 Arrive back at the trailhead.

21 A. Murray Young Path via Canon Brook Trail

This less-traveled trail makes for a rigorous loop up Dorr Mountain, particularly since you need to first hike 1.1 miles to reach the trailhead and then climb steeply up from the gorge between Cadillac and Dorr Mountains. But the solitude on this memorial path and views from atop Dorr are worth it.

Distance: 4.8-mile lollipop
Hiking time: About 4 to 5 hours
Difficulty: Strenuous
Trail surface: Granite steps, forest floor, rock ledges
Best season: Spring through fall

Other trail users: Hikers climbing Cadillac Mountain
Canine compatibility: Leashed dogs permitted
Map: USGS Acadia National Park and Vicinity
Special considerations: No facilities

Finding the trailhead: Drive about 2.6 miles south of downtown Bar Harbor on ME 3, past the Sieur de Monts park entrance and the Tarn parking lot, to the second gravel pullout south of the mountain pond, on the right (west) side of ME 3. There is also a paved pullout on the east side of ME 3 here. The Island Explorer's Sand Beach and Loop Road lines stop at Sieur de Monts, requiring a 1.1-mile hike to the Canon Brook trailhead via the Kane and Jesup Paths. GPS: N44 20.53' / W68 12.07'

The Hike

There are no spectacular vistas on this wooded trail until you tag on the short, steep climb up to Dorr Mountain at the end. But recent rehabilitation of the garden-like stepping stones in the lower sections of the path provides for a perspective that's just as awe-inspiring, in a different way.

Follow the Canon Brook Trail, on the right (west) side of ME 3, for 1.1 miles south and west around the base of Dorr and beyond the junction with the Dorr South Ridge Trail. The A. Murray Young trailhead is on the right (north) side of the intersection with the Canon Brook Trail.

Hard to get to because of the 1.1 miles required on the Canon Brook Trail, the A. Murray Young Path gives you the chance of making it most of the way up Dorr without crowds of other hikers. But you'll most likely have plenty of company once you reach the summit, especially during summer.

The trail heads north from the Canon Brook Trail, crossing from one side of the brook that drains from the mountains to the other. At one such crossing near the start, a plaque reads, "In Memory of Andrew Murray Young, who loved this island where God has given of his beauty with a lavish hand."

Occasionally the trail goes along flat stones laid in garden-path style and up stone steps. Ascending steadily, it passes some nice cascades two-thirds of the way up. After

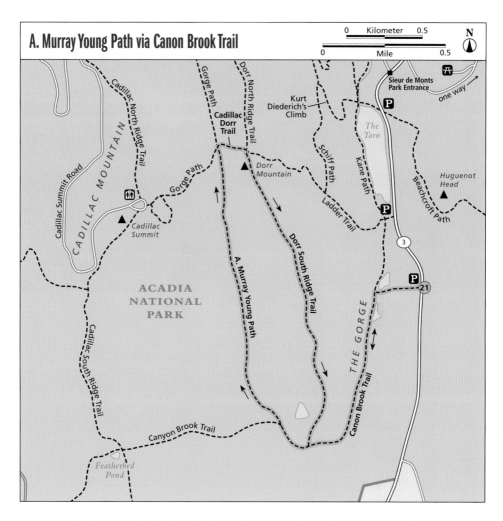

0   Kilometer   0.5   N

0   Mile   0.5

Sieur de Monts Park Entrance

Cadillac North Ridge Trail

Cadillac Summit Road

Gorge Path

Dorr North Ridge Trail

Cadillac Dorr Trail

Kurt Diederich's Climb

Schiff Path

Kane Path

The Tarn

Huguenot Head ▲

Beachcroft Path

one way

CADILLAC MOUNTAIN

▲ Dorr Mountain

Gorge Path

Ladder Trail

▲ **Cadillac Summit**

A. Murray Young Path

Dorr South Ridge Trail

3

ACADIA NATIONAL PARK

THE GORGE

21

Canon Brook Trail

Cadillac South Ridge Trail

Canyon Brook Trail

Featherbed Pond

you reach the top of the brook, the trail gets rocky and steep, staying that way for the last 0.25 mile or so. You're basically climbing up a rockslide between Cadillac and Dorr. There are nice views behind you, south to the Gulf of Maine.

At 2.2 miles (1.1 miles from its trailhead), the A. Murray Young Path officially ends at the top of the gorge, at a junction with Gorge Path, which turns left (west) here, up Cadillac. Continue straight (south) less than 50 feet along the Gorge Path, then turn right (east) to make the short but steep climb up Dorr. It used to be a four-way intersection at the top of the gorge, with the spur to Cadillac directly across from the spur to Dorr. But a major 2014 trail rehabilitation project rerouted the junction, slightly staggering where the mountaintop spurs came in, to bring it back to its historic offset alignment.

At 2.4 miles reach Dorr's ridge and the intersection with Dorr South and North Ridge Trails and Schiff Path. Turn right (south) onto Dorr South Ridge Trail.

The sound of cascades and birdsong may be the only thing breaking the silence along the A. Murray Young Path.

Reach 1,270-foot Dorr Mountain, with its 360-degree views, at 2.5 miles. Continue straight (south) down the open Dorr South Ridge Trail until it dead-ends at the Canon Brook Trail at 3.8 miles. Turn left (east) onto the Canon Brook Trail.

At 4.5 miles, reach a junction with Kane Path. Bear right (east) to stay on the Canon Brook Trail to return to the ME 3 pullout parking area at 4.8 miles.

Miles and Directions

0.0   Start at the Canon Brook trailhead, on the right (west) side of ME 3 south of the Tarn. Head west toward the base of Dorr.

0.3   Reach a junction with the Kane Path. Turn left (south) and continue following Canon Brook Trail around the ridge of Dorr.

1.0   Reach a junction with Dorr South Ridge Trail coming in on the right (north). Stay straight (west).

1.1   Arrive at the A. Murray Young Path trailhead and turn right onto the path.

2.2   Reach a junction with Gorge Path, which turns left (west) here up Cadillac, and also continues straight (south). Follow the Gorge Path straight for less than 50 feet to a spur to Dorr Mountain. Turn right (east) on the spur to head steeply up Dorr.

2.4   Attain the ridge of Dorr and the intersection with Dorr South and North Ridge Trails and Schiff Path. Turn right (south) onto Dorr South Ridge Trail.

2.5   Summit Dorr Mountain. Continue straight on Dorr South Ridge Trail.

3.8   The Dorr South Ridge Trail dead-ends at the Canon Brook Trail. Turn left (east) onto the Canon Brook Trail to loop back.

4.5   At the junction with Kane Path, bear right (east) to stay on the Canon Brook Trail.

4.8   Arrive back at the Canon Brook trailhead.

22 Kebo Mountain Loop via Hemlock and Stratheden Paths

With the recent opening of the Kebo Brook Trail providing valuable connections, it's now possible to loop up 407-foot Kebo Mountain and make use of a couple of the lesser used routes from Sieur de Monts, of Hemlock and Stratheden Paths. You may see remnants of trees that burned in the 1947 fire, limited but close-up views of the Porcupine Islands, or even a barred owl.

Distance: 2.7-mile lollipop
Hiking time: About 2 to 2.5 hours
Difficulty: Moderate
Trail surface: Forest floor, rock ledges
Best season: Spring through fall
Other trail users: Hikers climbing Dorr, dog walkers, joggers and area residents

Canine compatibility: Leashed dogs permitted on trail (but not in the Wild Gardens of Acadia, Nature Center, or Abbe Museum)
Map: USGS Acadia National Park and Vicinity
Special considerations: Seasonal restrooms are available at the Sieur de Monts parking area

Finding the trailhead: From downtown Bar Harbor head south on ME 3 for about 2 miles and turn right (northwest) into the park's Sieur de Monts entrance, then a quick left (west) into the Sieur de Monts parking area. Walk away from the restrooms toward the far (northwestern) end of the parking lot and pick up the Hemlock Path at what looks like a gravel road. The Island Explorer's Sand Beach and Loop Road lines stop at Sieur de Monts. GPS: N44 21.46' / W68 12.27'

The Hike

This circuit takes you from Sieur de Monts to the low summit of Kebo Mountain, incorporating trails that date back a century as well as the newly opened Kebo Brook Trail. Although the views are limited on Kebo, you may get a peek of a Porcupine Island through the trees, or ripening wild Maine blueberries along the trail.

Both the Hemlock and Stratheden Paths had their start as part of a century-old network connecting downtown Bar Harbor to what was yet to become Acadia National Park. With the reopening of the historic Great Meadow Loop, the new Kebo Brook Trail, and the Island Explorer bus in season, it's even possible to access this circuit from Bar Harbor, without ever needing to drive.

Begin at the far (northwest) end of the Sieur de Monts parking area by picking up the Hemlock Path, an old gravel road. Pass Jesup Path and its boardwalk at 0.1 mile, and stay straight on Hemlock until you reach a junction with the Stratheden Path at 0.4 mile. Turn left onto what is now called the Hemlock Trail because of its rougher nature. At 0.6 mile, turn right onto the Kebo Mountain Trail.

Hemlock Path makes for a pleasant woods walk.

A short scramble takes you to a rocky knob. Walk along the ridge to the Kebo summit at 1.2 miles. Peer between the trees and you may get views west to the north ridge of Cadillac, and northeast to Bald Porcupine Island.

Descend to the one-way Park Loop Road at 1.5 miles and cross over—be careful; watch for traffic!—to connect with the Kebo Brook Trail. Turn right onto the Kebo Brook Trail, and at 1.6 miles turn right to cross back over the Park Loop Road and hook up with Stratheden Path, a well-graded woods walk dating back to the 1890s.

Stratheden originally began at the Kebo Valley Golf Club, but that section has been lost with the passage of time. The path was reopened by the National Park Service in the 1990s after being closed for four decades.

The trail's unusual name stems from strath, a Scottish Gaelic word for a low-lying grassland along a river valley, and Eden, the former name for Bar Harbor. Considering that the original trail skirted the marshy Great Meadow on its way from Bar Harbor to Sieur de Monts, Stratheden is a fitting moniker. There's even a stone inscribed with the name of the path still in the woods.

Take Stratheden until it ends at the junction with Hemlock Path, at 2.3 miles. Stay straight on Hemlock Path and return to the Sieur de Monts parking area at 2.7 miles.

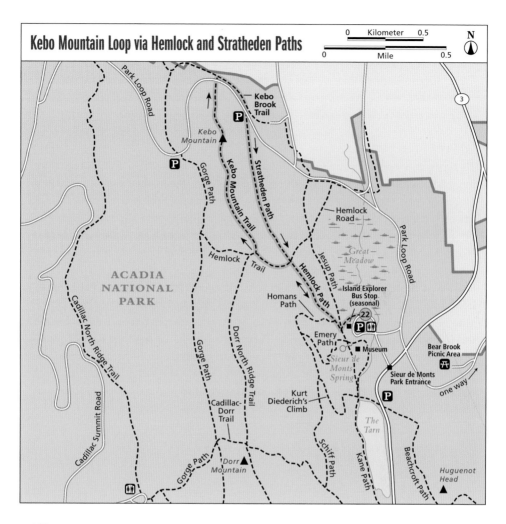

Kebo Mountain Loop via Hemlock and Stratheden Paths

Miles and Directions

0.0 Start at the Hemlock Path trailhead at a gravel road, on far (northwestern) corner of the Sieur de Monts parking area.

0.1 Reach a junction with Jesup Path. Go straight (northwest) to follow Hemlock Path.

0.4 Reach a junction with Stratheden Path. Turn left (west) on a rougher section that's now called Hemlock Trail.

0.6 Reach a junction with Dorr Mountain North Ridge Trail coming in on the left, and Kebo Mountain Trail on the right. Turn right (north) onto Kebo Mountain Trail.

1.2 Arrive at Kebo Mountain summit. Continue straight (north) to descend.

1.5 Arrive at Park Loop Road. Cross road to pick up Kebo Brook Trail. Turn right (east) on Kebo Brook Trail.

1.6 Reach junction with Stratheden Path across Park Loop Road. Turn right (south), cross road and pick up Stratheden.

2.3 Arrive at junction with Hemlock Path. Go straight (southeast) on Hemlock Path.

2.6 Reach a junction with Jesup Path. Stay straight (southeast) to return to Sieur de Monts parking area.

2.7 Arrive back at the Hemlock Path trailhead.

Options

To access this circuit by walking from Bar Harbor, head west on Park Street from the town ball fields. Turn left (south) onto Glen Mary Road, then right (west) onto Norris Avenue, then left (south) onto Spring Street. Follow Spring Street for 0.2 mile, cross over Cromwell Harbor Road and turn right (west) onto the Great Meadow Loop. Follow the Great Meadow Loop for 0.3 mile as it parallels Cromwell Harbor Road, then turn left (south) on the trail as it parallels Kebo Street.

At the junction with the Kebo Brook Trail in 0.2 mile, turn right (west) and follow that well-graded route for 0.2 mile, to the junction with Stratheden Path, on the left (south) across the Park Loop Road. Cross the road and follow Stratheden for 0.7 mile until it ends at a junction. Turn right (west) onto the Hemlock Trail and reach the Kebo Mountain Trail in 0.2 mile. Turn right (north) to head up Kebo Mountain, reaching the summit in 0.6 mile. Continue straight (north) to descend to the Park Loop Road in 0.3 mile. Cross the road to pick up the Kebo Brook Trail. Turn right (east) on Kebo Brook Trail and follow it straight for 0.3 mile back to the Great Meadow Loop. From there, retrace your steps back to Bar Harbor.

23 Great Meadow Loop and Jesup Path to Sieur de Monts

This is a woods, wetlands, and field loop hike. It takes you by Sieur de Monts Spring and the newly rehabilitated Spring Pool, the Wild Gardens of Acadia, the Nature Center, and the Abbe Museum. You'll hear birdsong and get open views of Huguenot Head and Champlain and Dorr Mountains along Great Meadow. And you can re-create the historic experience of walking between Bar Harbor and the park, like the residents and visitors of yore.

Distance: 4.2 miles out and back, or 2.1 miles one-way if you take the Island Explorer back to Bar Harbor Village Green
Hiking time: About 2 to 3 hours
Difficulty: Easy
Trail surface: Forest floor, graded gravel path, wooden boardwalk and bridges
Best season: Spring through fall, particularly early morning or late afternoon in summer to avoid the crowds

Other trail users: Dog walkers, joggers, area residents
Canine compatibility: Leashed dogs permitted on trail (but not in the Wild Gardens of Acadia, Nature Center, or Abbe Museum)
Map: USGS Acadia National Park and Vicinity
Special considerations: Graded gravel and wooden boardwalk surfaces make part of the walk wheelchair and baby-stroller accessible. Seasonal restrooms are at the ball fields and Sieur de Monts parking area.

Finding the trailhead: From downtown Bar Harbor head south on ME 3 for about half a mile, turn right (west) onto Park Street, and park by the ball fields. Walk west on Park Street to begin the hike. The closest Island Explorer stop is Bar Harbor Village Green. During peak season you can reduce the hiking distance by half, by taking the Island Explorer at Sieur de Monts on the return. GPS: N44 22.58' / W68 12.11'

The Hike

This walk from Bar Harbor to Sieur de Monts, the historic heart of Acadia, may very well be one of the best hikes to mark Acadia's Centennial.

The Great Meadow Loop, partly on park land and partly on private property, is just one of the village connector trails re-created as part of the $13 million Acadia Trails Forever initiative, a joint effort of the Friends of Acadia and the National Park Service.

The idea: to provide options for walking between town and the mountains, ponds, and sea, as was the case during the days of the nineteenth- and early-twentieth-century rusticators, or artists, tourists, and summer residents, who would think nothing of walking 5, 10, or 15 miles in a day.

First created nearly one hundred years ago by George B. Dorr and others as part of a garden path that connected to downtown Bar Harbor, Jesup Path connects the

Apple blossoms frame a view of Champlain from Jesup Path.

Great Meadow Loop to Sieur de Monts. And Sieur de Monts is where Acadia all began in 1916 as a national monument, with Dorr as its first superintendent.

The hike described here begins by the Bar Harbor ball fields and could just as easily be done in reverse starting at the easy-to-reach Sieur de Monts parking area. But as part of Centennial efforts, park officials encourage visitors to walk south from Bar Harbor as the rusticators did. From the ball fields, walk west on Park Street, turn left (south) on Ledgelawn Avenue and follow it for 0.4 mile as it crosses over Cromwell Harbor Road by the former public works yard and becomes Great Meadow Drive. Turn right at a wooden bridge on the right (west) and turn quickly left (south) onto the Great Meadow Loop as it circles around Kebo Valley Golf Course. Follow the trail south for 0.4 mile as it meanders through the woods and crosses Ledgelawn Avenue a couple of times. As it nears the Park Loop Road, the trail bears right (west) to parallel the Park Loop Road for 0.3 mile.

Just before the Great Meadow Loop reaches a junction with Kebo Street and turns away from the Park Loop Road, cross to the left (south) over the one-way Park Loop Road (watch for traffic on the right) to pick up Jesup Path. This well-graded path takes you by the Great Meadow, across Hemlock Path a couple of times, on the way to Sieur de Monts.

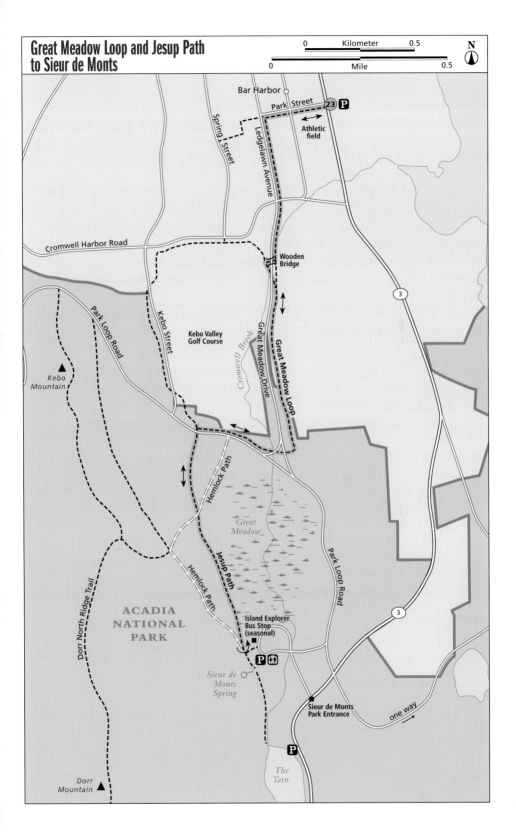

Great Meadow Loop and Jesup Path to Sieur de Monts

Kilometer

0   0.5

0   Mile   0.5

N

Bar Harbor

Park Street

23 P

Athletic field

Spring Street

Ledgelawn Avenue

Cromwell Harbor Road

Wooden Bridge

Kebo Street

Kebo Valley Golf Course

Cromwell Brook

Great Meadow Drive

Great Meadow Loop

3

Park Loop Road

Kebo Mountain

Hemlock Path

Jesup Path

Great Meadow

Park Loop Road

3

Dorr North Ridge Trail

Hemlock Path

ACADIA NATIONAL PARK

Island Explorer Bus Stop (seasonal)

P

Sieur de Monts Spring

Sieur de Monts Park Entrance

one way

Dorr Mountain ▲

P

The Tarn

You'll find plenty of birds and flowering plants along the marshy "meadow," especially in spring. As you head south on Jesup Path, look across the Great Meadow toward the Sieur de Monts area for open views of Huguenot Head and Champlain Mountain to the east (left) and Dorr Mountain to the west (right).

At the end of Jesup Path's long boardwalk, cross over Hemlock Path and head straight toward Sieur de Monts. Here you will find a rock inscribed with the words "Sweet Waters of Acadia" near the Sieur de Monts Spring House built by Dorr in 1909. You'll also find a Dorr memorial plaque.

Over the last several years, with the Centennial in mind, officials have worked toward rehabilitating the Spring Pool to Dorr's original landscaped vision. They've removed invasive plants, reset large stones, and replaced the spring-fed pool's gravel to better support spawning native brook trout.

The Spring Pool is a fitting place to reflect on Acadia's Centennial and Dorr, all the park has meant for generations past, and what it can mean for generations to come.

Return the way you came, for a 4.2-mile round-trip, or catch the Island Explorer in season to your next destination.

Miles and Directions

0.0 Start at Park Street and head west, with the Bar Harbor ball fields on your left.

0.2 Turn left onto Ledgelawn Avenue.

0.3 Cross over Cromwell Harbor Road and stay straight as Ledgelawn becomes Great Meadow Drive.

0.6 Turn right (west) across a wooden bridge and quickly left (south) to follow Great Meadow Loop as it circles Kebo Valley Golf Course and crosses Great Meadow Drive a couple of times on its way toward the Park Loop Road.

1.0 Follow Great Meadow Loop right (west) as it parallels the Park Loop Road.

1.3 Just before the Great Meadow Loop reaches the junction with Kebo Street, cross left (south) over the one-way Park Loop Road (watch for traffic on the right) to pick up Jesup Path on the other side. Head straight (south) on Jesup Path.

1.6 Cross over Hemlock Path.

2.0 At the end of the long boardwalk, cross over Hemlock Path again and continue straight (southeast) on Jesup Path.

2.1 Reach Sieur de Monts. Instead of retracing your steps, you can take the Island Explorer bus In season on the return, or explore other hiking options.

4.2 Arrive back at the trailhead.

Cadillac Mountain Area

24 Cadillac North Ridge Trail

The open north ridge of Cadillac Mountain provides expansive views of Frenchman Bay, Bar Harbor, and the Porcupine Islands. In season, naturalists and volunteers help spot migrating raptors at perhaps the prettiest hawk–watching site in North America.

Distance: 4.4 miles out and back
Hiking time: About 3 to 4 hours
Difficulty: Moderate
Trail surface: Granite steps, forest floor, rock ledges
Best season: Spring through fall, particularly early morning or late afternoon in summer to avoid the crowds atop Cadillac

Other trail users: Participants in annual Hawk-Watch, mid-August through mid-October
Canine compatibility: Leashed dogs permitted
Map: USGS Acadia National Park and Vicinity
Special considerations: No facilities at the trailhead; seasonal gift shop and restrooms at the summit. A couple sections of the trail come close to Cadillac Mountain Road.

Finding the trailhead: From the park's visitor center, drive south on the Park Loop Road for about 3 miles and turn left (east) at the sign for Sand Beach. Follow the one-way Park Loop Road for 0.3 mile. The trailhead is on the right (south) side of the loop road. Limited parking is available along the side of the Park Loop Road. The Island Explorer's Loop Road line stops at the trailhead, but you can't take the bus down from Cadillac, since it doesn't go up the summit road. GPS: N44 22.42' / W68 13.46'

The Hike

Cadillac North Ridge Trail follows old Native American footpaths and nears the route of a former buckboard road up spectacular 1,530-foot Cadillac Mountain, the highest point on the Atlantic coast.

Like many of the ridge trails in Acadia, this one traverses exposed granite ledges much of the way, offering grand scenery. Here the views include Bar Harbor, Frenchman Bay, Schoodic Peninsula, and a series of distinctive rocky islands, beginning with Bar Island and extending into the bay with the Porcupines.

This is one of the oldest trails on Mount Desert Island. Recreational hikers ascended the mountain as early as the 1850s, when there was a survey station on the peak. In the late 1800s, a large hotel graced the summit. The trail was rerouted in the 1930s to accommodate the Cadillac Mountain Road.

If you hike during summer, be prepared for crowds at the summit and the sound and smell of cars, buses, and RVs on the way up. The trail comes close to the auto road in two places.

Late summer goldenrod frames the panorama from the Cadillac North Ridge Trail.

The blue-blazed trail begins off the Park Loop Road with a series of four stone steps. Immediately there are views of Bar Harbor and the islands to the left and behind you, or north and northeast. At 0.1 mile the trail turns sharply right, dipping down into a cool grove of birches and evergreens.

Rising moderately, the southbound trail offers views of the low-lying Kebo Mountain to the left (east), Eagle Lake to the southwest, and Cadillac Mountain to the south–southeast. The trail levels off briefly, then begins rising again, offering clear views of Cadillac and the neighboring 1,270-foot Dorr Mountain.

At 0.6 mile the trail comes close to the summit road, paralleling it through the woods. At 1.1 miles it begins climbing steeply through a birch forest up a series of more than one hundred stone steps.

You clear tree line at 1.2 miles. Even though the trail has already offered glimpses of Bar Harbor and Frenchman Bay, the view here is even more breathtaking. At 1.3 miles the trail comes within view of the summit road, at a point where it looks like a Stonehenge of sorts with its border of huge granite rocks. This is a tricky spot. Do not follow a well-worn footpath to the road. Instead stay to the left, away from the road, and follow the blue blazes.

The trail soon turns sharply left near a scenic road turnout and leaves the road behind. For the final assault up the pink granite of Cadillac Mountain, follow the Bates-style cairns that mark the trail.

At 2.2 miles reach the summit parking area and the panoramas of Cadillac, including not only Frenchman Bay and Bar Harbor but also Dorr Mountain and the Gulf of Maine to the east and the Beehive and Otter Cliff to the southeast.

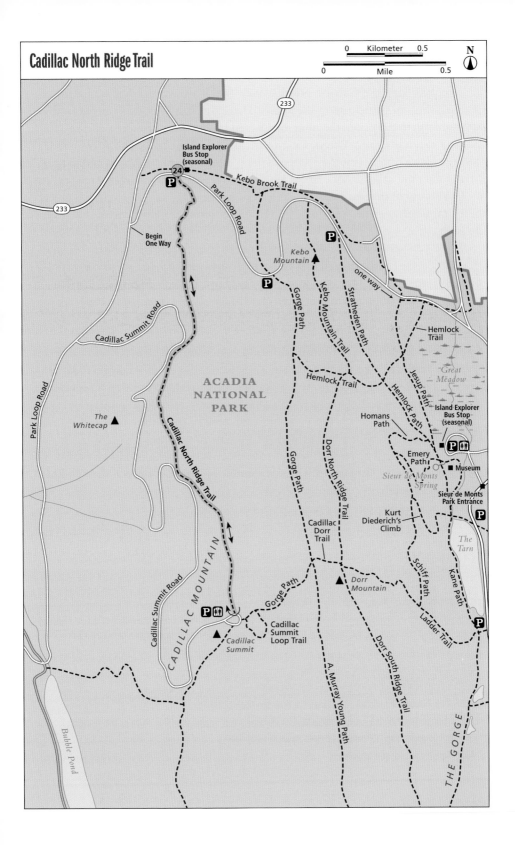

Cadillac North Ridge Trail

0 Kilometer 0.5

0 Mile 0.5

N

233

Island Explorer
Bus Stop
(seasonal)

24

P

Kebo Brook Trail

Park Loop Road

Begin
One Way

Kebo
Mountain

P

one way

Cadillac Summit Road

P

Gorge Path

Kebo Mountain Trail

Stratheden Path

Hemlock
Trail

Great
Meadow

ACADIA
NATIONAL
PARK

Hemlock Trail

Jesup Path

The
Whitecap

Cadillac North Ridge Trail

Park Loop Road

Gorge Path

Dorr North Ridge Trail

Hemlock Path

Homans
Path

Island Explorer
Bus Stop
(seasonal)

P

Emery
Path

Museum

Sieur de Monts
Spring

Sieur de Monts
Park Entrance

P

Cadillac
Dorr Trail

Kurt
Diederich's
Climb

The
Tarn

P

C A D I L L A C   M O U N T A I N

Dorr
Mountain

Schiff Path

Kane Path

P

Gorge Path

Cadillac Summit Road

P

Cadillac
Summit

Cadillac
Summit Loop Trail

Gorge Path

A. Murray Young Path

Dorr South Ridge Trail

Ladder Trail

P

Bubble Pond

T H E   G O R G E

You can take the easy 0.3-mile Cadillac Summit Loop Trail that leads off the east end of the parking area and learn about the geology of Mount Desert Island.

If you're hiking the Cadillac North Ridge Trail between mid-August and mid-October, you can participate in the annual HawkWatch, a joint effort between the park's interpretive division, the nonprofit Schoodic Institute's bird ecology program and the Friends of Acadia. The viewing area is just before the trail ends at the summit. During a HawkWatch session we dropped in on, Tony Linforth, an Acadia park ranger there at the time, called it "one of the best bird-watching spots in North America."

The beauty of the place is undeniable. And unlike many other such watch posts, there's no need to crane your neck. From this location you mostly look down on the birds.

While you stare out over the vast expanse of Frenchman Bay, kestrels—a type of small falcon—sharp-shinned hawks, northern harriers, ospreys, and other predator birds come soaring from the north and east down the coastline, using drafts and thermals to gain altitude. You don't even need binoculars. Using landmarks such as Ironbound Island, the four Porcupines—Sheep, Burnt, Long, and Bald—Egg Rock, Turtle Island, or Schoodic Peninsula, you can pinpoint the birds and alert others to confirm your finds. Interpretive naturalists and volunteers will identify them for you.

There might be twenty birds over the bay at one time, but volunteers like Ed Hawkes, a master bird carver from Bar Harbor, are careful to count each bird only once. They tally about 2,600 migrating raptors each year, recording them on a chart. Sharp-shinned hawks are the most common, followed by the pointy-winged kestrels, which are headed to winter homes, perhaps a utility pole in Texas.

When we stopped by one early August afternoon, a sharp-shinned hawk provided us with quite a thrill, flapping its wings in four or five quick bursts and then gliding right over our heads.

Angi King Johnston, an interpretive naturalist and former Acadia park ranger who was keeping track of the raptors when we stopped by in 2014, said HawkWatch shows the beauty of citizens taking part in a science project. "It's the brilliance of HawkWatch," she said, standing over Frenchman Bay one day. "I could not do my job without all the extra help." Return the way you came.

Miles and Directions

0.0 Start at the Cadillac North Ridge trailhead, on the right (south) side of the one-way Park Loop Road.

0.6 Trail nears the Cadillac Summit Road.

1.1 Climb steeply up a long series of stone steps.

1.3 Trail nears the summit road again; follow the trail to the left.

2.2 Reach the Cadillac summit. (**Option:** Walk along the northeastern portion of the parking lot to reach the 0.3-mile Cadillac Summit Loop Trail.)

4.4 Arrive back at the trailhead.

25 Cadillac Summit Loop Trail

Located at the top of Acadia's highest mountain, this short and easy trail offers maybe the best views in the park and plaques that identify more than forty islands, peaks, and other key points off its slopes. On a sunny day this loop is the best place for any hiker to get some bearings before exploring the rest of Acadia. The trail is often busy during peak summer months, since cars and buses can drive up the summit road.

Distance: 0.3-mile loop
Hiking time: About 30 minutes
Difficulty: Easy
Trail surface: Paved walkway
Best season: Spring through fall, particularly early morning or late afternoon in summer to avoid the crowds
Other trail users: Hikers coming from Gorge Path or Cadillac North Ridge or Cadillac South

Ridge Trail, visitors with wheelchairs or baby strollers, birders
Canine compatibility: Leashed dogs permitted
Map: USGS Acadia National Park and Vicinity
Special considerations: Seasonal restrooms and gift shop at the summit. The walkway is designed to be partially accessible for visitors with wheelchairs or baby strollers. The 3.5-mile paved auto road to the summit is a winding and narrow route.

Finding the trailhead: From the park visitor center, drive south on the Park Loop Road for about 3.5 miles, and turn left (east) at the sign for Cadillac Mountain. Ascend the winding summit road to the top. The paved walkway begins off the eastern side of the parking lot, across from the summit gift shop. The Island Explorer bus does not go up Cadillac, but the Loop Road line has a Cadillac North Ridge stop, where the 2.2-mile moderately difficult Cadillac North Ridge Trail takes you to the top and a connection with the Cadillac Summit Loop Trail. GPS: N44 21.09' / W68 13.28'

The Hike

You gain a new appreciation for 1,530-foot-high Cadillac Mountain on this trail, with plaques describing the history and features of Mount Desert Island and the spectacular views from Acadia's highest summit.

One display explains the geological essence of Acadia—the pink granite with its three main minerals. Another commemorates Stephen Tyng Mather, a wealthy entrepreneur, leading advocate for creation of the National Park Service in 1916, and its first director. Yet others, newly designed and put on display in 2015, describe everything from the night sky over Acadia to those who helped found the park a century ago, from George B. Dorr to Charles Eliot.

A top feature of this hike is a circular viewing area with two plaques that pinpoint about forty highlights of the sweeping views, allowing anyone to find spots such as the Turtle Island, Frenchman Bay, Schoodic Peninsula, Porcupine Islands, Seawall, Baker Island, and the Gulf of Maine.

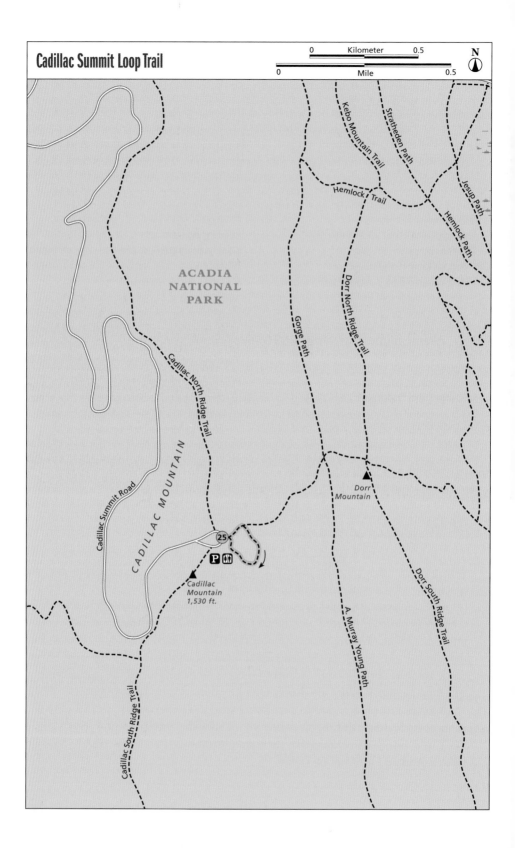

0   Kilometer   0.5

0   Mile   0.5

N

Kebo Mountain Trail

Stratheden Path

Jesup Path

Hemlock Trail

Hemlock Path

ACADIA
NATIONAL
PARK

Gorge Path

Dorr North Ridge Trail

Cadillac North Ridge Trail

Cadillac Summit Road

CADILLAC MOUNTAIN

Dorr
Mountain

Dorr South Ridge Trail

25

P

Cadillac
Mountain
1,530 ft.

A. Murray Young Path

Cadillac South Ridge Trail

Rainbow beyond Cadillac.

Aside from the vistas described on the plaques, you may also see bald eagles and turkey vultures soaring above Cadillac, especially during the annual HawkWatch late August through mid-October, when migrating raptors like kestrels, peregrine falcons, and sharp-shinned hawks can be spotted.

You may also see three-toothed cinquefoil, low-bush blueberries, and other greenery on the summit, as described in one of the new plaques, entitled "Not so Barren." A tiny white flower known as mountain sandwort, the pink blooms of rhodora, and even a couple of small birch trees can also be found along the walkway, proof of the success of restoration efforts over the past decade. Wooden barricades and signs reminding hikers to stay on the trail and solid rock are part of the continued revegetation program.

The peak of Cadillac, as marked by the US Geological Survey, is actually off the Cadillac South Ridge Trail, near an antenna behind the gift shop, but the best views are from the loop trail.

There are two access points to the paved summit loop trail off the eastern edge of the parking area, marked by signs on wood posts. The access point on the left (northeast), near the handicapped parking spots, is also the start of a ramp for visitors with wheelchairs and baby strollers to reach the accessible circular viewing area.

The trail, originally built by the Civilian Conservation Corps, the Depression-era public work relief program, is tinged to match the pink Cadillac granite and features several sets of granite boulders for steps. Even though the trail is easy, watch your footing; people have gotten injured along the walkway, which can be uneven in spots.

Because of its grand vistas and easy access, the trail can get very crowded in summer. Early and late in the day are best. But there can be small crowds at sunrise, especially at the times of year when the sun's rays first hit the United States atop Cadillac, the eastern seaboard's highest mountain. And there can even be a motor brigade heading up for the sunset, as we found one afternoon as dusk approached.

Miles and Directions

0.0 Start at the Cadillac Summit Loop trailhead, with two access points located at the eastern edge of the parking area, across from the summit shop. The left (northeastern) trail entrance connects to a ramp that allows wheelchair and baby stroller access to a circular viewing area.

0.3 Complete the loop at the trailhead.

26 Gorge Path

Rising from the wet and wooded depths of the ravine between Cadillac and Dorr Mountains to the spectacular views of the highest peak in Acadia, Gorge Path provides the starkest contrast between dark forest and open summit of all the trails up Cadillac. If you hike during the park's busy season, you couldn't find more of a difference between the tranquility of lower Gorge Path and the hubbub atop Cadillac. A major restoration effort in 2014 has brought the path back to its former glory, with some of the finest stonework anywhere in the Acadia trail system.

Distance: 3.8 miles out and back
Hiking time: About 4 to 5 hours
Difficulty: Strenuous
Trail surface: Granite steps, forest floor, rock ledges, log boardwalk
Best season: Spring through fall, particularly early morning or late afternoon in summer to avoid the crowds atop Cadillac

Other trail users: Hikers climbing Dorr
Canine compatibility: Leashed dogs permitted but not recommended on upper Gorge Path to the top of Cadillac
Map: USGS Acadia National Park and Vicinity
Special considerations: No facilities at the trailhead; seasonal gift shop and restrooms at the summit

Finding the trailhead: From the park's visitor center, drive south on the Park Loop Road for about 3 miles, and turn left (east) at the sign for Sand Beach. Follow the one-way Park Loop Road for 0.8 mile. The trailhead is on the right (south), just after the road crosses a stone bridge, with stone steps leading down below the bridge. Limited parking is available along the right (south) side of the Park Loop Road. The closest Island Explorer stop is Cadillac North Ridge on the Loop Road line, where you can take the new Kebo Brook Trail 0.4 mile east, then south 0.4 mile on the northernmost section of the Gorge Path, to the trailhead at the Park Loop Road. You can also ask the bus driver to let you off at the Gorge Path trailhead on the Park Loop Road, if it is safe to do so. GPS: N44 22.21' / W68 13.18'

The Hike

First described in the 1870s as a path that allows "youth and enthusiasm . . . to find scope for their ambition," Gorge Path is still a challenge for the most ambitious hiker today.

It's also an engineering marvel and an aesthetic wonder, especially after a 2014 rehabilitation, funded in part by an $800,000 federal grant that allowed for the largest Acadia trail crew since the Civilian Conservation Corps, and the Acadia Trails Forever endowment, consisting of $4 million in park user fees and appropriations and $9 million in donations from the nonprofit Friends of Acadia.

A new village connector, the Kebo Brook Trail, even allows people to re-create the Bar Harbor-to-Cadillac forays of yore via Gorge Path, or to get off the Island Explorer at the Cadillac North Ridge stop and access Gorge Path without having to walk the Park Loop Road.

The recently rehabilitated Gorge Path takes you up the gap between Cadillac and Dorr Mountains.

In recent years, substantial erosion and collapsing stonework had made the Gorge Path a difficult hike, with loose gravel, exposed roots and crooked steps. The 2014 rehabilitation has returned the lower end of the path to its historic garden-like approach, and the steep climb to Cadillac to a less eroded aspect.

A total of 118 feet of causeway, 3 stone drains, 590 square feet of retaining wall, 440 stepping stones and 1,200 feet of stone paving were rehabilitated or built along the Gorge Path, according to Gary Stellpflug, Acadia trails foreman.

The hike begins by descending from the Park Loop Road along stone steps, a recently reconfigured section that follows the original 1870s route of the Gorge Path. Admire the wooden balustrade, the stone bridge and the stepping stones, a harbinger of more gorgeous path to come.

The northernmost section of Gorge Path that leads to the Kebo Brook Trail goes off to the right (north), under the bridge. Head straight ahead up the stone steps and follow the path as it curves south from the Park Loop Road.

Follow blue blazes and cairns, walk along log bridges, and hop across brook beds on newly relaid stepping stones.

Pass a junction at 0.4 mile with the Hemlock Trail, which heads to the left (east) toward Kebo Mountain Trail, Dorr North Ridge Trail, and the Sieur de Monts Spring area. We saw a pileated woodpecker here once.

As the path steepens, roughly paralleling the brook that runs down the ravine, the gorge between Cadillac and Dorr narrows and the brook forms small waterfalls and cascades.

At one of these cascades a plaque set into a cliff on the Cadillac Mountain side of the gorge reads: "In loving memory of Lilian Endicott Francklyn, 1891–1928. This trail is endowed by her friends." The plaque, which had become loose and was removed in fall 2012, was lovingly cleaned and given a fresh coat of wax by the park staff, and reinstalled in 2014. Francklyn, who died in her eighth month of pregnancy, was a descendant of William H. Seward, secretary of state under President Abraham Lincoln. Gorge Path is one of a number of memorial trails sprinkled throughout Acadia, a reminder of the history that runs long and deep here. The path continues, crossing the brook a few more times, and climbs steeply up a long series of stone steps until it rises above the brook. Finally leveling off at a birch grove at the top of the gorge, the path reaches a junction with a spur to Dorr Mountain that heads left (east) at 1.5 miles.

It used to be a four-way intersection at the top of the gorge, with the spur to Cadillac directly across from the spur to Dorr. But the 2014 Gorge Path rehabilitation rerouted the junction, slightly staggering where the mountaintop spurs came in, to bring it back to its historic offset alignment.

Stay straight (south) on Gorge Path and in less than 50 feet, turn right (west) and climb precipitously up Cadillac Mountain, ending at the summit at 1.9 miles.

Return the way you came.

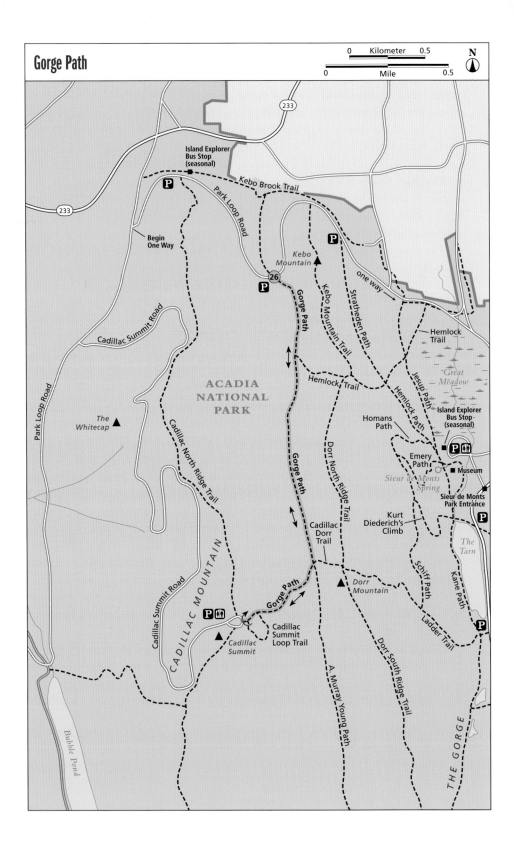

Gorge Path

0   Kilometer   0.5

0   Mile   0.5

N

233

233

Island Explorer
Bus Stop
(seasonal)

Kebo Brook Trail

P

Begin
One Way

Park Loop Road

Kebo
Mountain

one way

26

P

Cadillac Summit Road

Gorge Path

Kebo Mountain Trail

Stratheden Path

Hemlock
Trail

ACADIA
NATIONAL
PARK

Park Loop Road

The
Whitecap

Cadillac North Ridge Trail

Hemlock Trail

Great
Meadow

Jesup Path

Island Explorer
Bus Stop
(seasonal)

Homans
Path

Hemlock Path

P

Gorge Path

Dorr North Ridge Trail

Emery
Path

Museum

Sieur de Monts
Spring

Sieur de Monts
Park Entrance

Cadillac
Dorr
Trail

Kurt
Diederich's
Climb

P

The
Tarn

CADILLAC MOUNTAIN

Cadillac Summit Road

P

Gorge Path

Dorr
Mountain

Schiff Path

Kane Path

Cadillac
Summit
Loop Trail

Cadillac
Summit

Ladder Trail

P

Bubble Pond

A Murray Young Path

Dorr South Ridge Trail

THE GORGE

Miles and Directions

0.0 Start at the Gorge Path trailhead, on the right (south) side of the one-way Park Loop Road, just after the road crosses a stone bridge.

0.4 Pass the junction with the Hemlock Trail, coming in from the left (east).

1.5 Reach a spur to Dorr Mountain on the left (east). Stay straight (south) and reach a junction with the A. Murray Young Path, which goes down the other side of the gorge, in less than 50 feet. Turn right (west) and follow Gorge Path to the top of Cadillac.

1.9 Summit Cadillac, and reach the junction with the Cadillac Summit Loop Trail, a 0.3-mile paved route with interpretive plaques describing scenery and history.

3.8 Arrive back at the trailhead.

27 Cadillac South Ridge Trail and Eagles Crag Loop

One of the longest trails in Acadia, this hike provides fine views along Cadillac's open south ridge, the chance to see raptors soar at Eagles Crag, and a pleasant place to rest on benches along a mountain pond called the Featherbed. First described in an 1870s guidebook, the Cadillac South Ridge Trail has long been an important part of the extensive trail network on Mount Desert Island.

Distance: 7.0 miles out and back
Hiking time: About 4 to 5 hours
Difficulty: Moderate
Trail surface: Granite steps, wooden bridges, forest floor, rock ledges
Best season: Spring through fall, particularly early morning or late afternoon in summer to avoid the crowds atop Cadillac

Other trail users: Hikers on Canon Brook or Cadillac West Face Trail; motorists who park at the Blue Hill Overlook and get out to explore
Canine compatibility: Leashed dogs permitted
Map: USGS Acadia National Park and Vicinity
Special considerations: No facilities at the trailhead; seasonal gift shop and restrooms at the summit

Finding the trailhead: From downtown Bar Harbor, head south 5 miles on ME 3 toward Seal Harbor. The trailhead is on the right, after the Blackwoods Campground entrance. Park at a gravel pullout on the right (north) side of ME 3. The Island Explorer's Sand Beach line stops at Blackwoods Campground. GPS: N44 18.46' / W68 12.52'

The Hike

Like the Cadillac North Ridge Trail, the South Ridge Trail is a gradual climb, but it has the advantage of not coming close to the Cadillac Mountain Road until near the end.

The trail, which can also be picked up via an extension from the Blackwoods Campground, begins by going over a few log bridges and ascending gradually. At 0.9 mile it reaches the junction with the south end of the 0.3-mile Eagles Crag Loop. Turn right (east) onto Eagles Crag to enjoy the clifftop panorama, including the Cranberry Isles, Otter Point, and the village of Otter Creek to the south and southeast and Frenchman Bay, Champlain, and the Beehive to the north and northeast.

Continue around on the Eagles Crag Loop until it intersects back with the Cadillac South Ridge Trail at 1.2 miles. Turn right (north) back onto the ridge. From here until you attain the summit, the trail, marked by Bates-style cairns, offers open views of the Cranberry Isles, the mountain pond called the Bowl, the 520-foot Beehive, Egg Rock in the distance, and the great length of the Schoodic Peninsula. A little higher are some gorgeous sweeping views of islands; Pemetic Mountain, the fourth highest peak in the park; and Dorr Mountain, the third highest.

At 2.4 miles reach the Featherbed, a perfect spot to rest and have lunch. Hand-hewn wooden benches here offer a place to sit and take in the views around the small

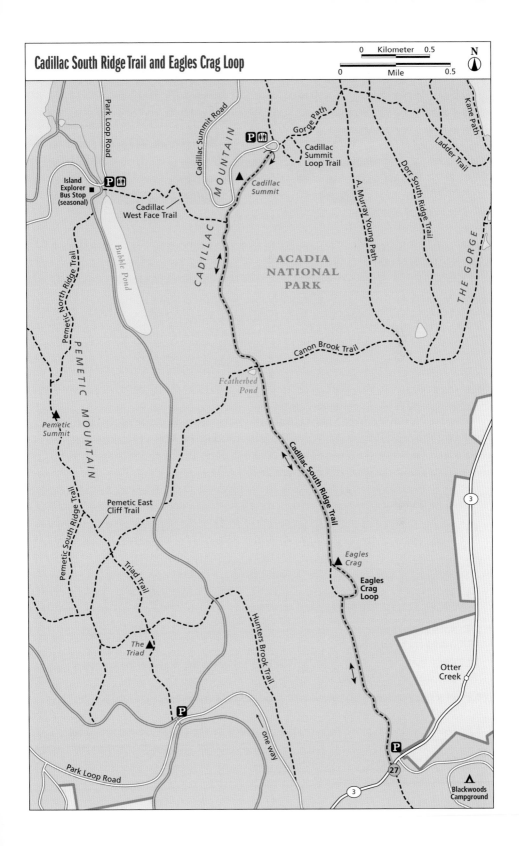

Cadillac South Ridge Trail and Eagles Crag Loop

0   Kilometer   0.5
0   Mile   0.5

N

Park Loop Road

Cadillac Summit Road

CADILLAC MOUNTAIN

Gorge Path

P

Cadillac Summit Loop Trail

Kane Path

Ladder Trail

Island Explorer Bus Stop (seasonal)

P

Cadillac West Face Trail

Cadillac Summit

A Murray Young Path

Dorr South Ridge Trail

CADILLAC

ACADIA NATIONAL PARK

THE GORGE

Bubble Pond

Pemetic North Ridge Trail

PEMETIC MOUNTAIN

Canon Brook Trail

Featherbed Pond

Pemetic Summit

Cadillac South Ridge Trail

3

Pemetic South Ridge Trail

Pemetic East Cliff Trail

Eagles Crag

Eagles Crag Loop

Triad Trail

Hunters Brook Trail

The Triad

Otter Creek

P

one way

Park Loop Road

27

3

Blackwoods Campground

A bench along the Featherbed provides a respite along the Cadillac South Ridge Trail.

mountain pond, listen to the birdsong, and watch for wildlife. The Canon Brook Trail, which leads east to ME 3 and west to a carriage road, also intersects here.

Continue north, up steep rock. If the conditions are right, you can turn around and see the moon reflected in the Featherbed below, as we did late one summer afternoon.

At 3.1 miles the Cadillac West Face Trail comes in on the left (west). The views here are dramatic, with the Bubbles and Pemetic Mountain visible to the west and the Cranberry Isles to the south.

At 3.2 miles, as the trail nears the summit road, bear right (northeast) before the road. Climb up a rock face using a conveniently placed iron rung, and follow the trail as it basically parallels the auto road to the top.

The trail crosses left over a gravel road near the end, reaching the summit parking area next to the gift shop at 3.5 miles. Before returning the way you came, cross the parking area and walk the short Cadillac Summit Loop Trail for mountaintop views and to learn about the geology of Mount Desert Island.

Miles and Directions

0.0 Start at the Cadillac South Ridge trailhead, on the right (north) side of ME 3 after the Blackwoods Campground entrance.

0.9 Reach the southern junction with the 0.3-mile Eagles Crag Loop. Turn right (east) to take the side loop for fine views from Cadillac's south ridge.

1.2 Return to the Cadillac South Ridge Trail at the northern end of the Eagles Crag Loop. Turn right (north) back onto the ridge trail.

2.4 Arrive at the Featherbed and the junction with the Canon Brook Trail. Continue straight (north) on the ridge trail.

3.1 Reach the junction with the Cadillac West Face Trail, which comes in from the left (west). Stay straight (north) on the ridge trail.

3.2 Bear right (northeast) to continue on the ridge trail as it nears the summit road and the Blue Hill Overlook parking area.

3.5 Reach Cadillac's summit. The trail crosses left over a gravel road near the end and comes out at the summit parking lot next to the gift shop. (***Option:*** Cross the parking lot to take the 0.3-mile Cadillac Summit Loop Trail.)

7.0 Arrive back at the trailhead.

28 Cadillac West Face Trail

This rugged climb, once known as the Steep Trail, can be treacherous, especially when wet, because it doesn't have the man-made handholds and footholds that distinguish other Acadia cliffside routes. It's the shortest but steepest route up Cadillac and begins by rising swiftly from Bubble Pond. The loop described here provides a gentler descent, down Cadillac's south ridge, to a little-used part of the Canon Brook Trail and back to Bubble Pond on a carriage road.

Distance: 5.0-mile lollipop, including the 0.8-mile round-trip spur to Cadillac and 1.5 miles back on a carriage road
Hiking time: About 4 to 5 hours
Difficulty: Strenuous
Trail surface: Granite steps, forest floor, rock ledges
Best season: Spring through fall, particularly early morning or late afternoon in summer to avoid the crowds atop Cadillac

Other trail users: Hikers climbing the Cadillac South Ridge and Canon Brook Trails; bicyclists or walkers along the carriage road
Canine compatibility: Leashed dogs permitted but not recommended
Map: USGS Acadia National Park and Vicinity
Special considerations: Chemical toilet and picnic table near the trailhead at Bubble Pond; seasonal gift shop and restrooms on Cadillac's summit

Finding the trailhead: From the park's visitor center, drive south on the Park Loop Road for 5 miles, past the Cadillac Mountain Road entrance, to the Bubble Pond parking area (not the Bubble Rock parking area farther south). Walk toward Bubble Pond and bear left (northeast). Cross the outlet of the pond to the trailhead on the northeast shore of the pond. The Island Explorer's Loop Road and Jordan Pond lines stop at the Bubble Pond parking area. GPS: N44 20.58' / W68 14.25'

The Hike

The Cadillac West Face Trail begins as a rocky path taking you up to a huge cedar grove. Watch carefully for cairns and blue blazes marking the way—it is easy to lose your way here. At one point you need to hoist yourself up a difficult rock face.

Soon you get views of Bubble Pond down to your right (west) and Pemetic Mountain to the southwest. The rugged trail continues steeply up, and the views of Bubble Pond and Pemetic keep getting more expansive.

After a series of switchbacks, you see your first glimpse of Eagle Lake to the northwest. Then you see the Cranberry Isles to the south. The trail begins to moderate as you approach the ridge. A wide-open cliff face (be careful, especially when conditions are wet) gives you the best views yet.

As you near the ridge, you'll see an array of islands—even Isle au Haut, another island component of Acadia, in the distance to the southwest. You can gaze out over the expansive waters of Eagle Lake and see Sargent Mountain rising to the west, the cliffs of Penobscot Mountain, and the wilderness of Pemetic Mountain.

The Cadillac West Face Trail, the most difficult way up the highest mountain in Acadia, starts at Bubble Pond.

At 0.9 mile reach the junction with the Cadillac South Ridge Trail. This is a lovely place to watch a sunset, but if that's your plan, it's best to have a car at the nearby Blue Hill Overlook parking area on the Cadillac Mountain Road rather than risk getting stuck on the ridge after dark.

Turn left (north) onto the Cadillac South Ridge Trail. As the trail nears the summit road by the Blue Hill Overlook, bear right (northeast) and follow the trail as it parallels the road to the summit parking lot. Reach the 1,530-foot peak at 1.3 miles, with its grand views of Bar Harbor, Frenchman Bay, and the surrounding mountains.

To loop back, turn around and go down the Cadillac South Ridge Trail. Stay straight (south) on the ridge trail and pass the junction with the Cadillac West Face Trail. Reach the mountain pond known as the Featherbed and the intersection with the Canon Brook Trail at 2.4 miles from the start. (If you opted not to add the 0.8-mile round-trip spur to Cadillac, this point is reached 1.6 miles from the start.)

Turn right (west) onto the Canon Brook Trail, along a little-used section that used to be called the Pond Trail. This segment of the Canon Brook Trail gets steep and features iron rungs and stone steps.

Reach a carriage road in 3.5 miles from the start (2.7 miles from the start if you didn't hike up to Cadillac). Turn right (north) onto the carriage road and walk 1.5 miles, returning to the Bubble Pond parking area after a total hiking distance of 5.0 miles with the Cadillac spur, or 4.2 miles without it.

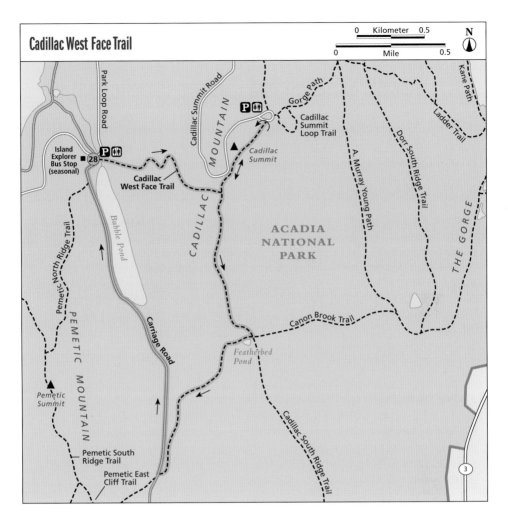

Cadillac West Face Trail

0 Kilometer 0.5
0 Mile 0.5

N

Miles and Directions

0.0 Start at the Cadillac West Face trailhead, on the northeast shore of Bubble Pond, reached from the parking area by heading left (northeast) along the pond and crossing its outlet.

0.9 Reach the junction with the Cadillac South Ridge Trail. Turn left (north) for the spur to summit Cadillac. (**Option:** Turn right [south] toward the mountain pond known as the Featherbed to shorten the overall hike distance to 4.2 miles.)

1.3 Attain Cadillac's summit. Turn around and return down the Cadillac South Ridge Trail.

1.7 Pass the junction with the Cadillac West Face Trail, and continue straight (south) down the ridge.

2.4 Reach the Featherbed and the junction with the Canon Brook Trail. Turn right (west) onto the Canon Brook Trail.

3.5 Turn right (north) onto the carriage road.

5.0 Arrive back at the Bubble Pond parking area.

Pemetic, Triad, and Day Mountain Area

29 Pemetic Northwest Trail (Bubbles–Pemetic Trail)

This shortest and steepest route up Pemetic, which means "range of mountains" in the Wabanaki language, gives quick access to open views of mountains and sea, and even of bald eagles soaring on thermals high above. A fork in the trail provides the option of following a high road along a ledge or a low road into a ravine.

Distance: 1.2 miles out and back

Hiking time: About 1.5 to 3 hours

Difficulty: Strenuous

Trail surface: Forest floor, rock ledges, wooden bridges and steps

Best season: Spring through fall, particularly early morning or late afternoon in summer to avoid the crowds

Other trail users: Hikers climbing Pemetic North Ridge Trail

Canine compatibility: Leashed dogs permitted but not recommended

Map: USGS Acadia National Park and Vicinity

Special considerations: No facilities at the trailhead; chemical toilet at Jordan Pond north lot and full seasonal facilities at the Jordan Pond House, both a short drive or Island Explorer bus ride away

Finding the trailhead: From the park's visitor center, drive south on the Park Loop Road for about 6 miles, past the Cadillac Mountain entrance and the Bubble Pond parking lot, to the Bubble Rock parking lot on the right (west) side of the road. The trailhead is on the east side of the Park Loop Road, across from the Bubble Rock parking lot. There's a new Island Explorer stop at the Bubble Rock parking lot on the Jordan Pond and Loop Road lines, but you may still need to ask the bus driver to let you off. GPS: N44 20.28' / W68 15.00'

The Hike

Retaining the name Native Americans used to call Mount Desert Island, Pemetic Mountain provides a 360-degree panorama from atop its 1,248-foot summit. To the north is Eagle Lake; to the west lie Jordan Pond and Penobscot Mountain. To the south are the Cranberry Isles, and Cadillac Mountain rises to the east.

The Pemetic Northwest Trail, formerly known as the Bubbles–Pemetic Trail, is just one of several trails up the fourth-highest peak in Acadia, some dating as far back as the late 1800s, but it's the steepest, gaining almost 800 feet elevation in 0.5 mile.

From this perch atop Pemetic, look down upon the Bubbles and Eagle Lake.

From the trailhead, cross a log bridge and take a sharp right up a pile of granite blocks, following the cairns. In late May, blue marsh violets bloom between the cracks in the pink granite along here, creating a colorful show.

At 0.1 mile take another sharp right (south) at the top of large boulders, just before a giant cedar grove. The trail can be difficult to follow here, so watch carefully for cairns. The trail zigzags. At 0.2 mile you'll come to a set of logs nailed into a rock face. Use them as handrails to pull yourself up the increasingly steep trail.

Reach a fork in the trail marked by a cryptic sign at 0.3 mile. One symbol points to the bottom of a ravine; the other steers hikers along the ledges overlooking the rocky chasm. We recommend the upland route because it avoids what can be a wet, rocky ravine and a climb back up on a precariously perched log ladder.

Continue climbing along log-and-stone steps. At 0.5 mile you reach a junction with the Pemetic North Ridge Trail (Pemetic Northeast Face Trail). Bear right (south) onto the ridge trail and reach the summit at 0.6 mile.

Return the way you came.

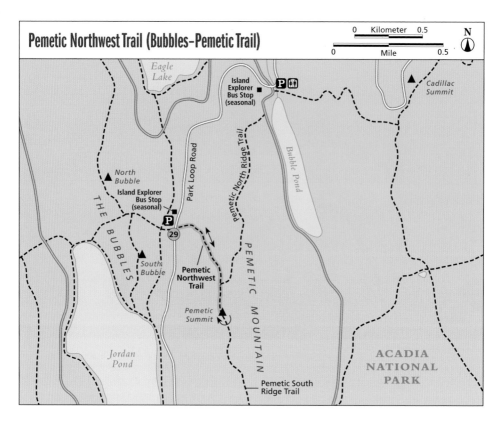

Pemetic Northwest Trail (Bubbles–Pemetic Trail)

Miles and Directions

0.0 Start at the Pemetic Northwest trailhead, on the east side of the Park Loop Road, across from the Bubble Rock parking area.

0.1 Take a sharp right (south) at the top of large boulders, before a giant cedar grove.

0.3 Come to a signed fork. You have a choice between climbing up a steep ravine (left) or taking the recommended parallel upland route along a ledge (right).

0.5 Reach the junction with the Pemetic North Ridge Trail. Bear right (south) onto the ridge trail.

0.6 Attain the Pemetic summit.

1.2 Arrive back at the trailhead.

30 Pemetic North and South Ridge Trails (Pemetic Northeast Face and Southwest Trails)

Hike along the Pemetic ridge, north and south, and reward yourself not only with its vistas but also with a stopover at the Jordan Pond House for its signature afternoon tea and popovers. If the Island Explorer bus is running, you can get to this route car-free or take the bus one-way back to the trailhead parking area.

Distance: 3.1 miles one way
Hiking time: About 2.5 to 3.5 hours, plus a 5- to 10-minute bus ride
Difficulty: Moderate to strenuous
Trail surface: Forest floor, rock ledges
Best season: Spring through fall, particularly early morning or late afternoon in summer to avoid the crowds

Other trail users: Hikers climbing Pemetic Northwest or East Cliff Trail
Canine compatibility: Leashed dogs permitted
Special considerations: Chemical toilet and picnic table near the trailhead at Bubble Pond; full facilities available seasonally at trail's end at the Jordan Pond House

Finding the trailhead: From the park's visitor center, drive south on the Park Loop Road for 5 miles, past the Cadillac Mountain Road entrance, to the Bubble Pond parking area (not the Bubble Rock parking area farther south). Walk toward Bubble Pond and bear right to the Pemetic North Ridge (Pemetic Northeast Face) trailhead, on the northwest shore of the pond. The Island Explorer's Loop Road and Jordan Pond lines stop at the Bubble Pond parking area. GPS: N44 20.55' / W68 14.30'

The Hike

The growing popularity of the fare-free Island Explorer, which runs from late June through early October, creates plenty of opportunities for accessing Acadia's trails without a car—or for hiking long one-way trips and taking the bus back to the start.

This route, along Pemetic's ridge and over to the Jordan Pond House, is one example of a trip perfectly complemented by a ride on the Island Explorer. You can drive or take the bus from Bar Harbor to the trailhead at Bubble Pond, hike along Pemetic's ridge, and end the trip with lunch, afternoon tea and popovers, or an early dinner at the Jordan Pond House. Then catch the bus back to your car, to town, or to the next trailhead.

The combinations of long one-way hikes and car-free trips are limited only by your imagination. Just remember to have an Island Explorer schedule in your daypack and a watch to keep track of time so that you don't miss the last bus of the day for your destination.

The Pemetic North Ridge Trail (Pemetic Northeast Face Trail) begins at the Bubble Pond parking area. Before you hit the trail, take a look at the unique Bubble Pond Bridge on the carriage road here. Of the seventeen bridges on the carriage

The expansive views along the Pemetic South Ridge Trail include the Cranberry Isles.

roads, it's the only one made through and through with compressed rock. The cores of the other bridges are built with mortar.

From the pond, bear right along the shore and pick up the trailhead on the northwest shore. At 0.1 mile cross a carriage road and enter the woods. You may even see a downy woodpecker in this stretch.

The trail immediately starts climbing Pemetic's wooded northeast face. Cadillac Mountain comes into view to the left (east) through the trees. Cadillac is so close here, you can see cars going up the mountain's road.

The trail reaches a ridge and then goes up and down wooded and rocky knobs. At 1.0 mile reach the junction with the Pemetic Northwest Trail (Bubbles–Pemetic Trail) coming in from the right (north). Bear left (south) to continue on the Pemetic North Ridge Trail.

Reach the summit of 1,248-foot Pemetic and the junction with the Pemetic South Ridge Trail at 1.1 miles. Once we watched in awe as a mature bald eagle soared on thermals, clearly identifiable by its white head and tail. The peak was fairly crowded, and we were the first to spot the magnificent bird. Sometimes it's easy to confuse bald eagles with turkey vultures, but a more experienced birder on the summit confirmed our sighting.

Views here include Cadillac Mountain to the northeast; the Triad, Day Mountain, and the Cranberry Isles to the south; Jordan Pond and Penobscot and Sargent Mountains to the west; and the twin rounded mountains known as the Bubbles to the northwest.

Go straight (south) on the Pemetic South Ridge Trail and get some wide-open views of islands, Northeast Harbor, and Southwest Harbor with all the watercraft.

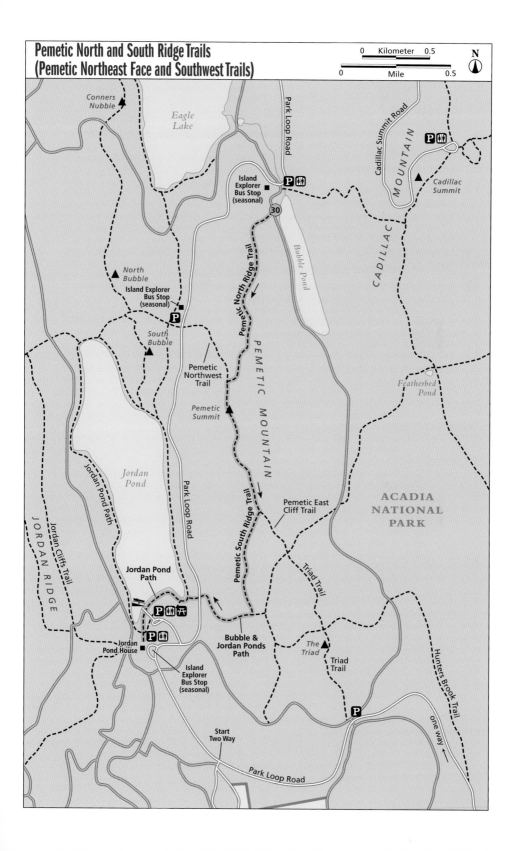

Pemetic North and South Ridge Trails
(Pemetic Northeast Face and Southwest Trails)

Kilometer 0 0.5
Mile 0 0.5
N

Conners Nubble

Eagle Lake

Park Loop Road

Cadillac Summit Road

CADILLAC MOUNTAIN

P

Cadillac Summit

Island Explorer Bus Stop (seasonal)

P

30

Bubble Pond

North Bubble

Island Explorer Bus Stop (seasonal)

P

South Bubble

Pemetic North Ridge Trail

PEMETIC MOUNTAIN

Pemetic Northwest Trail

Featherbed Pond

Pemetic Summit

Jordan Pond

Park Loop Road

Pemetic South Ridge Trail

Pemetic East Cliff Trail

ACADIA NATIONAL PARK

JORDAN RIDGE

Jordan Cliffs Trail

Jordan Pond Path

Jordan Pond Path

P

Triad Trail

P

Bubble & Jordan Ponds Path

The Triad

Triad Trail

Jordan Pond House

P

Island Explorer Bus Stop (seasonal)

Hunters Brook Trail

Start Two Way

P

one way

Park Loop Road

One time as we were heading down the ridge, we came almost eye to eye with a turkey vulture hovering against the wind.

Miles and Directions

0.0   Start at the Pemetic North Ridge (Pemetic Northeast Face) trailhead, on the northwest shore of Bubble Pond.

0.1   Cross a carriage road.

1.0   Reach the junction with the Pemetic Northwest Trail (Bubbles-Pemetic Trail), and bear left (south) to continue on the ridge.

1.1   Summit Pemetic and reach the junction with Pemetic South Ridge Trail (Pemetic Southwest Trail). Continue straight (south) on the ridge trail.

1.7   Reach the junction with the Pemetic East Cliff Trail, coming in on the left (east). Bear right (southwest) to continue on the Pemetic South Ridge Trail.

2.3   Reach the end of the Pemetic South Ridge Trail at a junction with the Bubble & Jordan Ponds Path. Turn right (west) toward Jordan Pond.

2.7   Cross the Park Loop Road and continue west toward Jordan Pond, picking up Jordan Pond Path and following it to the Jordan Pond House.

3.1   Arrive at the Jordan Pond House, where you can have lunch, afternoon tea and popovers, or dinner. Then take the Island Explorer bus back to the Bubble Pond parking area, Bar Harbor, or your next destination on the bus line.

31 Triad and Pemetic East Cliff Trails (Pemetic Mountain Trail)

This is the longest way up Pemetic, first meandering over the partly wooded 698-foot Triad summit before bringing you up steep cliffs and along the ridge to the fourth-highest peak in Acadia. This hike has one of the more out-of-the-way trailheads, making it a route less traveled.

Distance: 3.6 miles out and back
Hiking time: About 2.5 to 3.5 hours
Difficulty: Moderate to strenuous
Trail surface: Wooden bridges, forest floor, rock ledges
Best season: Spring through fall

Other trail users: Hikers climbing the Pemetic South Ridge Trail
Canine compatibility: Leashed dogs permitted
Map: USGS Acadia National Park and Vicinity
Special considerations: No facilities

Finding the trailhead: From the Sieur de Monts park entrance, head south on the one-way Park Loop Road 8 miles, going under the ME 3 overpass to the next overpass, where the Day Mountain carriage road goes over the Park Loop Road. Park in the gravel pullout along the Park Loop Road just before the Day Mountain carriage road overpass. Look for a wooden sign that says "Path to Carriage Road" on the right (north) side. Take the path up. The Triad (Pemetic Mountain) trailhead is diagonally left across the carriage road. The Island Explorer's Loop Road line stops at Wildwood Stables, near the Day Mountain carriage road overpass on the Park Loop Road. GPS: N44 18.57' / W68 14.03'

The Hike

From the trailhead at the carriage road, climb gradually 0.4 mile to the summit of the Triad, with its limited views south to most of the Cranberry Isles and better views north to Pemetic Mountain. Smack in the middle of Pemetic and Day Mountains, the Triad can be a peaceful perch, even on a summer weekend, as we discovered on a recent trip.

A plaque set in a rock just below the peak carries the name of one of the old memorial paths that used to crisscross this area, the Van Santvoord Trail. The memorial path is no longer marked, but the plaque keeps alive the memory of John V. Van Santvoord, a New York banker, owner of a Hudson River boat company, and chairman of a village path committee in the early 1900s.

At 0.5 mile reach the junction with the Hunters Brook Trail. Jog to the left (west) and turn right (north) to continue on the Triad Trail.

At 0.9 mile reach the four-way intersection with the Bubble & Jordan Ponds Path (Pond Trail). Go straight (northwest) to pick up the Pemetic East Cliff Trail (Pemetic Mountain Trail).

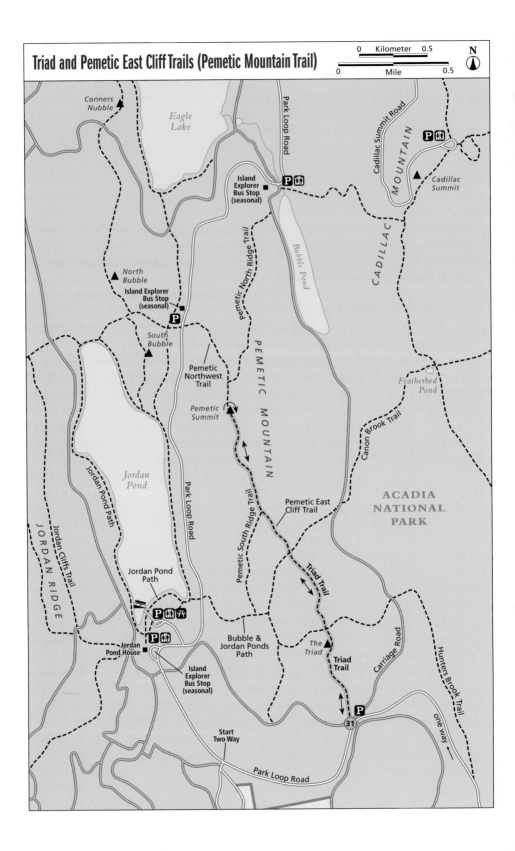

Triad and Pemetic East Cliff Trails (Pemetic Mountain Trail)

0   Kilometer   0.5

0   Mile   0.5

N

Conners Nubble

Eagle Lake

Park Loop Road

Cadillac Summit Road

CADILLAC MOUNTAIN

Cadillac Summit

Island Explorer Bus Stop (seasonal)

Pemetic North Ridge Trail

Bubble Pond

North Bubble

Island Explorer Bus Stop (seasonal)

South Bubble

Pemetic Northwest Trail

PEMETIC MOUNTAIN

Featherbed Pond

Pemetic Summit

Canon Brook Trail

Jordan Pond

Park Loop Road

Pemetic South Ridge Trail

Pemetic East Cliff Trail

ACADIA NATIONAL PARK

Jordan Pond Path

JORDAN RIDGE

Jordan Cliffs Trail

Jordan Pond Path

Triad Trail

Bubble & Jordan Ponds Path

The Triad

Triad Trail

Carriage Road

Hunters Brook Trail

Jordan Pond House

Island Explorer Bus Stop (seasonal)

31

one way

Start Two Way

Park Loop Road

The trail between the Triad and Pemetic summits offers views of Cadillac and colorful flora.

You'll soon start the steep climb up the rocky cliffs of Pemetic. The trail is tricky here. There are some spots where the trail goes straight up cliffs and rock faces, hard as that may be to believe at first.

At 1.2 miles attain the ridge at the junction with the Pemetic South Ridge Trail (Pemetic Southwest Trail). Bear right (north) to continue straight up the open ridge, where you get hints of the panorama to come. Reach the summit, with its 360-degree views, at 1.8 miles. Eagle Lake is visible to the north, and Jordan Pond and Penobscot Mountain are to the west. South are the Cranberry Isles, and east is Cadillac Mountain.

Return the way you came.

Miles and Directions

0.0 Start at the Triad (Pemetic Mountain) trailhead, diagonally left across the Day Mountain carriage road from where a path leads up from the Park Loop Road.

0.4 Summit the Triad.

0.5 Reach the junction with the Hunters Brook Trail (Triad-Hunters Brook Trail). Jog to the left (west) and turn right (north) to continue toward Pemetic.

0.9 Reach the junction with the Bubble & Jordan Ponds Path (Pond Trail). Go straight (northwest) to pick up the Pemetic East Cliff Trail (Pemetic Mountain Trail).

1.2 Bear right (north) at the junction with the Pemetic South Ridge Trail (Pemetic Southwest Trail) and continue on the ridge toward Pemetic.

1.8 Attain the Pemetic summit.

3.6 Arrive back at the trailhead.

32 Hunters Brook Trail (Triad–Hunters Brook Trail)

A little-traveled woods walk along Hunters Brook takes you up the Triad, a 698-foot peak with limited views of the Cranberry Isles to the south, beyond Day Mountain. You may even see the elusive spruce grouse.

Distance: 3.8 miles out and back
Hiking time: About 2.5 to 3.5 hours
Difficulty: Moderate
Trail surface: Forest floor, rock ledges
Best season: Spring through fall

Other trail users: Hikers climbing the Triad and Pemetic East Cliff Trails
Canine compatibility: Leashed dogs permitted
Map: USGS Acadia National Park and Vicinity
Special considerations: No facilities

Finding the trailhead: From the Sieur de Monts park entrance, head south on the one-way Park Loop Road for 7 miles. Park at a gravel pullout on the right (east) side of the road, just past the ME 3 overpass. The trailhead is on the right. The Island Explorer's Loop Road line stops at Wildwood Stables, about 1 mile farther down the Park Loop Road; ask if the bus driver can let you off at the Hunters Brook trailhead, just past the ME 3 overpass. GPS: N44 18.35' / W68 13.20'

The Hike

From the Park Loop Road, the trail starts out relatively flat along Hunters Brook. After a couple of brook crossings, the trail turns sharply left (west) just before crossing a carriage road at 1.4 miles.

The trail begins a sometimes steep climb toward the Triad, with sheer rock face in some areas. The woods here are so little traveled, don't be surprised if you come across a spruce grouse, as we did one spring. The bird is so uncommon, it can't be hunted in the state of Maine. And it's so well camouflaged and able to stay motionless for stretches at a time, it's easy to miss if you don't look about you.

At 1.8 miles reach the junction with the Triad and Pemetic East Cliff Trails, both once known as the Pemetic Mountain Trail. Turn left (south) on the Triad Trail, and reach the summit at 1.9 miles.

Return the way you came.

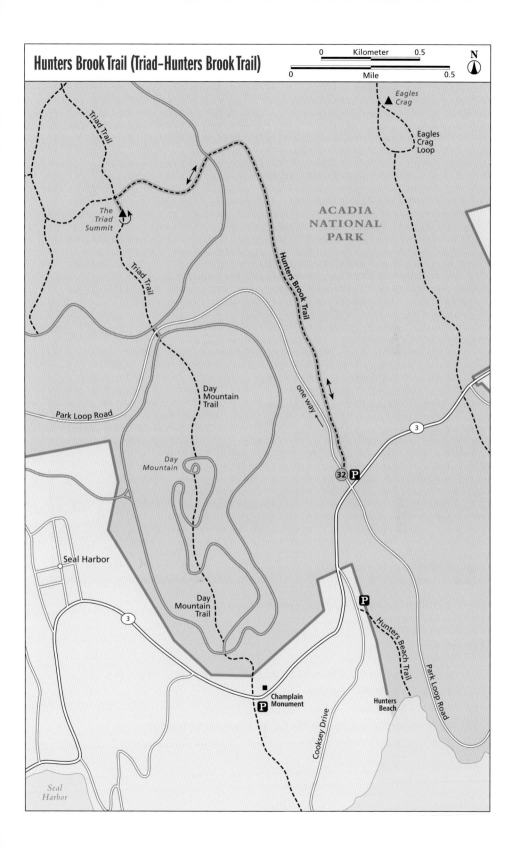

Hunters Brook Trail (Triad–Hunters Brook Trail)

0   Kilometer   0.5

0   Mile   0.5

N

Eagles Crag

Eagles Crag Loop

Triad Trail

ACADIA NATIONAL PARK

The Triad Summit

Triad Trail

Hunters Brook Trail

Day Mountain Trail

Park Loop Road

one way

Day Mountain

3

32 P

Seal Harbor

Day Mountain Trail

P

Hunters Beach Trail

Park Loop Road

3

Hunters Beach

Champlain Monument

P

Cooksey Drive

Seal Harbor

The elusive spruce grouse spotted along the secluded Hunters Brook Trail.

Miles and Directions

0.0 Start at the Hunters Brook trailhead, on the right (east) side of the one-way Park Loop Road just past the ME 3 overpass.

1.4 Cross a carriage road.

1.8 Reach the junction with the Triad Trail. Turn left (south) on the Triad Trail.

1.9 Summit the Triad.

3.8 Arrive back at the trailhead.

33 Hunters Beach Trail

This lovely short hike leads to a cobble beach on the Atlantic and the chance to explore an unusual sea cliff at low tide. The trail also offers some special views of Baker Island, Little Cranberry Island, and nearby ocean ledges.

Distance: 0.4 mile out and back
Hiking time: About 30 to 45 minutes
Difficulty: Easy
Trail surface: Wooden bridges, forest floor, cobble beach
Best season: Spring through fall

Other trail users: Local residents using nearby old village improvement association trails
Canine compatibility: Leashed dogs permitted
Map: USGS Acadia National Park and Vicinity
Special considerations: No facilities; limited parking

Finding the trailhead: From downtown Bar Harbor, head south on ME 3 toward Seal Harbor, and travel 0.6 mile past the Blackwoods Campground entrance. Turn left (southeast) at Cooksey Drive (no trucks, buses, trailers, or campers allowed on this road, which is labeled Sea Cliff Drive on some maps) and travel 0.2 mile to a small gravel parking area on the left (east) side of the road. The trailhead is on the southeastern end of the parking area. The Island Explorer does not stop here. GPS: N44 18.04' / W68 13.15'

Hunters Brook empties out to sea at this cobble beach.

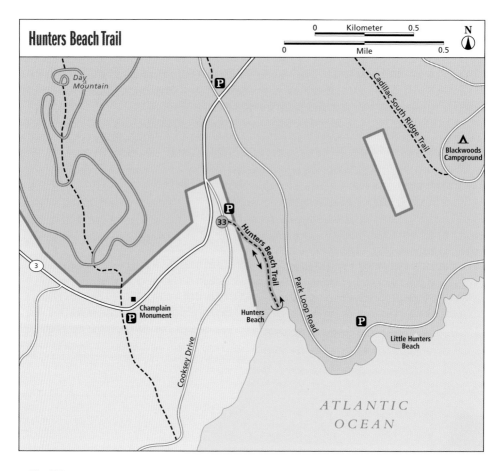

Hunters Beach Trail

Day Mountain

Cadillac South Ridge Trail

Blackwoods Campground

33

Hunters Beach Trail

3

Champlain Monument

Hunters Beach

Park Loop Road

Cooksey Drive

Little Hunters Beach

ATLANTIC OCEAN

The Hike

To reach the cobble beach and sea cliff, start on a wide pine-needle-covered path and then descend slightly to a footbridge. Hunters Brook, with large boulders scattered all over, can be seen flowing to your left (east).

A short boardwalk provides easy access over the brook to the end of the trail and Hunters Beach.

This could be one of the best spots in Acadia to step along a cobble and boulder beach and get close to some cliffs and ocean waves.

The trail, which dates back to the 1890s, is not well publicized, and it can seem remote. At certain times you might have this beach all to yourself or share it with only a few other visitors or seabirds known as common eiders.

To the left, facing the Atlantic, pink and black granite cliffs rise from the shore. At low tide only, you can walk along an inlet and between the amazing volcanic cliffs with their pillars and jagged rock.

Caution: Watch the tide if you walk along this tiny inlet, or you might get trapped by the rushing waves.

Take some time to enjoy the views south over the ocean to Bunker Ledge with its monument, the circular Baker Island, and adjacent Little Cranberry Island. Take away pictures and memories, not beach cobbles or anything else you find along the trail.

Miles and Directions

0.0 Start at the Hunters Beach trailhead, on the southeastern end of the trailhead parking area on Cooksey Drive.

0.2 Reach the cobble beach, with a sea cliff to the left (east) worth exploring at low tide.

0.4 Arrive back at the trailhead.

34 Little Hunters Beach

The jagged, pink granite cliffs off this cobble beach are reminiscent of the cliffs on Isle au Haut, a remote island that is part of the park. Little Hunters Beach features a seasonal brook that rushes to the sea, smooth cobblestones, and views of Little Cranberry Island. This is a good place to see tidal pools at low tide or the pounding ocean at high tide.

Distance: 0.2 mile out and back
Hiking time: About 15 minutes
Difficulty: Easy to moderate
Trail surface: Wooden stairs, cobble beach, rock ledges
Best season: Spring through fall

Other trail users: Motorists stopping along the Park Loop Road
Canine compatibility: Leashed dogs permitted
Map: USGS Acadia National Park and Vicinity
Special considerations: No facilities

Finding the trailhead: From the park's visitor center, drive south on the Park Loop Road for about 3 miles and turn left (east) at the sign for Sand Beach. Follow the one-way Park Loop Road, going 4.3 miles beyond Sand Beach and 1.6 miles beyond Otter Cove. Drive past three parking turnouts after Otter Cove, one after another, and park at the next pullout on the right (north) side of the Park Loop Road, near a stone bridge. The stairs down to the beach are on the left (south) side of the Park Loop Road. There is no nearby Island Explorer stop. GPS: N44 17.55' / W68 12.41'

The Hike

The walk begins along a charming wooden stairway, with thirty-five steps and double-log hand railings. To the right, depending on the season and any rainfall, a brook comes rushing out from under a stone-faced bridge on the Park Loop Road.

It may be Little Hunters Beach, but the scenery is large.

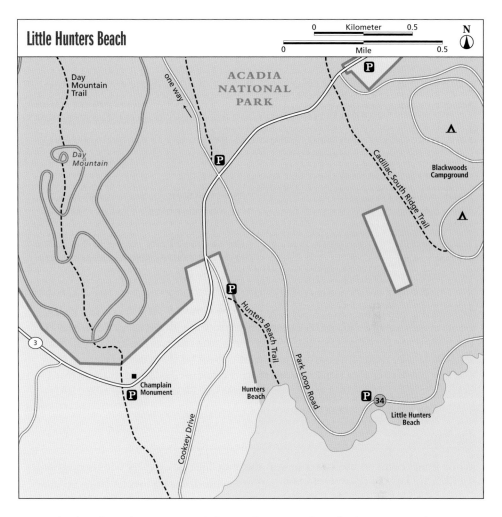

The beach is about 100 yards long. It's a nice place for listening to the ocean waves, exploring the tidal line, or examining some ancient, rounded cobblestones.

There are also great views of some good-size sea-stained pink cliffs, Baker Island, and Little Cranberry Island.

The beach is best explored at low tide or during calm seas. Heed the sign: "Do Not Remove Beach Stones."

Miles and Directions

0.0 Start at the stairs down to Little Hunters Beach, on the left (south) side of the Park Loop Road.

0.1 Reach the shoreline.

0.2 Arrive back at the top of the stairs.

35 Day Mountain Trail

Of all the trails in Acadia, this one offers the closest views of the Cranberry Isles. It also features an off-the-beaten-path monument to French explorer Samuel Champlain, who gave Mount Desert Island its name. There are options to loop up or down portions of the Day Mountain carriage road, the last to be built in Acadia and the only one that goes up a summit.

Distance: 1.6 miles out and back
Hiking time: About 1 to 2 hours
Difficulty: Moderate
Trail surface: Carriage road, granite steps, forest floor, rock ledges
Best season: Spring through fall

Other trail users: Horse-drawn carriage; bicyclists and walkers on Day Mountain carriage road
Canine compatibility: Leashed dogs permitted
Map: USGS Acadia National Park and Vicinity
Special considerations: No facilities

Finding the trailhead: From downtown Bar Harbor, head south on ME 3 toward Seal Harbor. Go 1.3 miles beyond the Blackwoods Campground entrance to a parking area on the left (south) side of ME 3, at a pedestrian crosswalk. The trailhead is across the road and heads north from ME 3. Be careful crossing what can be a high-speed roadway. The Island Explorer does not go by here, but the Loop Road line stops at Wildwood Stables, near the Day Mountain carriage road overpass on the Park Loop Road, at the other end of the trail. GPS: N44 17.58' / W68 13.41'

The Hike

Good things come in small packages, as this little hike proves. Day Mountain is only 583 feet high and a mere 0.8 mile from the trailhead, but it provides close-up views of the Cranberry Isles to the south and affords spectacular sunsets to the west.

The opportunity to learn some history, see a horse-drawn carriage, pick some wild blueberries, or loop up or down along portions of the easier Day Mountain carriage road makes it a good hike for children and teenagers, too, as we discovered when hiking this trail with our nieces Sharon and Michelle.

First, there's a history lesson:

In the woods just to the northeast of the trailhead is a hidden monument with these words inscribed in front: "In honor of Samuel de Champlain. Born in France 1567. Died at Quebec 1635. A soldier, sailor, explorer and administrator who gave this island its name." On the back are excerpts from Champlain's September 5, 1604, journal entry, explaining why he used the phrase "Île des Monts Déserts," or Island of Barren Mountains, to describe this place.

The monument was erected to mark the 300th anniversary of Champlain's discovery, before the idea of Acadia National Park even existed. Initially located overlooking

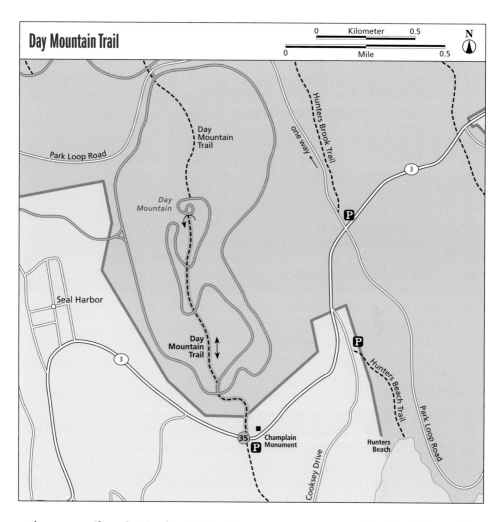

Kilometer 0 0.5

Mile 0 0.5

N

Day Mountain Trail

Park Loop Road

Day Mountain

Hunters Brook Trail

one way

3

P

Seal Harbor

Day Mountain Trail

P

3

Hunters Beach Trail

Park Loop Road

35 Champlain Monument
P

Hunters Beach

Cooksey Drive

the ocean off nearby Cooksey Drive, the monument was moved in the 1970s to this spot near the Day Mountain trailhead.

Next there's a chance to see a horse-drawn carriage coming from nearby Wildwood Stables, as the trail soon takes you to the first crossing of the Day Mountain carriage road at 0.2 mile. The intersection here is also a crossroads for bicyclists, so be careful as you continue on the hiking trail.

Cross the carriage road twice more, at 0.5 mile and at 0.6 mile. You can get some wonderful views along the road toward Otter Point to the east, the Cranberry Isles to the south, and Somes Sound to the west.

Then there's the opportunity to pick some wild Maine blueberries, if you hit the trail at the right time. On that unusually hot July day that we were hiking with our nieces, we were thankful for the juicy berries, ripe for the picking, to take our minds off the humidity.

The closest views of the Cranberry Isles from Acadia's peaks are right here on Day Mountain.

Reach the summit of Day Mountain at 0.8 mile, where you get even better views, including Gorham Mountain to the east. Return the way you came or, as the mood hits, loop back down along portions of the carriage road. (The east side of the Day Mountain carriage road system is the easier route.)

Because the trail can be steep and rocky, it's nice to have the more gradual carriage road option. Our niece Michelle, thirteen at the time, at first thought descending the smoother surfaced carriage road would be easier. But as she discovered on that hot day, the cool shade of the woods can be preferable.

It's easy to switch back and forth between carriage road and trail on the way up or down Day Mountain, another good thing about this little hike. If you take the Island Explorer bus to Wildwood Stables or park on the Park Loop Road near the Day Mountain carriage road overpass, you can hike south to the summit from the other end of the trail.

Miles and Directions

0.0 Start at the Day Mountain trailhead, on the north side of ME 3, across from the parking area. The Champlain Monument is on the right, just northeast of the trailhead.

0.2 Cross the carriage road to intersection No. 36, and pick up the trail across the intersection, on the left (northwest) side of the carriage road that goes up Day Mountain.

0.5 Cross the carriage road.

0.6 Cross the carriage road again.

0.8 Reach the Day Mountain summit, where the carriage road ends in a cul-de-sac.

1.6 Arrive back at the trailhead.

36 Bubble & Jordan Ponds Path (Pond Trail)

Part of a historic late-1800s loop trail connecting Bubble and Jordan Ponds, this hike harkens back to a different way of life and preferred mode of transportation, before carriage road and Park Loop Road construction impacted the route. You can still do a grand tour on foot from pond to pond, but you now have the option of hopping the Island Explorer bus back to the Jordan Pond House for afternoon tea and popovers.

Distance: 2.6 miles one-way, with the option to catch the Island Explorer bus back to the trailhead

Hiking time: About 2.5 to 3.5 hours, plus a 5- to 10-minute bus ride

Difficulty: Easy to moderate

Trail surface: Carriage road, granite steps, forest floor

Best season: Spring through fall

Other trail users: Bicyclists and walkers using the carriage road

Canine compatibility: Leashed dogs permitted

Map: USGS Acadia National Park and Vicinity

Special considerations: Full facilities available seasonally at the nearby Jordan Pond House

Finding the trailhead: From the park's visitor center, head south on the Park Loop Road for about 7.3 miles to a small pullout parking area on the right (west) side of the loop road, just before the Jordan Pond north lot and Jordan Pond House parking lot. The trailhead is east across the Park Loop Road from the small parking area. The Island Explorer's Loop Road and Jordan Pond lines stop at the Jordan Pond House near the trailhead and also at the Bubble Pond parking area at trail's end, so you don't even need a car to hike this trail. GPS: N44 19.25' / W68 14.54'

The Hike

Once a main thoroughfare in the footpath system connecting Bar Harbor to Jordan Pond to Seal Harbor, part of this trail was supplanted when John D. Rockefeller Jr. built the carriage road along Bubble Pond in the late 1920s.

Now that the park service is restoring some of the old routes and trail names, you can re-create the original pond-to-pond experience by walking along a portion of the carriage road and following a section of what used to be known as the Pond Trail as it gets returned to its historic name of Bubble & Jordan Ponds Path.

Heading east-southeast from the Jordan Pond area toward Pemetic ridge and the wooded valley between Pemetic and Cadillac Mountains, Bubble & Jordan Ponds Path begins along a relatively flat section of woods then climbs moderately.

At 0.4 mile you'll come to an intersection with the Pemetic South Ridge Trail (Pemetic Southwest Trail), which leads left (north) to Pemetic Mountain. Continue straight (northeast) on Bubble & Jordan Ponds Path, passing a spur at 0.5 mile that leads right (southeast) to the Triad.

Don't let the weathered sign with the outdated name of "Pond Trail" at the start throw you off the Bubble & Jordan Ponds Path.

At 0.8 mile reach the intersection with the Pemetic East Cliff Trail coming in from the left and the Triad Trail coming in from the right (both trails were formerly known as the Pemetic Mountain Trail). Stay straight (northeast) to continue on Bubble & Jordan Ponds Path.

At 1.1 miles reach the carriage road. Turn left (north) and stay on the road to Bubble Pond, bypassing the section of the Canon Brook Trail (also formerly known as the Pond Trail) that heads right (east) off the road and on to Cadillac ridge and the Featherbed.

At 2.6 miles reach the Bubble Pond parking area. If the Island Explorer is running, you can catch either the Loop Road or Jordan Pond line south to the Jordan Pond House area to return to your car or get afternoon tea and popovers.

Miles and Directions

0.0 Start at the Bubble & Jordan Ponds Path (Pond Trail) trailhead, east across a small pullout parking area on the Park Loop Road, just before the Jordan Pond north lot and Jordan Pond House parking lot.

0.4 Reach the junction with the Pemetic South Ridge Trail that leads left (north) to Pemetic Mountain; continue straight (northeast).

0.5 Pass a spur that leads right (southeast) to the Triad; continue straight (northeast).

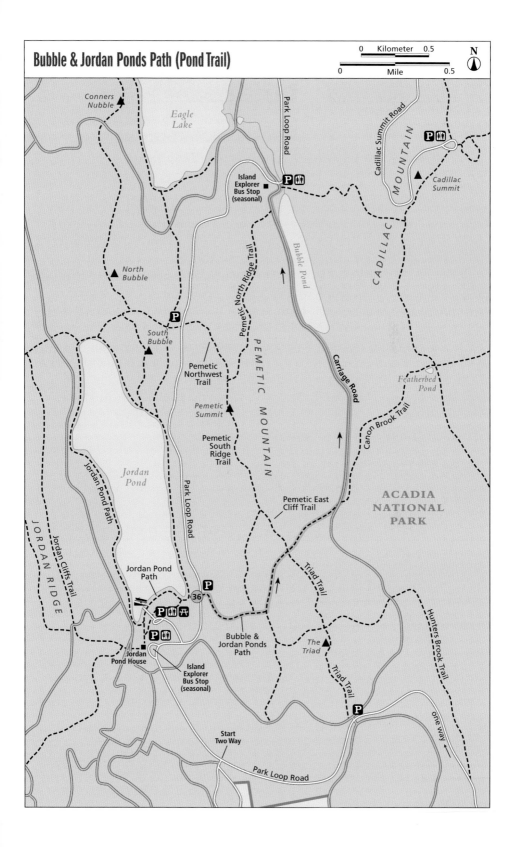

Bubble & Jordan Ponds Path (Pond Trail)

0 Kilometer 0.5

0 Mile 0.5

N

Conners Nubble

Eagle Lake

Park Loop Road

Cadillac Summit Road

CADILLAC MOUNTAIN

P

Cadillac Summit

Island Explorer Bus Stop (seasonal)

P

North Bubble

Pemetic North Ridge Trail

Bubble Pond

PEMETIC MOUNTAIN

P

South Bubble

Pemetic Northwest Trail

Carriage Road

Featherbed Pond

Pemetic Summit

Pemetic South Ridge Trail

Canon Brook Trail

Jordan Pond Path

Jordan Pond

Park Loop Road

Pemetic East Cliff Trail

ACADIA NATIONAL PARK

Jordan Cliffs Trail

JORDAN RIDGE

Jordan Pond Path

P 36

P

Triad Trail

Bubble & Jordan Ponds Path

Hunters Brook Trail

P

Jordan Pond House

Island Explorer Bus Stop (seasonal)

The Triad

Triad Trail

P

one way

Start Two Way

Park Loop Road

0.8 Reach the junction with the Pemetic East Cliff and Triad Trails; continue straight (northeast).

1.1 Reach the carriage road. Turn left (north) and stay on the carriage road, bypassing the section of the Canon Brook Trail (Pond Trail) that heads right (east) off the road toward Cadillac.

2.6 Reach the Bubble Pond parking area, where you can catch the Island Explorer's Loop Road or Jordan Pond line south back to the Jordan Pond House area.

Options

You can add a 1.1-mile one-way spur to the Featherbed—a restful mountain pond with benches to sit on along its banks—by taking the Canon Brook Trail (Pond Trail) east off the carriage road. This first takes you across a boggy area on log bridges before it climbs steeply up the Cadillac ridge. This section includes iron rungs and granite steps and is not recommended for dogs. The trail is little frequented until you get to the Featherbed and the crossroads with the Cadillac South Ridge Trail. Return to the carriage road and continue north on the road to Bubble Pond for a total 4.8-mile hike, assuming you can take the Island Explorer back to the Jordan Pond House area.

Or you can go up and over Pemetic Mountain to reach Bubble Pond instead of following the carriage road, for a 2.7-mile one-way trip. Turn left (north) onto the Pemetic South Ridge Trail at 0.4 mile, reach Pemetic in another 1.2 miles, then descend the Pemetic North Ridge Trail and arrive at the Bubble Pond parking area in another 1.1 miles.

Jordan Pond, Bubbles, and Eagle Lake Area

37 Jordan Pond Path (Jordan Pond Shore Trail)

On this hike you will have expansive views of Jordan Pond, the Bubbles, and Jordan Cliffs, as well as a chance to glimpse a colorful merganser duck or watch kayakers. The graded gravel path on the east side of the pond is particularly easy, and an amazing 4,000 feet of log bridges on the west side help smooth the way over what would otherwise be a potentially wet, rocky, and root-filled trail.

Distance: 3.3-mile loop
Hiking time: About 1.5 to 2 hours
Difficulty: Easy
Trail surface: Graded gravel path, rock slabs, forest floor, log bridges, log boardwalk
Best season: Spring through fall, particularly early morning or late afternoon in summer to avoid the crowds
Other trail users: Motorists using the Jordan Pond boat ramp road that crosses the trail to unload their canoes or kayaks, people walking their bikes to the nearby Jordan Pond House

Canine compatibility: Leashed dogs permitted on the trail but not in Jordan Pond
Map: USGS Acadia National Park and Vicinity
Special considerations: Chemical toilet at trailhead; full facilities available seasonally at the nearby Jordan Pond House. Certain sections of graded gravel path on east, west, and south sides of pond are accessible to wheelchairs and baby strollers. No swimming or dogs allowed in Jordan Pond, which serves as a public water supply.

Finding the trailhead: From the park's visitor center, drive south on the Park Loop Road for about 7.6 miles, and turn right (north) into the Jordan Pond north lot. Park in the lot on the right (north). Follow the boat ramp road down to the shore of the pond. The trailhead is on the right (east) and leads around the pond. The Island Explorer's Loop Road and Jordan Pond lines stop at the nearby Jordan Pond House. GPS: N44 19.22' / W68 15.13'

The Hike

A vigorous walk around Jordan Pond, topped by afternoon tea and popovers on the lawn of the Jordan Pond House—it's one of those special Acadia experiences.

The trail starts from the end of the boat ramp road at the Jordan Pond north parking lot and immediately offers a spectacular view of the rounded mountains known as the Bubbles, which lie across the pond. Bear right (east), circling the pond counterclockwise.

The first half of the trail is along the easy eastern shore with its graded gravel path, but be prepared for the western shore's rock slabs and long series of log bridges known as a bog walk. The rocks and log bridges can be slippery when wet. Wear proper footwear.

Late afternoon sun casts a warm glow over Jordan Pond and the Bubbles in the distance.

At 0.2 mile you reach the first of several trails that diverge from the Jordan Pond Path. Bear left at each of the junctions to continue paralleling the shore. The trail rounds a bend at the south end of the pond and crosses a rock path that was originally built in the early 1900s, providing pond and wetlands views.

At 0.3 mile pass the junction with the Bubble & Jordan Ponds Path (Pond Trail), which leads to trails up Pemetic Mountain. Stay along the eastern shore of the pond.

The trail now begins heading north. You will soon start seeing Jordan Cliffs to the west across the pond. There are plenty of boulders along the shore to sit on and admire the crystal-clear waters and the tremendous views. Jordan Pond serves as a public water supply, so no swimming is allowed.

After passing over a series of wooden bridges, you soon come up under the towering pinkish granite of South Bubble near the north side of the pond.

At 1.1 miles you reach Jordan Pond Carry and the Bubbles Trail (South Bubble Trail), which veer to the right (north) and lead, respectively, to Eagle Lake and South Bubble.

At 1.6 miles pass the junction with Bubbles Divide, a trail that heads right (northeast) up the gap between North and South Bubbles and allows access to the precariously perched Bubble Rock, which is visible from the Park Loop Road.

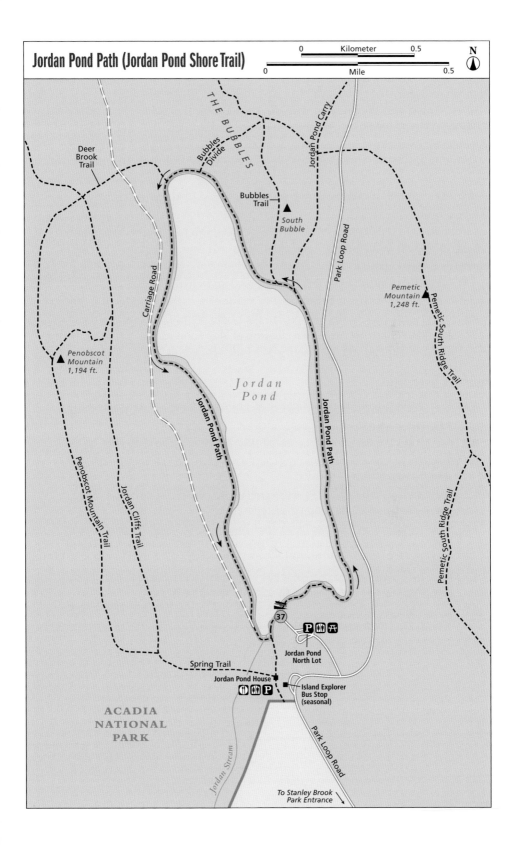

Jordan Pond Path (Jordan Pond Shore Trail)

0   Kilometer   0.5

0   Mile   0.5

N

THE BUBBLES

Bubbles Divide

Deer Brook Trail

Bubbles Trail

South Bubble

Jordan Pond Carry

Park Loop Road

Pemetic Mountain 1,248 ft.

Pemetic South Ridge Trail

Carriage Road

Penobscot Mountain 1,194 ft.

Jordan Pond

Jordan Pond Path

Jordan Pond Path

Penobscot Mountain Trail

Jordan Cliffs Trail

Pemetic South Ridge Trail

37

Jordan Pond North Lot

Spring Trail

Jordan Pond House

Island Explorer Bus Stop (seasonal)

ACADIA NATIONAL PARK

Jordan Stream

Park Loop Road

To Stanley Brook Park Entrance

You are now at the northernmost end of the pond and can get good views of the Jordan Pond House to the south and the Bubbles to the east. Cross a series of intricate wooden bridges—one rustic-style span has an archway in the middle.

At 1.7 miles pass the junction with the Deer Brook Trail, which leads up toward Penobscot Mountain and provides access to the Jordan Cliffs Trail and the beautiful double-arch Deer Brook Bridge, built in 1925 as part of the carriage road system.

Now begins the trail's traverse of the rougher western shore of the pond, with its rock slabs and long series of log bridges. After a bit of hide-and-seek with the shore and a stretch of rock hopping, you reach the log bridges that take you over fragile wetlands.

In addition to the dramatic views of the Bubbles, you may also catch a glimpse of a flock of seagulls or a common merganser, as we did. It is hard to miss a merganser, especially a female, with its rust-colored, crested head and pointed orange bill.

At 3.2 miles turn left onto the carriage road and cross a bridge. Then turn left again to follow the trail as it circles back to the Jordan Pond north lot at 3.3 miles. Just before you get back to the lot, you can turn right (south) and head up the hill to the Jordan Pond House for an Acadia tradition of afternoon tea and popovers, with a grand view of the pond and the Bubbles as nature's backdrop.

Miles and Directions

0.0   Start at the Jordan Pond Path trailhead. At the end of the boat ramp road, turn right along the graded gravel path and walk along the eastern shore of the pond.

0.2   Bear left at a junction and continue straight along the eastern shore of the pond.

0.3   Reach the junction with the Bubble & Jordan Ponds Path (Pond Trail); continue straight along the eastern shore of the pond.

1.1   Reach the junction with Jordan Pond Carry and the Bubbles Trail (South Bubble Trail); continue straight along the eastern shore of the pond.

1.6   Reach the junction with Bubbles Divide, which goes northeast through the gap between North and South Bubbles. Continue along the shore as the path rounds the north side of the pond.

1.7   Reach the junction with the Deer Brook Trail, which leads up Penobscot Mountain. Continue along the shore of the pond as the path now follows the west side.

3.2   Turn left onto the carriage road and cross a bridge. Turn left again to follow the path as it circles back to the Jordan Pond north lot.

3.3   Arrive back at the trailhead, completing the loop.

38 Jordan Stream Path

It's but a short woods walk from the Jordan Pond House along the meandering Jordan Stream to the highlight of this trail: a carriage road bridge made entirely of cobblestones rather than the cut granite of other bridges in the carriage road system. You may have company as you stop to admire the Cobblestone Bridge—this is a popular place for horse-drawn carriages to let off passengers.

Distance: 1.0 mile out and back
Hiking time: About 30 minutes to 1 hour
Difficulty: Easy to moderate
Trail surface: Wooden bridges, forest floor
Best season: Spring through fall

Other trail users: Passengers getting off a horse-drawn carriage to see Cobblestone Bridge
Canine compatibility: Leashed dogs permitted
Map: USGS Acadia National Park and Vicinity
Special considerations: Full facilities available seasonally at the Jordan Pond House

Finding the trailhead: From the park's visitor center, drive south on the Park Loop Road for about 7.6 miles, and turn right (north) into the Jordan Pond north lot. Park in the lot on the left (south) and follow signs to the Jordan Pond House. Walk past the Jordan Pond House and turn right (west) and follow a path marked "To Asticou, Spring Trail, Penobscot & Sargent Mtn Trails" down to a carriage road. The trailhead is across the carriage road on the left. The Island Explorer's Loop Road and Jordan Pond lines stop at the Jordan Pond House. GPS: N44 19.13' / W68 15.19'

The Hike

Even in its short distance, the Jordan Stream Path provides hikers with a historical flavor.

About one hundred years ago, the trail was laid out by the Seal Harbor Village Improvement Association as a scenic connector between the village and Jordan Pond. In the 1700s and earlier, it may have been part of a Native American canoe carry trail connecting Jordan Pond to the ocean. Today the trail takes park visitors by some of the carriage roads and stone bridges built in the early 1900s by industrialist and Mount Desert Island summer resident John D. Rockefeller Jr.

While the hike's destination, the Cobblestone Bridge, built in 1917 by Rockefeller, is much photographed now, it wasn't always so well loved, according to *Acadia's Carriage Roads*, by park naturalist Robert A. Thayer.

As George B. Dorr, Acadia's first park superintendent, commented soon after the bridge's construction: ". . . all have agreed in regretting it from the artistic standpoint, but vegetation now is closing in around it, and it will soon be little noticeable."

Cobblestone Bridge was the first bridge to be built along the carriage roads, in 1917, and is the only one to be made entirely of rounded boulders.

The Cobblestone Bridge is one of seventeen stone-faced bridges in the carriage road system, all but one financed by Rockefeller.

From the Jordan Stream Path trailhead at the carriage road behind the Jordan Pond House, follow the narrow path through the woods, paralleling the stream as it tumbles south toward the ocean. Part of the trail features neatly laid stepping-stones, making it seem like a garden path at times. Portions of the trail that had been eroded were about to be upgraded when we last hiked this route, with log planks stacked neatly, waiting to be put down as log boardwalks.

When you reach a junction with a carriage road at 0.2 mile, bear right (west) across a wooden bridge. Pick up the trail at the end of the bridge, heading left (south) down the other side of the stream.

The trail descends and gets rougher here. A series of wooden footbridges take you across stream tributaries.

At 0.5 mile the trail brings you to the base of the Cobblestone Bridge. The trail continues toward Seal Harbor across private land, making the bridge a natural stopping point.

Return the way you came.

Jordan Stream Path

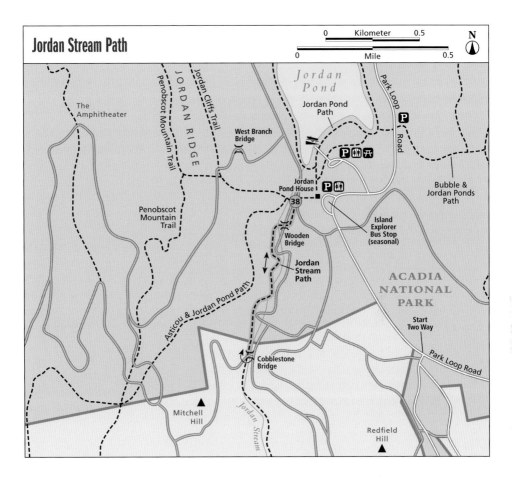

Miles and Directions

0.0   Start at the Jordan Stream Path trailhead, behind and to the left of the Jordan Pond House, across a carriage road.

0.2   Reach a junction with a carriage road. Cross a wooden bridge to the right (west) and continue south down the trail along the west bank of Jordan Stream.

0.5   Reach Cobblestone Bridge.

1.0   Arrive back at the trailhead.

39 Asticou & Jordan Pond Path (Asticou Trail)

After an extensive overhaul in 2014, Asticou & Jordan Pond Path is prepared to handle the use it did in the late 1800s, when it was a major walking route between Northeast Harbor and Jordan. This garden-style path is special by itself, but it also provides important access to a historic section of the Penobscot Mountain Trail and the Amphitheater Trail, which ascends toward Cedar Swamp and Sargent Mountains.

Distance: 2.6 miles out and back
Hiking time: About 1.5 to 2 hours
Difficulty: Easy
Trail surface: Graded gravel path, granite steps, wooden bridges, forest floor
Best season: Spring through fall

Other trail users: Joggers, users of nearby carriage roads
Canine compatibility: Leashed dogs permitted
Map: USGS Acadia National Park and Vicinity
Special considerations: Full facilities available seasonally at the Jordan Pond House

Finding the trailhead: From the park's visitor center, drive south on the Park Loop Road for about 7.6 miles and turn right (north) into the Jordan Pond north lot. Park in the lot on the left (south) and follow signs to the Jordan Pond House. Walk behind and to the right (west) of the Jordan Pond House and follow a path marked "To Asticou & Jordan Pond Path, Spring Trail, Penobscot & Sargent Mtn Trails" down to a carriage road. The trailhead, marked by a sign that reads "Sargent Mtn South Ridge Trail," is across the carriage road and wooden bridge, on the left. The Island Explorer's Loop Road and Jordan Pond lines stop at the Jordan Pond House. GPS: N44 19.12' / W68 15.20'

The Hike

This can be an easy hike. Or it can be more difficult if used as part of a climb up Penobscot, Cedar Swamp, or Sargent Mountain.

Leave the crowd at the Jordan Pond House behind, and take the graded gravel path into woods of striped maple and towering cedars and pines.

Also take some time to admire the craftsmanship and thoughtful labor involved in the 2014 restoration, funded in part by an $800,000 federal grant that allowed for the largest Acadia trail crew since the Civilian Conservation Corps, and the Acadia Trails Forever endowment, consisting of $4 million in park user fees and appropriations and $9 million in donations from the nonprofit Friends of Acadia.

Adhering to historical standards, trail crews upgraded and added new culverts, constructed new drains, reestablished stones along the trail edges and lay stone and logs to check erosion.

In the area known as Faint Hill, park crews studied old photos of a stairway before restoring or adding nearly 150 stone steps. In the same manner, they constructed five new, arched bridges that mirror the style of Acadia foot spans from an earlier era, according to Gary Stellpflug, Acadia trails foreman.

The Asticou & Jordan Pond Path is also good terrain for dogs. In fact, Acadia is among only a few national parks that allow dogs and other pets on trails as long as they are leashed.

During a recent hike on the path, Nicole Ramos said she was elated to bring Lucy, her Jack Russell terrier. If not for Acadia's pro-dog policy, "I'd probably be disappointed and maybe have to go somewhere else," she said.

At 1.1 miles cross a carriage road; at 1.2 miles cross a second carriage road. The even less-traveled Amphitheater Trail, up Cedar Swamp and Sargent Mountains, starts 0.3 mile to the right (northwest) along this carriage road.

At 1.3 miles reach a major junction, where gracious stepping stones take you across Little Harbor Brook, in place of a wooden bridge that was taken down in 2014 as being historically inaccurate. The recently reopened historic section of the Penobscot Mountain Trail heads right (north) just before this crossing over Little Harbor Brook. The private Harbor Brook Trail heads left (south) along the west side of the brook, on the other side of the brook crossing.

Although the Asticou & Jordan Pond Path continues west another 0.8 mile toward a junction with the Sargent South Ridge Trail, and another 0.3 mile beyond that to the Asticou Map House outside park borders, this is a natural turnaround point.

Return the way you came.

Gracious stepping-stones across Little Harbor Brook replaced a historically inaccurate bridge during major rehabilitation of the Asticou & Jordan Pond Path in 2014.

Asticou & Jordan Pond Path (Asticou Trail)

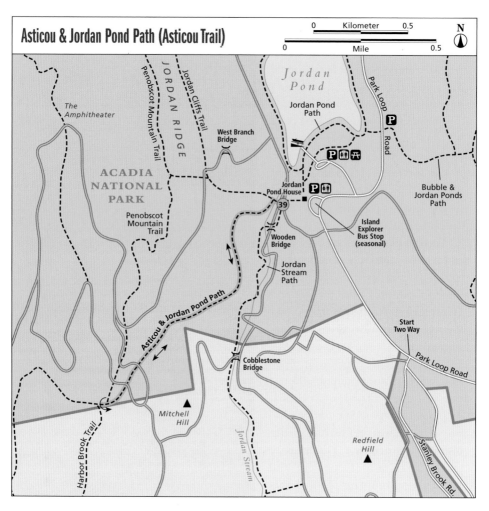

Miles and Directions

0.0 Start at the Asticou & Jordan Pond Path trailhead, behind and to the left of the Jordan Pond House, across a carriage road and wooden bridge.

1.1 Cross a carriage road.

1.2 Cross a second carriage road. To the right (northwest) 0.3 mile along the road is the Amphitheater trailhead for access to Cedar Swamp and Sargent Mountains. Continue straight (southwest) on the Asticou & Jordan Pond Path.

1.3 Reach a major junction, where stepping stones take you across Little Harbor Brook and the private Harbor Brook Trail heads to the left (south) along the west side of the brook. The recently reopened historic section of the Penobscot Mountain Trail heads to the right (north) just before this crossing over Little Harbor Brook. Although the path continues another 0.8 mile to a junction with the Sargent South Ridge Trail and another 0.3 mile beyond that to the Asticou Map House on private land, for this hike retrace your steps.

2.6 Arrive back at the trailhead.

40 Bubbles Divide (Bubble Rock Trail)

A moderate hike with some steep stretches brings you to 360-degree views from South Bubble and an up-close perspective of Bubble Rock, a precariously perched glacial erratic visible from the Park Loop Road that generations of hikers have playfully attempted to "push." From South Bubble, Jordan Pond and the Atlantic Ocean are to the south, North Bubble to the north, and Sargent and Penobscot Mountains to the west.

Distance: 1.0 mile out and back
Hiking time: 1 hour
Difficulty: Moderate to more challenging
Trail surface: Forest floor, rock ledges, log steps
Best season: Spring through fall, particularly early morning or late afternoon in summer to avoid the crowds

Other trail users: Hikers accessing North Bubble, Eagle Lake or Jordan Pond
Canine compatibility: Leashed dogs permitted
Map: USGS Acadia National Park and Vicinity
Special considerations: No facilities at trailhead; chemical toilet at Jordan Pond north lot and full seasonal facilities at Jordan Pond House, both a short drive or Island Explorer ride away

Finding the trailhead: From the park's visitor center, drive south on the Park Loop Road for about 6 miles, past the Cadillac Mountain entrance and the Bubble Pond parking lot, to the Bubble Rock parking lot on the right (west) side of the road. The trailhead departs from the Bubble Rock parking lot. There's a new Island Explorer stop at the Bubble Rock parking lot on the Jordan Pond and Loop Road lines, but you may still need to ask the bus driver to let you off. GPS: N44 20.27' / W68 15.00'

The Hike

By going up into the gap between South and North Bubbles, this historic trail, dating back to the late 1800s, provides the shortest ascent to either of the rounded mountains that overlook Jordan Pond. The trip also goes to Bubble Rock, a glacially deposited boulder known as an erratic, which sits atop South Bubble, and which generations of hikers have been photographed vainly trying to "push."

Heading west from the Bubble Rock parking lot, the trail crosses Jordan Pond Carry at 0.1 mile. At the junction with the northern section of the Bubbles Trail (North Bubble Trail) at 0.2 mile, stay straight. At the junction with the southern section of the Bubbles Trail at 0.3 mile, turn left (south) to South Bubble and Bubble Rock.

Follow the blue blazes and cairns along the trail and reach the 768-foot South Bubble summit at 0.5 mile. A sign points left (east) to nearby Bubble Rock, dumped

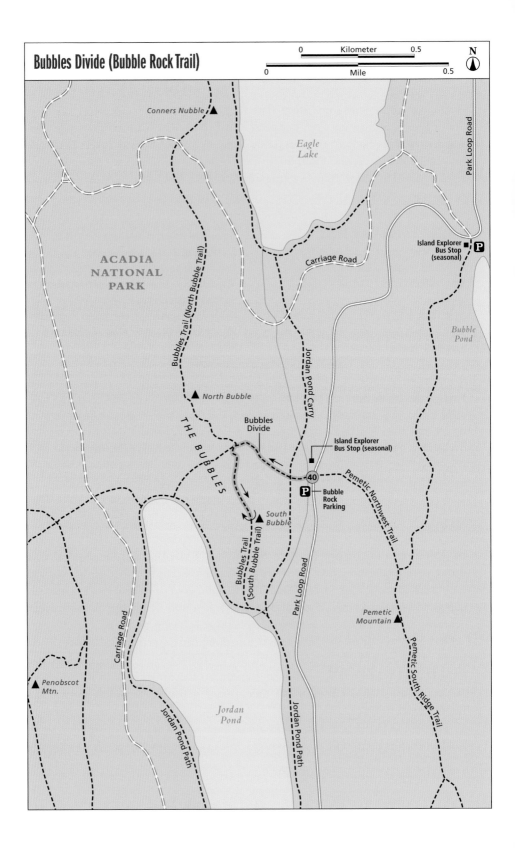

Bubbles Divide (Bubble Rock Trail)

Conners Nubble ▲

Eagle Lake

Park Loop Road

Island Explorer
Bus Stop
(seasonal) ■ 🅿

Carriage Road

**ACADIA
NATIONAL
PARK**

Bubble Pond

Bubbles Trail (North Bubble Trail)

North Bubble ▲

Bubbles
Divide

Island Explorer
Bus Stop (seasonal) ■

Jordan pond Carry

40

🅿 ▪ Bubble
Rock
Parking

Pemetic Northwest Trail

T H E   B U B B L E S

South
Bubble ▲

Bubbles Trail
(South Bubble Trail)

Pemetic
Mountain ▲

Park Loop Road

Penobscot
Mtn. ▲

Carriage Road

Jordan Pond Path

*Jordan
Pond*

Jordan Pond Path

Pemetic South Ridge Trail

0 — Kilometer — 0.5
0 — Mile — 0.5

N

here by glaciers countless years ago from a spot more than 20 miles to the northeast, according to the National Park Service.

Close inspection of the 100-ton rock reveals large black and white crystals that are unlike the native pink granite of Acadia, an indication that Bubble Rock came from afar. Generations ago, it was thought that floods of biblical proportions moved giant boulders around. But it was clues like Bubble Rock that led nineteenth-century scientist Louis Agassiz to theorize that massive glaciers once covered the earth.

Explore the views around and near the peak, in particular a breathtaking Jordan Pond overlook that's 0.1 mile south of the summit on the South Bubble Trail.

Return the way you came. Hardy hikers can make a 1.4-mile loop by heading steeply down the Bubbles Trail (South Bubble Trail) to the shores of Jordan Pond and turning sharply left (northeast) onto Jordan Pond Carry and then right (east) onto Bubbles Divide back to the parking lot.

Jordan Pond seems an extension of the Atlantic Ocean from this viewpoint just south of the South Bubble summit.

Miles and Directions

0.0 Start at the Bubbles Divide trailhead, departing from the Bubble Rock parking lot on the right (west) side of the Park Loop Road.

0.1 Cross the junction with Jordan Pond Carry.

0.2 Reach the junction with the northern section of the Bubbles Trail (North Bubble Trail), which comes in from the right (north). Stay straight.

0.3 Turn left (south) onto the southern section of the Bubbles Trail (South Bubble Trail).

0.5 Reach the South Bubble summit and Bubble Rock.

1.0 Arrive back at the trailhead.

41 Jordan Pond Carry to Eagle Lake and Bubbles Trails Loop

Get some quiet views of a scenic lake and impressive peaks in one loop. First walk along a pre–Revolutionary War canoe carry trail and hug the shores of Eagle Lake, then climb over Conners Nubble and North Bubble before circling back to the start.

Distance: 3.6-mile loop
Hiking time: About 2 to 3 hours
Difficulty: Moderate
Trail surface: Granite steps, wooden bridges, forest floor, rock ledges
Best season: Spring through fall
Other trail users: Hikers climbing Bubbles Divide to South Bubble and Bubble Rock; bicyclists and walkers at carriage road crossings

Canine compatibility: Leashed dogs permitted
Map: USGS Acadia National Park and Vicinity
Special considerations: No facilities at the trailhead; chemical toilet at Jordan Pond north lot and full seasonal facilities at the Jordan Pond House, both a short drive or Island Explorer ride away. No swimming or dogs are allowed in Eagle Lake, which serves as a public water supply.

Finding the trailhead: From the park's visitor center, drive south on the Park Loop Road for about 6 miles, past the Cadillac Mountain entrance and the Bubble Pond parking lot, to the Bubble Rock parking lot on the right (west) side of the road. The trail departs from the Bubble Rock parking lot. There's a new Island Explorer stop at the Bubble Rock parking lot on the Jordan Pond and Loop Road lines, but you may still need to ask the bus driver to let you off. GPS: N44 20.27' / W68 15. 00'

The Hike

This loop hike offers the chance to stroll along the quiet western shore of Eagle Lake, climb the less-known Conners Nubble, and pick plump wild blueberries.

Even during the height of Acadia's busy season, you can get solitude on this route, as we discovered with our nieces Sharon and Michelle one July, when we had the Nubble and its blueberries all to ourselves.

From the Bubble Rock parking area, head west to hook up with Jordan Pond Carry at 0.1 mile. Turn right (north) onto Jordan Pond Carry, toward Eagle Lake. Cross a carriage road at 0.5 mile, and reach the southern tip of the lake at 0.6 mile. Turn left (west) here onto the Eagle Lake Trail.

As the trail hugs the southern shore of the second-largest lake in Acadia, it heads in and out of the woods and goes by a sandy beach.

Continue following the shore, even if it means crossing over fields of rocks. The path gets rougher and more difficult here, as you start skirting the western bank, but you may also find flat rocks to sit on for a rest or bite of lunch. Our nieces enjoyed

North Bubble overlooks Jordan Pond and the glacial moraine that Jordan Pond House sits on.

such a respite here, and they found looking east across Eagle Lake at the tiny-looking cars driving up Cadillac's mountain road to be an interesting perspective.

You'll cross the base of a rock slide. After a little uphill section takes you inland into a birch grove the trail levels off.

At 1.7 miles reach the junction with the Bubbles Trail (North Bubble Trail). (If you come to a carriage road, you've overshot the Bubbles Trail and will need to backtrack a little.) Turn sharply left (south) onto the Bubbles Trail, and head toward Conners Nubble and the North Bubble summit.

At 2.1 miles reach the 588-foot summit of Conners Nubble. Enjoy its spectacular 360-degree views north and northeast to Frenchman Bay and Porcupine Islands, east to Eagle Lake and Cadillac Mountain, west to Sargent and Penobscot Mountains, and south and southeast to the Bubbles and Pemetic Mountain.

If you're hiking with youngsters at the right season, they'll be pleasantly diverted by the sun-ripened blueberries near the top of the Nubble.

Sharon and Michelle, 15 and 13 at the time and not used to hiking uphill on a hot day, found plenty of energy to engage in their newfound talent—blueberry picking and tasting. In fact, Michelle became so engrossed that we momentarily lost sight of her. "Where's your sister?" we asked Sharon. "Eating," she replied.

Descend Conners Nubble and cross a carriage road at 2.2 miles. Continue straight (south) on the Bubbles Trail, and begin the climb to the North Bubble. Look back as you climb and you'll see the beehive-like appearance of Conners Nubble to the

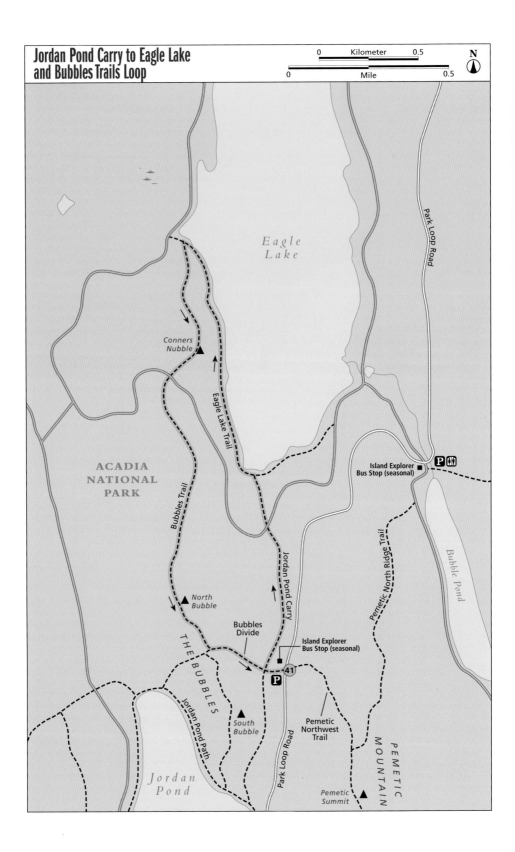

Kilometer

0   0.5

Mile

0   0.5

N

Eagle
Lake

Park Loop Road

Conners
Nubble

Eagle Lake Trail

Island Explorer
Bus Stop (seasonal)

P

ACADIA
NATIONAL
PARK

Bubbles Trail

Jordan Pond Carry

Pemetic North Ridge Trail

Bubble Pond

North
Bubble

Bubbles
Divide

Island Explorer
Bus Stop (seasonal)

41

P

THE BUBBLES

Jordan Pond Path

South
Bubble

Park Loop Road

Pemetic
Northwest
Trail

PEMETIC
MOUNTAIN

Jordan
Pond

Pemetic
Summit

north, as well as Eagle Lake and Frenchman Bay. You'll also have views of Cadillac Mountain to the east, and plenty of blueberry picking in season along the North Bubble ridge.

At 3.0 miles reach the summit of North Bubble, at 872 feet the higher of the two distinctive little mountains known as the Bubbles. From here you can see South Bubble, Jordan Pond, and the Cranberry Isles to the south.

Descend to the gap between North and South Bubbles, and turn left (east) onto Bubbles Divide at 3.3 miles. Cross the intersection with Jordan Pond Carry at 3.5 miles, and return to the Bubble Rock parking area at 3.6 miles.

Miles and Directions

0.0 Start at the Bubble Rock parking area, and head west on Bubbles Divide (Bubble Rock Trail) toward the junction with Jordan Pond Carry.

0.1 Turn right (north) onto Jordan Pond Carry, toward Eagle Lake.

0.5 Cross a carriage road.

0.6 Reach the south shore of Eagle Lake. Turn left (west) onto the Eagle Lake Trail, and parallel the shore.

1.7 Turn sharply left (south) at the junction onto the Bubbles Trail (North Bubble Trail).

2.1 Reach the summit of Conners Nubble.

2.2 Cross another carriage road to continue south on the Bubbles Trail.

3.0 Reach the summit of North Bubble.

3.3 At the junction with Bubbles Divide (Bubble Rock Trail), turn left (east).

3.5 Pass the intersection with Jordan Pond Carry, and continue straight (east).

3.6 Arrive back at the Bubble Rock parking area.

Penobscot, Sargent, and Parkman Mountain Area

42 Spring Trail (Penobscot Mountain Trail)

The Spring Trail is the park's most popular way to climb Penobscot Mountain, a peak with unbeatable views. The hike goes up the steep southeast side of the mountain, with some boulder climbing and narrow crevices making it especially challenging, and takes you by a stone bench with views of Jordan Pond below.

Distance: 1.0 mile out and back, plus an optional 2.0-mile round-trip climb to Penobscot Mountain
Hiking time: About 1–3 hours, depending on whether you add on Penobscot
Difficulty: Moderate to strenuous
Trail surface: Granite steps, wooden bridges, forest floor, rock ledges
Best season: Spring through fall

Other trail users: Hikers accessing Jordan Cliffs or Penobscot and Sargent Mountains; yoga enthusiasts
Canine compatibility: Leashed dogs permitted but not recommended
Map: USGS Acadia National Park and Vicinity
Special considerations: Full facilities available seasonally at the Jordan Pond House

Finding the trailhead: From the park's visitor center, drive south on the Park Loop Road for about 7.6 miles and turn right (north) into the Jordan Pond north lot. Park in the lot on the left (south) and follow signs to the Jordan Pond House. Walk past the Jordan Pond House and turn right (west) and follow a path marked "To Asticou, Spring Trail, Penobscot & Sargent Mtn Trails" down to a carriage road. The trailhead is across the carriage road to the right. The Island Explorer's Loop Road and Jordan Pond lines stop at the Jordan Pond House. GPS: N44 19.14' / W68 15.19'

The Hike

The Spring Trail is part of the rich history of the Jordan Pond House. The trail was laid out and built by Thomas McIntire, who began serving tourists at the Jordan Pond House in 1895. The trail's ease of access from the Jordan Pond House and its open views make this a well-frequented way up Penobscot Mountain. It is also part of the most traveled route up Sargent Mountain. Formerly called the Penobscot Mountain Trail, it has been restored to its historic name.

The trail begins behind the Jordan Pond House, across a carriage road and to the right.

At 0.3 mile pass the junction with the Jordan Cliffs Trail and the spring that gives this trail its name and cross a carriage road about 0.1 mile south of the West Branch Bridge, one of the unique stone spans that dot the Acadia landscape.

Begin the climb up Penobscot along stone steps that rise sharply on the west side of the carriage road. Switchbacks take you along a ledge with an elaborate system of wooden and iron handrails. You'll be amazed at the high cliffs in this area.

After climbing about thirty large pink granite steps, the trail reaches a flat open rock ledge with a man-made granite bench that is at least forty years old. Take a seat and enjoy a great spot for appreciating the awesome beauty of the park. Here you can see the blue expanse of Jordan Pond and then North Bubble and South Bubble side by side. The wide span of Pemetic Mountain fills the sky across the pond. We've seen yoga enthusiasts taking in the scenery near this ledge too.

At 0.5 mile reach the intersection with the Penobscot Mountain Trail. The recently reopened historic southern section of the Penobscot Mountain Trail comes in from the left, while the northern section heads

Hold on tightly to the iron and wood railings.

off toward the peak to the right (north). For an optional 2.0-mile round-trip climb to Penobscot and its open ridge with views south to the Cranberry Isles, bear right (north) on the Penobscot Mountain Trail.

Return the way you came.

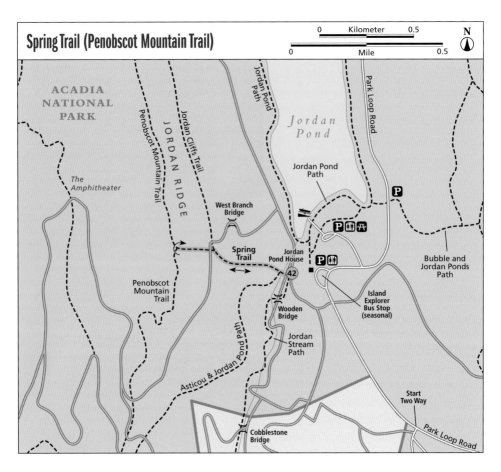

Spring Trail (Penobscot Mountain Trail)

Miles and Directions

0.0 Start at the Spring trailhead, behind the Jordan Pond House, across a carriage road and to the right.

0.3 Pass the junction with the Jordan Cliffs Trail heading off to the right (north), and cross a carriage road near the West Branch Bridge. Start climbing the Penobscot southeast face on stone steps on the west side of the road.

0.5 Reach the intersection with the original route of the Penobscot Mountain Trail. (*Option:* Bear right (north) to reach Penobscot Mountain in 1.0 mile.)

1.0 Arrive back at the trailhead.

43 Penobscot Mountain Trail via Asticou & Jordan Pond Path

Beginning at a revived section of the historic ridge trail to 1,194-foot Penobscot Mountain, this route is reached after first walking more than a mile along the garden-like Asticou & Jordan Pond Path. You'll find more solitude going up this way than along the Spring Trail that more directly connects the Jordan Pond House to Penobscot.

Distance: 7.0 miles out and back
Hiking time: About 3.5 to 4.5 hours
Difficulty: Moderate to strenuous
Trail surface: Granite steps, forest floor, rock ledges
Best season: Spring through fall

Other trail users: None
Canine compatibility: Leashed dogs permitted
Map: USGS Acadia National Park and Vicinity
Special considerations: Full facilities available seasonally at the Jordan Pond House

Finding the trailhead: From the park's visitor center, drive south on the Park Loop Road for about 7.6 miles and turn right (north) into the Jordan Pond north lot. Park in the lot on the left (south) and follow signs to the Jordan Pond House. Walk past the Jordan Pond House and turn right (west) and follow a path marked "To Asticou, Spring Trail, Penobscot & Sargent Mtn Trails" down to a carriage road. The trailhead for the Asticou & Jordan Pond Path, marked by a sign that reads "Sargent Mtn South Ridge Trail," is across the carriage road and wooden bridge, on the left. Follow the Asticou & Jordan Pond Path. Cross two more carriage roads, and at 1.3 miles in on the Asticou & Jordan Pond Path reach the Penobscot Mountain trailhead just before Little Harbor Brook. The Penobscot Mountain Trail heads right (north) along the east side of Little Harbor Brook. The Island Explorer's Loop Road and Jordan Pond lines stop at the Jordan Pond House. GPS at start: N44 19.12' / W68 15.20'

The Hike

After a 1.3-mile stroll from the Jordan Pond House along the graded gravel Asticou & Jordan Pond Path, reach the recently reopened historic start of the Penobscot Mountain Trail. Take the trail right (north), cross a couple of carriage roads in quick succession and then climb steeply up Penobscot, while taking in the views of the Cranberry Isles.

Switch back into the shade of some pine and maple trees, and continue to climb along upgraded stone steps. Reach some open rock slabs with higher views of Baker Island and the other Cranberry Isles.

Soon Jordan Pond comes into sight, just before you reach the junction of the Spring Trail, coming in from the right (east) at 2.5 miles. Bates-style cairns are the guide along open rock slabs, with views of Jordan Pond to the east and the Amphitheater formation and the south ridge of Sargent Mountain to the west.

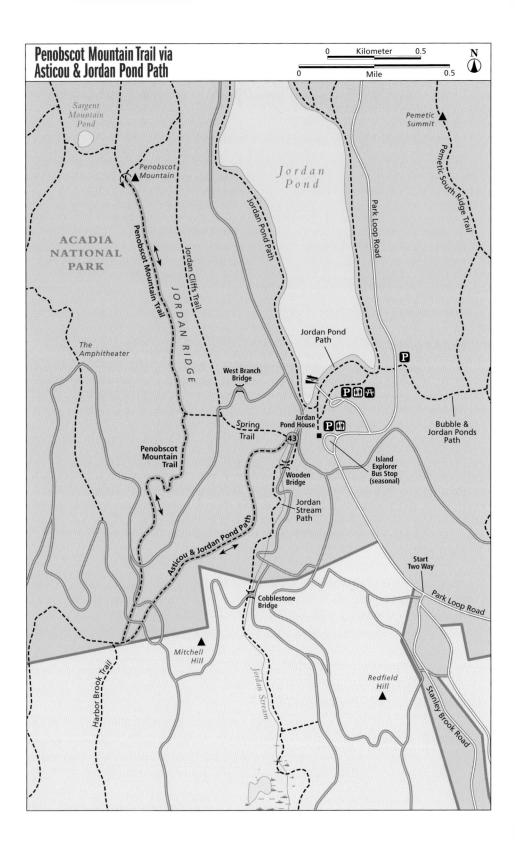

Penobscot Mountain Trail via Asticou & Jordan Pond Path

0   Kilometer   0.5

0   Mile   0.5

N

Sargent Mountain Pond

Pemetic Summit

Penobscot Mountain

Pemetic South Ridge Trail

ACADIA NATIONAL PARK

Penobscot Mountain Trail

Jordan Cliffs Trail

J O R D A N   R I D G E

Jordan Pond Path

Jordan Pond

Park Loop Road

The Amphitheater

Jordan Pond Path

P

West Branch Bridge

P

Spring Trail

Penobscot Mountain Trail

Jordan Pond House

43

P

Bubble & Jordan Ponds Path

Wooden Bridge

Jordan Stream Path

Island Explorer Bus Stop (seasonal)

Asticou & Jordan Pond Path

Start Two Way

Park Loop Road

Cobblestone Bridge

Mitchell Hill

Harbor Brook Trail

Jordan Stream

Redfield Hill

Stanley Brook Road

The open ridge of Penosbscot Mountain lets you see clear to the Cranberry Isles and beyond.

At 3.5 miles reach the 1,194-foot summit of Penobscot, with its broad vistas. To the south are the Cranberry Isles, east are Pemetic and Cadillac Mountains, north is Sargent Mountain, the second highest peak in Acadia, and west are Norumbega and Parkman Mountains and Bald Peak. There are truly magnificent views of Southwest Harbor and the islands beyond, such as Swans Island.

Return the way you came.

Miles and Directions

0.0 Start at the Asticou & Jordan Pond Path trailhead, behind and to the left of the Jordan Pond House, across a carriage road and wooden bridge.

1.1 Cross a carriage road.

1.2 Cross a second carriage road. To the right (northwest) 0.3 mile along the road is the Amphitheater trailhead for access to Cedar Swamp and Sargent Mountains. Continue straight (southwest) on the Asticou & Jordan Pond Path.

1.3 Reach the Penobscot Mountain trailhead, on the right (north) just before Little Harbor Brook. Go right (north) on the Penobscot Mountain Trail.

2.5 Reach the junction of the Spring Trail coming in from the Jordan Pond House. Turn left (north) to continue on the Penobscot Mountain Trail.

3.5 Summit Penobscot, where trails head northwest up to Sargent Mountain, or northeast down to Jordan Pond.

5.7 Arrive back at the Penobscot Mountain trailhead, and turn left (northeast) onto the Asticou & Jordan Pond Path.

7.0 Arrive back at the Jordan Pond House.

44 Jordan Cliffs Trail via Spring Trail

A dramatic climb along Jordan Cliffs, this trail provides breathtaking views of Jordan Pond, the Bubbles, and surrounding scenery and features iron rungs and exposed ledges. The cliffs are a favorite nesting area for peregrine falcons, so sections of the trail may be closed at certain times of the year.

Distance: 3.5-mile loop
Hiking time: About 2.5 to 3.5 hours
Difficulty: Strenuous to expert only
Trail surface: Iron rungs, granite steps, wooden bridges, forest floor, rock ledges
Best season: Late summer to fall to avoid peregrine falcon nesting season

Other trail users: Hikers climbing to Penobscot
Canine compatibility: Dogs prohibited
Map: USGS Acadia National Park and Vicinity
Special considerations: Full facilities available seasonally at the Jordan Pond House

Finding the trailhead: From the park's visitor center, drive south on the Park Loop Road for about 7.6 miles and turn right (north) into the Jordan Pond north lot. Park in the lot on the left (south) and follow signs to the Jordan Pond House. Walk past the Jordan Pond House and turn right (west) and follow a path marked "To Asticou, Spring Trail, Penobscot & Sargent Mtn Trails" down to a carriage road to access the Spring Trail. Follow the Spring Trail (Penobscot Mountain Trail) across the carriage road to the right, and reach the Jordan Cliffs trailhead in 0.3 mile. The Island Explorer's Loop Road and Jordan Pond lines stop at the Jordan Pond House. GPS at start: N44 19.14' / W68 15.19'

The Hike

The best time to climb the Jordan Cliffs Trail is earlier in the day, before the sun starts sinking behind the Penobscot ridge. The best season is late summer into fall to avoid the possibility of the trail being closed for peregrine falcon nesting season. These occasional closures help the success of Acadia's reintroduction program, which between 1991 and 2015 had resulted in more than 120 peregrine falcon chicks fledging, or able to fly, from cliffside nests.

Jordan Cliffs, in fact, was where the Acadia peregrine program got its start as a "hacking" site. By placing and raising captive-bred chicks on these rock faces beginning in the 1980s, officials hoped this area would be "imprinted" on the young falcons as home so that they would return to breed as adults. One of those original young falcons nested in 1991, the first to do so in Acadia in thirty-five years. Since then, falcons born on Jordan Cliffs have been found in Washington, D.C., and Vermont.

From behind and to the right (west) of the Jordan Pond House, follow the Spring Trail (Penobscot Mountain Trail) across the carriage road to the right, and reach the Jordan Cliffs trailhead in 0.3 mile.

Hikers need the assistance of that iron rung to make it up the cliffs that peregrine falcons so easily soar above.

The trail starts easily enough from the junction with the Spring Trail, crossing a carriage road. Then you see a sign that warns about exposed cliffs and fixed iron rungs. This is not a trail for people afraid of heights. The trail may not be as challenging as the Precipice off Champlain Mountain, but it's close.

Ascending then leveling off along the cliffs, the trail soon begins offering its spectacular vistas. To the south is an open view of the Cranberry Isles, and to the east is

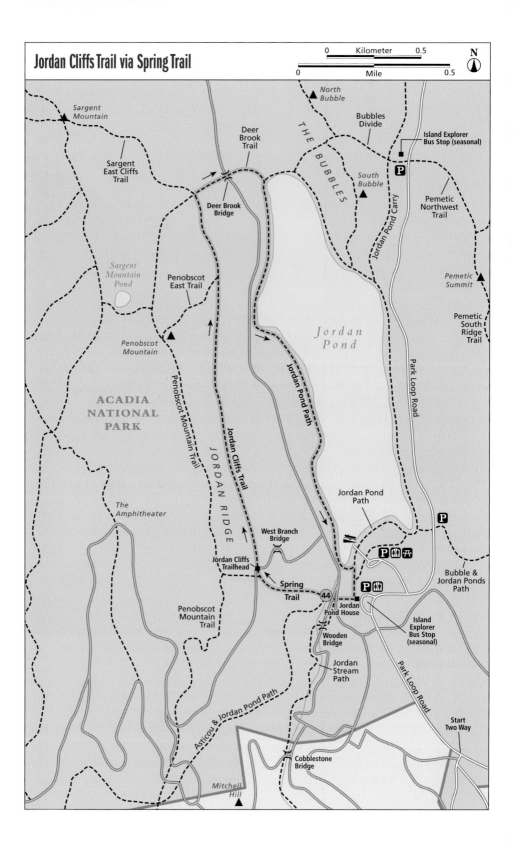

Jordan Cliffs Trail via Spring Trail

0   Kilometer   0.5

0   Mile   0.5

N

Sargent
Mountain

Sargent
East Cliffs
Trail

Deer
Brook
Trail

North
Bubble

THE BUBBLES

Bubbles
Divide

Island Explorer
Bus Stop (seasonal)

P

South
Bubble

Pemetic
Northwest
Trail

Deer Brook
Bridge

Sargent
Mountain
Pond

Penobscot
East Trail

Jordan
Pond

Jordan Pond Carry

Pemetic
Summit

Pemetic
South
Ridge
Trail

Penobscot
Mountain

Penobscot Mountain Trail

ACADIA
NATIONAL
PARK

Jordan Cliffs Trail

JORDAN RIDGE

Jordan Pond Path

Park Loop Road

The
Amphitheater

Jordan Pond
Path

P

West Branch
Bridge

P

Bubble &
Jordan Ponds
Path

Jordan Cliffs
Trailhead

Spring
Trail

44

P

Penobscot
Mountain
Trail

Jordan
Pond House

Island
Explorer
Bus Stop
(seasonal)

Wooden
Bridge

Jordan
Stream
Path

Asticou & Jordan Pond Path

Park Loop Road

Start
Two Way

Cobblestone
Bridge

Mitchell
Hill

Jordan Pond, forming a fantastic backdrop for photos or video. Across the pond, the Bubbles and Pemetic Mountain soon come into sight to the northeast.

We once met a Colorado couple mid-cliff here who were visiting Acadia for the first time and said the terrain reminded them of home. "It's kind of like the Rockies."

The trail features a variety of handrails, iron rungs, and stone steps to help you through some tricky spots on the rock face. You even need to cross a suspended one-log bridge nearly as narrow as a gymnast's balance beam, with thirty-two carved-out notches for footholds. It's at least reassuring to know the park service has rebuilt the intricate log bridge—and that there are log handrails.

Following the bridge is a stretch of exposed cliffs with dramatic views toward Jordan Pond. Finally clearing the exposed ledges, you come to a shady resting spot directly across from South Bubble—a good place to catch your breath and get a pat on the back for safely negotiating one of Acadia's more difficult cliff trails.

Reach a junction with the Penobscot East Trail at 1.5 miles, which heads left (southwest) toward Penobscot Mountain. Go straight (north) to continue along the Jordan Cliffs Trail, descending all the way.

At 1.7 miles reach the intersection with the Deer Brook Trail and Sargent East Cliffs Trail. Turn right (northeast) to head down on the Deer Brook Trail toward Jordan Pond.

At 1.8 miles cross a carriage road by the double-arched Deer Brook Bridge. Reach the shores of Jordan Pond at 2.0 miles, and turn right (south) to head toward the Jordan Pond House, returning at 3.5 miles.

Miles and Directions

0.0 Start at the trailhead for Spring Trail (Penobscot Mountain Trail), behind the Jordan Pond House, across a carriage road and to the right.

0.3 Reach the Jordan Cliffs trailhead.

0.4 Cross the carriage road.

1.5 Reach the junction with the Penobscot East Trail, which heads 0.5 mile left (southwest) up Penobscot. Stay straight (north).

1.7 Reach the junction with the Deer Brook and Sargent East Cliffs Trails. Turn right to head northeast down the Deer Brook Trail toward Jordan Pond. (Sargent East Cliffs Trail goes to Sargent Mountain in 0.8 mile.)

1.8 Cross a carriage road by the Deer Brook Bridge.

2.0 Reach Jordan Pond. Turn right (south) to head along the western shore of the pond, creating a loop without needing to rehike the Spring Trail.

3.5 Arrive back at the Jordan Pond House.

45 Deer Brook Trail via Jordan Pond Path

It's not the most scenic or accessible route up Penobscot Mountain, but the hike does offer a perspective on the carriage road system's Deer Brook Bridge that eludes some park users. On foot it's amazing to see the bridge's towering double-arched construction, the only such carriage road span in Acadia. On a bicycle or horse-drawn carriage, it's easy to miss the unusual architecture below.

Distance: 5.2 miles out and back
Hiking time: About 3 to 3.5 hours
Difficulty: Moderate to strenuous
Trail surface: Forest floor, rock ledges
Best season: Spring through fall

Other trail users: Hikers on the Sargent East Cliffs or Jordan Cliffs Trail
Canine compatibility: Leashed dogs permitted
Map: USGS Acadia National Park and Vicinity
Special considerations: Full facilities available seasonally at the nearby Jordan Pond House

Finding the trailhead: From the park's visitor center, head south on the Park Loop Road for about 7.6 miles and turn right (north) into the Jordan Pond north lot. Park in the lot on the right. Follow the boat ramp road down to the shore of the pond. The trailhead for Jordan Pond Path is on the right (east) and leads around the pond. Follow Jordan Pond Path to the right (northeast) for 1.7 miles, halfway around to the northwestern shore of Jordan Pond. The Deer Brook trailhead is on the right (northwest). The Island Explorer's Loop Road and Jordan Pond lines stop at the nearby Jordan Pond House. GPS at start: N44 19.22' / W68 15.13'

The Hike

A less-traveled route up Penobscot Mountain, this trail follows Deer Brook steeply up through the woods and includes some potentially tricky brook crossings. It offers solitude and a chance to explore the lovely double-arched Deer Brook Bridge, built in 1925. And it's the beneficiary of a National Park Service Centennial Challenge grant in 2015, with $50,000 federal funds matched by $50,000 from the nonprofit Friends of Acadia, for badly needed erosion control and rehabilitation.

From the end of the boat ramp, take Jordan Pond Path to the right (northeast) for 1.7 miles, halfway around the pond, to the Deer Brook trailhead on the right (northwest).

Leave the shore of Jordan Pond and climb on stone steps along the brook, with its strong cascades. In 1.9 miles reach the unusual Deer Brook Bridge. The bridge, built by master masons under the personal oversight of John D. Rockefeller Jr., is 78 feet long and 22.4 feet high. Take a look around and notice if the bridge's dark granite matches the area as intended by Rockefeller and his architect.

Cross the carriage road diagonally to the left and ascend. Deer Brook flows through a large chasm here. Soon the trail cuts through a wooded area of tall spruce and pine.

Stay straight (southwest) at 2.0 miles, through the intersection where the Jordan Cliffs and Sargent East Cliffs Trails come in. Continue climbing steeply.

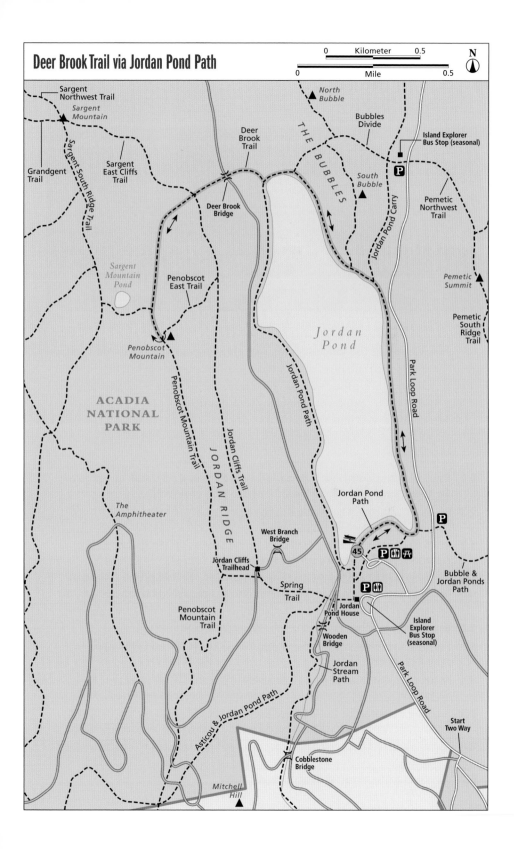

The year of construction, 1925, is set into the circular medallion of the Deer Brook Bridge.

At 2.5 miles reach the junction with a spur to Sargent Mountain Pond and the Sargent South Ridge Trail. Bear left (southeast), and reach the open 1,194-foot summit of Penobscot in 2.6 miles, with its 360-degree views. Here is where the Penobscot East Trail and the Penobscot Mountain Trail also meet.

Return the way you came.

Miles and Directions

0.0 Start at the Jordan Pond Path trailhead. At the end of the boat ramp road, turn right along the graded gravel path and walk along the eastern shore of the pond.

0.3 Reach the junction with the Bubble & Jordan Ponds Path (Pond Trail); continue straight along the eastern shore of the pond.

1.1 Reach the junction with Jordan Pond Carry and the Bubbles Trail (South Bubble Trail); continue straight along the eastern shore of the pond.

1.6 Reach the junction with Bubbles Divide, which goes northeast through the gap between North and South Bubbles. Continue along the shore as the path rounds the north side of the pond.

1.7 Reach the Deer Brook trailhead, and turn right (northwest) onto the trail.

1.9 Reach the Deer Brook Bridge and a carriage road. Cross over the road and continue straight (southwest).

2.0 Reach the junction with the Jordan Cliffs Trail coming in from the left (south) and the Sargent East Cliffs Trail coming in from the right (north). Continue straight (southwest).

2.5 Reach the junction with a spur to Sargent Mountain Pond that goes to the right (west) and hooks up with the Sargent South Ridge Trail. Bear left (southeast) to continue to Penobscot.

2.6 Summit Penobscot, and reach the junction with the Penobscot East and Penobscot Mountain Trails.

5.2 Arrive back at the Jordan Pond Path trailhead.

46 Sargent East Cliffs Trail via Jordan Pond Path and Deer Brook Trail

Accessed from the Deer Brook Trail, this is a recently reopened route up Sargent Mountain, at 1,373 feet the park's second-highest peak. The approximately 90-year-old trail, tastefully refurbished with some unique historic-style cairns, offers jaw-dropping views of Cadillac Mountain rising above North and South Bubbles, Conners Nubble, and Eagle Lake.

Distance: 5.4 miles out and back
Hiking time: About 2.5 to 3.5 hours
Difficulty: Moderate to strenuous
Trail surface: Granite steps, forest floor, rock ledges
Best season: Spring through fall

Other trail users: Hikers climbing the Jordan Cliffs Trail or Penobscot Mountain
Canine compatibility: Leashed dogs permitted
Map: USGS Acadia National Park and Vicinity
Special considerations: Full facilities available seasonally at the nearby Jordan Pond House

Finding the trailhead: From the park's visitor center, head south on the Park Loop Road for about 7.6 miles and turn right (north) into the Jordan Pond north lot. Park in the lot on the right. Follow the boat ramp road down to the shore of the pond. The trailhead for Jordan Pond Path is on the right (east) and leads around the pond. The Island Explorer's Loop Road and Jordan Pond lines stop at the nearby Jordan Pond House. GPS at start: N44 19.22' / W68 15.13'

The Hike

Sargent East Cliffs Trail is a steep and rewarding hike of less than 1.0 mile along a historic trail to the wide-open peak of Sargent Mountain.

But before you get there, you need to first walk along the eastern shore of Jordan Pond for 1.7 miles, starting at the Jordan Pond Path trailhead at the foot of the boat ramp. Then you need to turn right (northwest) onto the Deer Brook Trail, until you reach the Sargent East Cliffs trailhead at 2.0 miles. Leaving the Deer Brook Trail, ascend immediately to the right (northwest) along stone steps and switchback up the mountain. Soon there are views of Jordan Pond; the Bubbles; and Penobscot, Cadillac, and Pemetic Mountains.

The trees disappear behind you and the trail traverses an open granite face, with blue blazes and Bates-style cairns directing the way.

Thomas McIntire, owner of what was once known as the Jordan Pond Tea House, helped build this trail, maybe in the early 1920s. The trail was closed in the mid-1990s when it became badly eroded. The park service reopened it about a decade later and tagged it with the historic name. It had previously been considered the northern end of the Jordan Cliffs Trail.

The pink of rhodora and granite complement each other along the Sargent East Cliffs Trail.

One thing is for sure as you ascend up the eastern face of Sargent: There's no need to go to the peak for fantastic views. There are also lots of places to sit, get some peace, and enjoy the scenery.

Before reaching the summit, the trail bears left through a thicket of trees. The climbing gets a little difficult over the rocks before the trail bursts into the open again just below the peak.

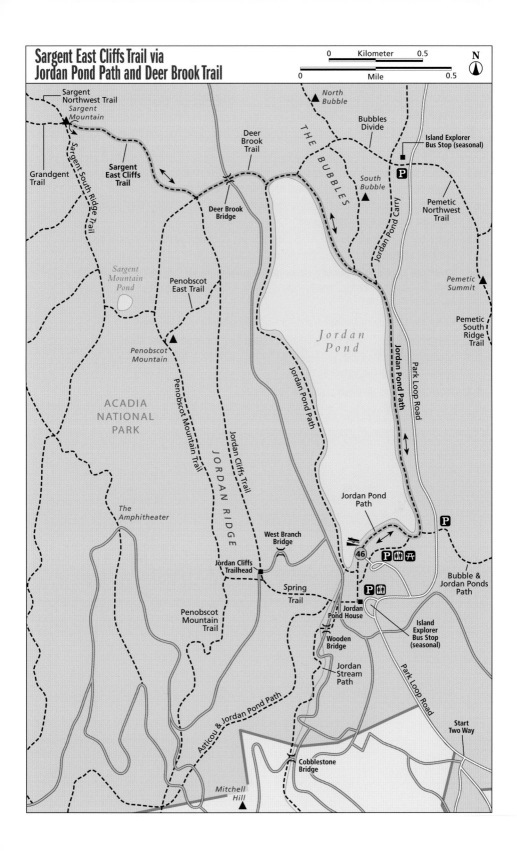

Sargent East Cliffs Trail via Jordan Pond Path and Deer Brook Trail

0   Kilometer   0.5

0   Mile   0.5

N

Sargent
Northwest Trail

*Sargent
Mountain*

Deer
Brook
Trail

*North
Bubble*

Bubbles
Divide

Island Explorer
Bus Stop (seasonal)

**Sargent
East Cliffs
Trail**

THE BUBBLES

*South
Bubble*

Jordan Pond Carry

P

Pemetic
Northwest
Trail

Grandgent
Trail

Sargent South Ridge Trail

Deer Brook
Bridge

Penobscot
East Trail

*Sargent
Mountain
Pond*

*Jordan
Pond*

*Pemetic
Summit*

Pemetic
South
Ridge
Trail

Penobscot
Mountain

Penobscot Mountain Trail

ACADIA
NATIONAL
PARK

JORDAN RIDGE

Jordan Cliffs Trail

Jordan Pond Path

Jordan Pond
Path

Jordan Pond Path

*The
Amphitheater*

West Branch
Bridge

P

P

Bubble &
Jordan Ponds
Path

Jordan Cliffs
Trailhead

46

P

Spring
Trail

Penobscot
Mountain
Trail

P

Jordan
Pond House

Island
Explorer
Bus Stop
(seasonal)

Park Loop Road

Wooden
Bridge

Asticou & Jordan Pond Path

Jordan
Stream
Path

Start
Two Way

Park Loop Road

Cobblestone
Bridge

*Mitchell
Hill*

Atop Sargent you can see in all directions. Somes Sound and Western Mountain are to the west, the Cranberry Isles and the Gulf of Maine to the south, Pemetic and Cadillac Mountains to the east, and the Porcupine Islands and Frenchman Bay to the northeast.

Miles and Directions

0.0 Start at the Jordan Pond Path trailhead. At the end of the boat ramp road, turn right along the graded gravel path and walk along the eastern shore of the pond.

0.3 Reach the junction with the Bubble & Jordan Ponds Path (Pond Trail); continue straight along the eastern shore of the pond.

1.1 Reach the junction with Jordan Pond Carry and the Bubbles Trail (South Bubble Trail); continue straight along the eastern shore of the pond.

1.6 Reach the junction with Bubbles Divide, which goes northeast through the gap between North and South Bubbles. Continue along the shore as the path rounds the north side of the pond.

1.7 Reach the Deer Brook trailhead, and turn right (northwest) onto the trail.

2.0 Reach the Sargent East Cliffs trailhead, and turn right (northwest) onto the trail.

2.7 Summit Sargent Mountain and reach the junction with the Sargent Northwest, Sargent South Ridge, and Grandgent Trails.

5.4 Arrive back at the trailhead for Jordan Pond Path.

47 Sargent Mountain Loop via Giant Slide and Grandgent Trails

This strenuous loop combines sections of a few trails for a traverse along huge boulders and rock slabs at the bottom of a giant slide and then up the open summit of Sargent, Acadia's second-highest peak. You'll also bag less-visited Gilmore Peak, nestled between Sargent and Parkman Mountains.

Distance: 5.5-mile lollipop
Hiking time: About 3.5 to 4.5 hours
Difficulty: Moderate to strenuous
Trail surface: Ravine, granite steps, wooden bridges, forest floor, rock ledges
Best season: Spring through fall

Other trail users: Hikers climbing Gilmore Peak
Canine compatibility: Leashed dogs permitted but not recommended on the Giant Slide Trail
Map: USGS Acadia National Park and Vicinity
Special considerations: No facilities

Finding the trailhead: From Bar Harbor head west on ME 233 for 4 miles, then turn left (south) onto ME 198 for 0.9 mile. The recently moved Giant Slide trailhead is on the left (east) side of ME 198; park along the highway. The Island Explorer does not have a stop here, although the Brown Mountain line travels ME 198 on its way between Bar Harbor and Northeast Harbor; ask to be let off at the trailhead if it is safe to do so. GPS: N44 21.01' / W68 18.06'

The Hike

Deceivingly easy at first, the hike begins relatively flat.

The Giant Slide Trail starts by winding through a mossy forest and along some extensive trail work to protect the terrain—dozens of sections of log bridges, each 6 to 7 feet long, known as bog walks. Soon you'll climb a short series of granite steps to an amazing sea-green-colored, lichen-terraced landscape. Here a sign cautions "Fragile Habitat: Please Stay on the Trail" before it explains how lichen is made up of two different plants, alga and fungus, and can take decades to recover if trampled.

After crossing a carriage road at 0.7 mile and following the trail to the right (southeast), you start the challenging climb up through the beginnings of the Giant Slide, around and under large boulders and slabs, squeezing through crevices and clambering by trees and ferns growing on rocks on the thinnest cover of soil. If you hike after heavy rains, Sargent Brook's cascades and waterfalls can make for a wet and wonderful show along here, but the footing can be treacherous.

At 1.4 miles reach the junction with the Parkman Mountain Trail coming in on the right (west) and the Sargent Northwest Trail (Sargent North Ridge Trail) on the left (east). The Giant Slide Trail goes straight ahead at this junction, through a narrow, seemingly impassable, passageway between two rock walls (you'll be squeezing

Don't bump your head on the rock overhang as you make your way along the Giant Slide Trail.

through there on the way back). Turn left here to take the Sargent Northwest Trail up the steep face of Sargent.

The Sargent Northwest Trail brings you immediately across what can be a wide, rushing Sargent Brook after heavy rains. Ascend steeply as the trail switchbacks through the forest.

At 1.7 miles cross a carriage road, climb stone steps, and continue along the Sargent Northwest Trail on the other side. As the trail keeps going up steeply, you get your first views to the left (west) of Eagle Lake. If you hike this trail in late spring, you'll also see an explosion of purple flowers known as rhodora. In late summer there's a burst of goldenrods.

The trail dips then ascends along an open ridge with views all around. Keep your eyes out for the distinctive Bates-style cairns that mark the trail, especially along the bare rock ledges, to avoid losing your way.

At 2.4 miles reach the 1,373-foot summit of Sargent, second highest behind only Cadillac. Here you get spectacular 360-degree views of Somes Sound and Western Mountain to the right (west), the Cranberry Isles and the Gulf of Maine to the south, Pemetic and Cadillac Mountains to the east, and Porcupine Islands and Frenchman Bay to the northeast.

The area around Sargent Mountain is also noted for its red mountain cranberries—called lingonberries in certain parts of Europe, as a family we met here told us while they picked the berries in early August. Look closely, because the tiny berries are buried behind thick green leaves.

The summit also marks the junction of the Sargent East Cliffs, Sargent South Ridge, and Grandgent Trails. Take the rightmost trail (Grandgent) to head west off Sargent and loop back via Gilmore Peak and the Giant Slide Trail.

The Grandgent Trail is another one of Acadia's historic memorial paths, named for Charles Hall Grandgent, chair of Harvard's Romance language department, Southwest Harbor summer resident, and chair of the Southwest Harbor Village Improvement Association in the 1920s and 1930s.

At 2.7 miles reach the junction with the Maple Spring Trail. Turn right (west) to descend. At 3.2 miles, cross a brook on a nice footbridge to continue on the Grandgent Trail, and reach Gilmore Peak at 3.3 miles.

While this 1,036-foot peak is less visited than either the higher Sargent to the northeast or the more easily accessed Parkman Mountain or Bald Peak to the west and southwest, its views are definitely not second fiddle. From Gilmore—the lowest of the park's eight mountains 1,000 feet or higher—you can see west to Somes Sound, Echo Lake, and Long Pond, and east to Sargent.

Descend steeply down Gilmore along loose rock, reaching the junction with the Giant Slide Trail at 3.5 miles. Turn right (north) to loop back through the Giant Slide.

At 3.7 miles cross a carriage road diagonally to the right to continue northwest on the Giant Slide Trail. Follow Sargent Brook, crossing from one side to the other.

Sargent Mountain Loop via Giant Slide and Grandgent Trails

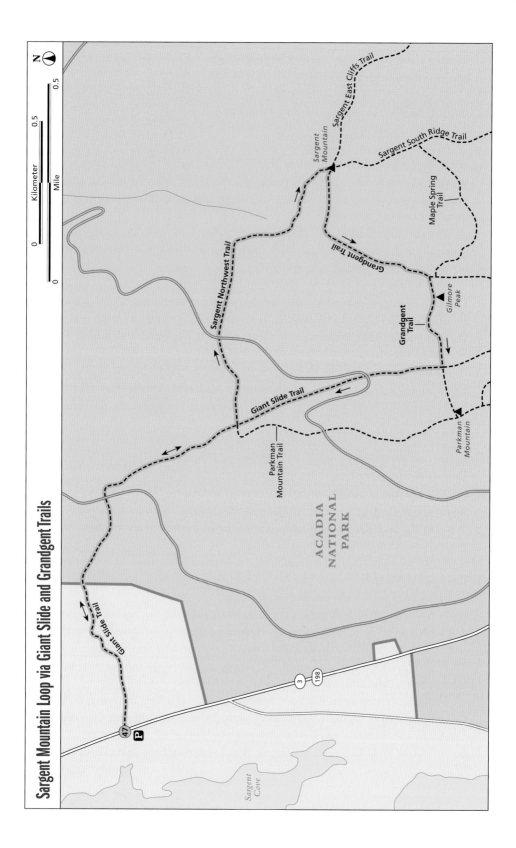

Watch your step on the moss-covered rocks, even as you admire a sheer rock wall that towers above on the right (east).

The trail gets rougher. Squeeze between the tumbled-down slabs of granite, and clamber over the boulders of Giant Slide. At 4.1 miles loop back to the junction with the Sargent Northwest Trail coming in from the east and Parkman Mountain Trail coming in from the west.

Stay straight (northwest) on the Giant Slide Trail, recrossing the first carriage road at 4.8 miles and looping back to the trailhead at 5.5 miles.

Miles and Directions

0.0 Start at the Giant Slide trailhead, on the east side of ME 198.

0.7 Cross a carriage road and follow the trail as it curves right (southeast).

1.4 Reach the junction with the Sargent Northwest Trail (Sargent Mountain North Ridge Trail) and Parkman Mountain Trail. Turn left (east) onto the Sargent Northwest Trail toward Sargent Mountain.

1.7 Cross a carriage road.

2.4 Summit Sargent and reach the junction with the Sargent East Cliffs, Sargent South Ridge, and Grandgent Trails. Turn right onto the Grandgent Trail and head west off the peak.

2.7 Reach the junction with the Maple Spring Trail. Turn right (west) and descend.

3.2 Cross a brook on a footbridge to continue on the Grandgent Trail.

3.3 Summit Gilmore Peak.

3.5 Reach the junction with the Giant Slide Trail. Turn right (north) to loop back.

3.7 Cross a carriage road.

4.1 Return to the junction with the Sargent Northwest and Parkman Mountain Trails. Go straight (northwest) to stay on the Giant Slide Trail.

4.8 Cross a carriage road and follow the trail as it curves left (west).

5.5 Arrive back at the Giant Slide trailhead.

48 Sargent South Ridge Trail via Carriage Road

A longer way up Sargent Mountain, this hike also includes a side trip to pleasant Cedar Swamp Mountain, a look down into a natural granite amphitheater between Sargent and Penobscot, and open ridgeline walking. Capping it off are the 360-degree views from the second-highest peak in Acadia.

Distance: 6.8 miles out and back
Hiking time: About 4 to 5 hours
Difficulty: Moderate
Trail surface: Forest floor, rock ledges
Best season: Spring through fall
Other trail users: Hikers climbing the Amphi-theater, Hadlock Brook, Maple Spring, or Penobscot Mountain Trail

Canine compatibility: Leashed dogs permitted
Map: USGS Acadia National Park and Vicinity
Special considerations: Chemical toilet at the carriage road parking lot near the Brown Mountain Gatehouse

Finding the trailhead: From Bar Harbor head west on ME 233 for 4 miles. Turn left (south) onto ME 198 and travel another 3.9 miles, past Upper Hadlock Pond on your left, to a carriage road parking lot on the left (east) side of ME 198 just before the Brown Mountain Gatehouse. The Island Explorer's Brown Mountain line stops here at the carriage road parking lot. GPS: N44 18.42' / W68 17.07'

The Hike

Most people who climb Sargent go up via the Spring and Penobscot Mountain Trails, preserving the solitude and beauty of the Sargent South Ridge Trail. As a result, you may see turkey vultures soaring on thermals or a cluster of pink lady's slippers or showy yellow-and-pink columbines.

This trail is where we were first amazed by Bates-style cairns, with rocks stacked like miniature architectural wonders, before we knew their historic significance or that they are named for Waldron Bates, chair of the Roads and Paths Committee of the Bar Harbor Village Improvement Association from 1900 to 1909.

Walk left (northeast) on the carriage road away from the gatehouse, which is now a private residence. Bear right (southeast) twice, at carriage road intersections No. 18 and No. 19, until you reach the trailhead on the left (north) in about 0.7 mile.

The trail heads north moderately up from the carriage road and soon hints at the dramatic views to come. It bears right and levels off and then ascends to an exposed pink granite ledge. The trail gently zigzags up the ridge of Sargent Mountain. Blueberry bushes line the path. In spring you can find columbine, with its delicate yellow-and-pink pipe-shaped flower; starflower, with its tiny six- or seven-pointed

Rhodora is native to the Northeast, and the passion for it is as old as the love for the hills of Mount Desert.

white flowers; and Canada dogwood, also known as bunchberry, with its four white petal–like bracts that appear to be a showy flower.

As the path takes you in and out of the woods and along exposed ledges, you get views of the Penobscot ridge to the right (east), the ocean behind you to the south, and Norumbega Mountain to the left (west).

You reach the first full view of the Penobscot summit as the trail brings you along the edge of the natural amphitheater formed by the Sargent and Penobscot ridges. You can peer down through the trees and see a carriage road cutting along the side of the Amphitheater. Along the ridge you get expansive views of Penobscot, the Amphitheater, the Gulf of Maine, and the Cranberry Isles.

At 2.1 miles a 0.1-mile spur heads left (west) to 942-foot Cedar Swamp Mountain, which can easily become a favorite. We stopped here twice on the same day and met a local couple who have summited Cedar Swamp countless times, even in winter.

But don't be surprised if you don't see a cedar swamp here. Gary Stellpflug, head of Acadia's trail crew, has a theory about that.

"Historically, Cedar Swamp Mountain was a half mile to the south on a nubble," according to trail maps of the late 1800s and early 1900s, where it's wetter and closer to Upper Hadlock Pond. Some later mapmaker may have put the summit higher on the ridge, thinking the peak couldn't have been on that lower bump.

"That's my guess," Stellpflug says. "It's purely a guess."

The history and the stories behind Acadia's trails are ever fascinating.

Come down from the mountain with no swamp and continue on the Sargent South Ridge Trail to Birch Spring, which is marked by a sign, so you can't miss it. The intersection with the Amphitheater Trail is also here, at 2.2 miles.

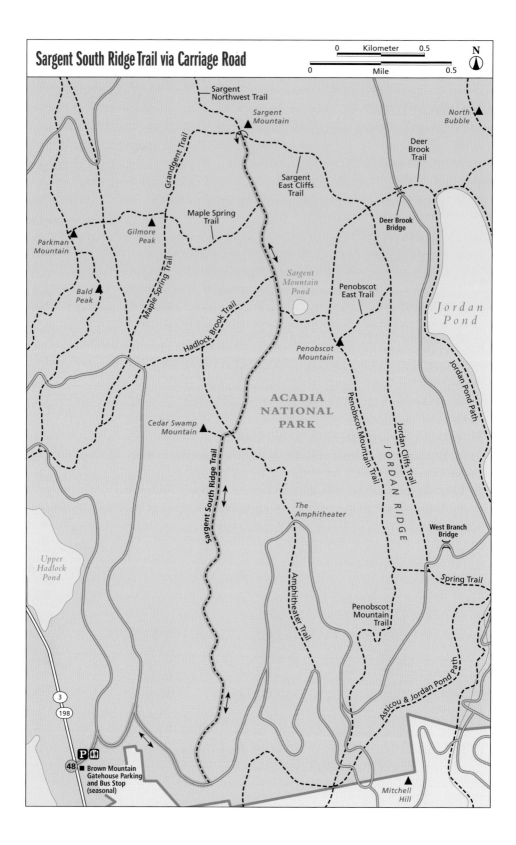

Sargent South Ridge Trail via Carriage Road

Sargent
Northwest Trail

Sargent
Mountain

North
Bubble

Grandgent Trail

Deer
Brook
Trail

Sargent
East Cliffs
Trail

Maple Spring
Trail

Deer Brook
Bridge

Parkman
Mountain

Gilmore
Peak

Maple Spring Trail

Sargent
Mountain
Pond

Penobscot
East Trail

Jordan
Pond

Bald
Peak

Hadlock Brook Trail

Penobscot
Mountain

Jordan Pond Path

ACADIA
NATIONAL
PARK

Cedar Swamp
Mountain

Sargent South Ridge Trail

Penobscot Mountain Trail

Jordan Cliffs Trail

JORDAN RIDGE

West Branch
Bridge

Upper
Hadlock
Pond

The
Amphitheater

Amphitheater Trail

Spring Trail

3
198

Penobscot
Mountain
Trail

Asticou & Jordan Pond Path

P

48   Brown Mountain
Gatehouse Parking
and Bus Stop
(seasonal)

Mitchell
Hill

The Sargent South Ridge Trail continues straight (northeast) up along woods and rocky ledges then ascends steeply up open rock slabs. Behind you, the ridge you just climbed snakes down toward the Gulf of Maine. You can also see the Cranberry Isles, Long Pond, and ME 3 to the south and Somes Sound and Norumbega to the west.

At 2.7 miles reach the junction with the Penobscot Mountain Trail, which heads east past Sargent Mountain Pond to the Penobscot summit. You're high enough on the open ridge of Sargent Mountain here to get views of Cadillac Mountain to the northeast and of Pemetic Mountain, which lies between Cadillac and Penobscot.

Continue straight (north) on the Sargent South Ridge Trail. Reach a junction at 2.9 miles with the Hadlock Brook Trail, which heads southwest toward ME 198, and at 3.1 miles, a junction with the Maple Spring Trail, which also heads toward ME 198.

At 3.4 miles, attain the 1,373-foot summit of Sargent to enjoy its 360-degree views. But tread carefully—Sargent and other Acadia summits are home to some unusual or rare subalpine plants, supported only by a thin layer of soil. Heavy foot traffic can kill the plants.

Trail workers are taking steps to protect the peaks. During a recent visit, Acadia trails foreman Stellpflug and Charlie Jacobi, resource specialist for Acadia, led a team to construct a causeway on the peak to direct hikers to stay on the trail instead of venturing onto the subalpine zone around the mountaintop. To build the causeway, the team used rocks and stones mostly from a massive cairn on Sargent. It was tough work, but maybe worth it if it helps save the popular peak from heavy hiking use.

Return the way you came.

Miles and Directions

0.0 Start at the Brown Mountain Gatehouse and walk left (northeast) on the carriage road, bearing right at intersections No. 18 and No. 19.

0.7 Reach the Sargent South Ridge trailhead, and turn left (north) onto the trail.

2.1 Reach the junction with the 0.1-mile spur to Cedar Swamp Mountain on the left (west).

2.2 Reach the junction with the Amphitheater Trail at Birch Spring. Stay straight (northeast) to continue on the Sargent South Ridge Trail.

2.7 Reach the junction with the Penobscot Mountain Trail, which leads right (east) past Sargent Mountain Pond to Penobscot Mountain. Stay straight (north) to continue toward Sargent.

2.9 Reach the junction with the Hadlock Brook Trail coming in on the left (west). Go straight (north) to continue toward Sargent.

3.1 Reach the junction with the Maple Spring Trail coming in on the left (west). Go straight (north) to continue toward Sargent.

3.4 Summit Sargent, and reach the junction with the Grandgent, Sargent East Cliffs, and Sargent Northwest Trails.

6.8 Arrive back at the gatehouse.

49 Amphitheater Trail via Asticou & Jordan Pond Path and Carriage Road

The Amphitheater Trail winds from Little Harbor Brook Bridge to 245-foot-long Amphitheater Bridge—the longest bridge in the carriage road system—and crosses a glacially carved valley between the Sargent and Penobscot ridges to Birch Spring. This trip takes you to the short spur up Cedar Swamp Mountain, but you can also make a longer day hike by adding Sargent or Penobscot.

Distance: 6.0 miles out and back
Hiking time: About 3.5 to 4.5 hours
Difficulty: Moderate to strenuous
Trail surface: Granite steps, forest floor, rock ledges
Best season: Spring through fall

Other trail users: Hikers climbing Sargent South Ridge Trail; bicyclists and walkers at carriage road crossings
Canine compatibility: Leashed dogs permitted
Map: USGS Acadia National Park and Vicinity
Special considerations: Full facilities available seasonally at the Jordan Pond House

Finding the trailhead: From the park's visitor center, drive south on the Park Loop Road for about 7.6 miles and turn right (north) into the Jordan Pond north lot. Park in the lot on the left (south) and follow signs to the Jordan Pond House. Walk past the Jordan Pond House and turn right (west) and follow a path marked "To Asticou, Spring Trail, Penobscot & Sargent Mtn Trails" down to a carriage road. The Asticou & Jordan Path trailhead, marked by a sign that says "Sargent Mtn South Ridge Trail," is across the carriage road and wooden bridge, on the left. The Island Explorer's Loop Road and Jordan Pond lines stop at the Jordan Pond House. GPS at start: N44 19.12' / W68 15.20'

The Hike

Before the carriage road system was built, the Amphitheater Trail was the only way to access this wilder side of Mount Desert Island, where eons ago the glaciers had carved a natural amphitheater.

Even today, if you walk this less-traveled trail, you'll experience the wilder side.

But first, take the well-graded Asticou & Jordan Pond Path, found behind and to the west of the Jordan Pond House, across a carriage road and wooden bridge. In 1.1 miles, cross a carriage road, and in 1.2 miles, come to another carriage road. Turn right (northwest) onto the carriage road here, and reach the Amphitheater trailhead at 1.5 miles.

The Amphitheater Trail starts at the Little Harbor Brook Bridge and the brook itself. The trail crosses from one side of the brook to the other.

Part of the Asticou & Jordan Pond Path that got a major overhaul in 2014.

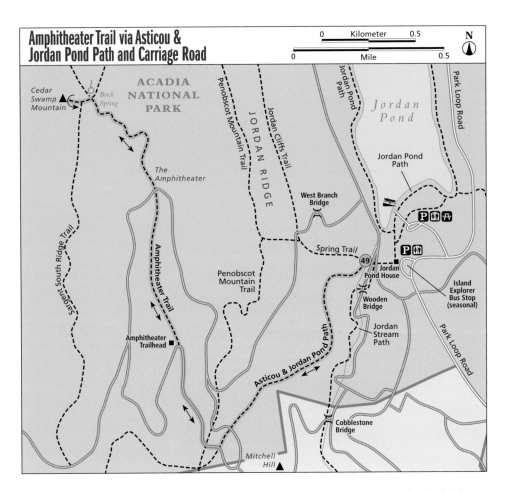

0   Kilometer   0.5

N

0   Mile   0.5

Cedar
Swamp ▲
Mountain

Birch
Spring

ACADIA
NATIONAL
PARK

Penobscot Mountain Trail

Jordan Cliffs Trail

J O R D A N   R I D G E

Jordan Pond Path

Jordan
Pond

Park Loop Road

The
Amphitheater

West Branch
Bridge

Jordan Pond
Path

Sargent South Ridge Trail

Amphitheater Trail

Spring Trail

49

Penobscot
Mountain
Trail

Jordan
Pond House

Island
Explorer
Bus Stop
(seasonal)

Amphitheater
Trailhead ■

Wooden
Bridge

Jordan
Stream
Path

Asticou & Jordan Pond Path

Park Loop Road

Cobblestone
Bridge

Mitchell
Hill ▲

At 2.3 miles reach the grand Amphitheater Bridge on a carriage road. The bridge towers above the trail and spans the long, rocky rim of the natural amphitheater, an open area walled by the west face of Penobscot and the east flank of Sargent's ridge.

Back in the 1920s the Amphitheater was a turning point in the struggle to protect the backcountry of Acadia. Activists who believed the area was sacred and should remain a place open to hikers only clashed with John D. Rockefeller Jr., who directed construction of the carriage road system and its bridges. At first Rockefeller agreed to leave the region untouched, and it remained a wilderness through most of the 1920s. In the end, Rockefeller decided to extend the carriage roads into the Amphi-theater, believing the section was important to his overall system and that people on horses or in horse-drawn carriages deserved access as much as hikers. The year 1931 is carved into stone railing on Rockefeller's bridge, dating his conquest of these woods.

You can turn around here if you want to make it a short trip. But if you like ridge and mountain views, cross the carriage road to continue north on the Amphitheater

Trail. The trail parallels the brook for a bit and then steeply ascends to open ledges. You get views behind you (south) to the Cranberry Isles.

At 2.9 miles reach the junction with the Sargent South Ridge Trail at Birch Spring. Turn left (west) onto the Sargent South Ridge Trail and clamber up some rock slabs. At 3.0 miles reach the short spur on the right (west) to 942-foot Cedar Swamp Mountain.

This peak is a great alternative to the taller Sargent. It provides views of Bald, Parkman, Gilmore, and Sargent to the north and northwest; Norumbega and Western Mountains to the west; and Penobscot Mountain to the east. A wooded part of Cedar Swamp Mountain blocks views to the south.

Return the way you came.

Miles and Directions

0.0 Start at the Asticou & Jordan Pond Path trailhead, behind and to the west of the Jordan Pond House, across a carriage road and wooden bridge.

1.1 Cross a carriage road.

1.2 Come to a second carriage road and turn right (northwest).

1.5 Reach the Amphitheater trailhead, on the right (north) side of the carriage road.

2.3 Reach the Amphitheater Bridge at a carriage road crossing. (**Option:** Turn around here for a 4.6-mile round-trip hike.)

2.9 Reach the junction with the Sargent South Ridge Trail at Birch Spring. Turn left (west) onto the Sargent South Ridge Trail.

3.0 Turn right (west) at the short spur to Cedar Swamp Mountain.

6.0 Arrive back at the Asticou & Jordan Pond Path trailhead.

Options

To loop back to Jordan Pond House via Penobscot rather than heading to Cedar Swamp, at Birch Spring, turn right (north) onto the Sargent South Ridge Trail. In 0.5 mile, turn right (east) at the junction with the spur to Sargent Mountain Pond, and head 0.3 mile to Penobscot. From there, head south on the Penobscot Mountain Trail, then east on the Spring Trail, to return to the Jordan Pond House. The entire loop is approximately 5.2 miles from start to finish.

If you want to continue on to Sargent Mountain before heading down over Penobscot, follow the Sargent South Ridge Trail north 1.2 miles from Birch Spring all the way up to that higher peak, passing the turnoffs to Sargent Pond and Hadlock Brook and Maple Spring Trails along the way. Then, to loop down over Penobscot, descend the Sargent summit back to the junction with the turnoff to Sargent Pond and turn left (east) for 0.3 mile to Penobscot Mountain. At the Penobscot summit, turn right (south) and follow the Penobscot Mountain and Spring Trails back down to the south shore of Jordan Pond. This entire hike totals 6.6 miles from start to finish.

50 Sargent Mountain via Hadlock Brook and Maple Spring Trails

By combining these two steep, less-traveled trails up to Sargent's ridge, you'll get to walk by the carriage roads' Waterfall and Hemlock Bridges, crisscross brooks, and admire the stonework, both natural in the form of Pulpit Rock and man-made in the form of granite steps. To loop up Sargent via the relatively less-steep way, this route goes up the Hadlock Brook Trail and comes down the Maple Spring Trail. There's still an elevation gain of more than 1,000 feet in just over 1.0 mile.

Distance: 4.2-mile lollipop
Hiking time: About 3 to 4 hours
Difficulty: Strenuous
Trail surface: Wooden bridges, granite steps, forest floor, rock ledges
Best season: Spring through fall
Other trail users: Hikers on Sargent South Ridge Trail; bicyclists and walkers at carriage road crossings

Canine compatibility: Leashed dogs permitted
Map: USGS Acadia National Park and Vicinity
Special considerations: No facilities at the Norumbega parking area; a chemical toilet at the nearby Parkman Mountain parking area. Bring insect repellent during mosquito season.

Finding the trailhead: From Bar Harbor head west on ME 233 for 4 miles. Turn left (south) onto ME 198 and travel nearly 3 miles, past the Parkman Mountain parking area, to the Norumbega Mountain parking area on the right. The Hadlock Brook trailhead is on the left (east) side of ME 198, across from the Norumbega Mountain parking area. The closest Island Explorer stop is north on ME 198 at the Parkman Mountain parking area, along the Brown Mountain line, but you can ask the bus driver to let you off at the Norumbega parking area if it is safe to do so. GPS: N44 19.33' / W68 17.28'

The Hike

These rough trails provide loop access to Sargent Mountain from the west and the chance to admire the Hadlock Falls in season at Waterfall Bridge and the flat-topped Pulpit Rock at the junction of the Maple Spring and Giant Slide Trails.

Because of all the water along these trails, mosquitoes can be fierce, especially near the Hadlock Brook trailhead, where the route skirts a marshland north of Upper Hadlock Pond. Bring repellent.

Stay on Hadlock Brook trail as the Parkman Mountain Trail heads left at 0.1 mile and the Bald Peak Trail heads left at 0.2 mile. Then cross the first carriage road. At 0.4 mile pass the junction with the Maple Spring Trail, where you'll be looping back.

Hikers come up the Sargent South Ridge, with Penobscot behind them.

At 0.8 mile you reach a fork in the Hadlock Brook Trail. Take the under-the-bridge route to the right for a unique perspective on the Waterfall Bridge and the 40-foot waterfall that is at its most powerful in spring after the snows melt.

Cross the carriage road at 0.9 mile and begin a rough, steep climb, repeatedly crossing Hadlock Brook. Reach the junction with a trail that leads to Birch Spring at 1.1 miles, coming in on the right (south). Continue climbing steeply on the Hadlock Brook Trail, past the tree line.

At 1.6 miles reach the junction with the Sargent South Ridge Trail. Turn left and head north on the ridge, passing the junction at 1.8 miles with the Maple Spring Trail, which you'll later descend.

Reach the spectacular Sargent Mountain summit at 2.1 miles, where a series of trails meet.

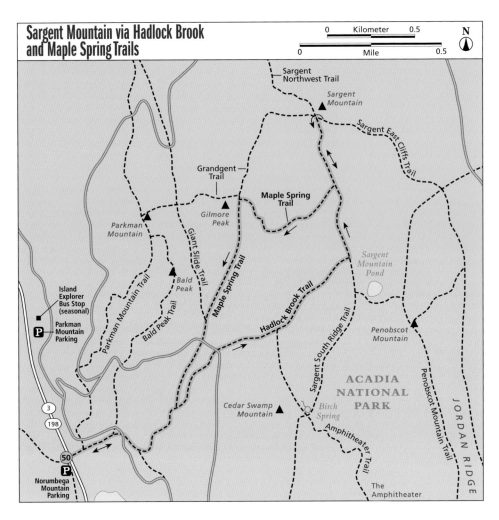

Kilometer 0.5

N

0 0.5

Mile

Sargent
Northwest Trail

Sargent
Mountain

Sargent East Cliffs Trail

Grandgent
Trail

Maple Spring
Trail

Gilmore
Peak

Parkman
Mountain

Giant Slide Trail

Sargent
Mountain
Pond

Island
Explorer
Bus Stop
(seasonal)

Parkman
Mountain
Parking

Parkman Mountain Trail

Bald
Peak

Maple Spring Trail

Bald Peak Trail

Hadlock Brook Trail

Sargent South Ridge Trail

Penobscot
Mountain

Penobscot Mountain Trail

JORDAN RIDGE

3

198

Cedar Swamp
Mountain

Birch
Spring

ACADIA
NATIONAL
PARK

50

Norumbega
Mountain
Parking

Amphitheater Trail

The
Amphitheater

To loop back down, head south down the ridge. At 2.4 miles turn right (southwest) at the junction onto the Maple Spring Trail, descending sharply. At 2.9 miles reach the junction with the Grandgent Trail, coming in on the right (north) and heading straight (west).

Turn left (south) to continue on the Maple Spring Trail. Reach the junction with the Giant Slide Trail at 3.4 miles. The natural rock formation known as Pulpit Rock is here, where Maple Spring and Giant Slide Trails meet.

At 3.5 miles reach the Hemlock Bridge and cross a carriage road to continue southwest on the Maple Spring Trail. At 3.8 miles connect back to the Hadlock Brook Trail, closing the loop. Bear right (southwest) to return to ME 198 and the Norumbega parking area at 4.2 miles.

Miles and Directions

0.0 Start at the Hadlock Brook trailhead, on the east side of ME 198, across from the Norumbega parking area.

0.1 Pass the Parkman Mountain trailhead on the left (north).

0.2 Pass the Bald Peak trailhead on the left (north) and cross a carriage road.

0.3 Bear left (northeast) to continue on the Hadlock Brook Trail.

0.4 Reach the junction with the Maple Spring Trail, which you'll be looping back on. Stay straight to continue northeast on the Hadlock Brook Trail.

0.8 Reach a fork in the trail, where you can choose to bear right, as suggested in the trail description, and go under the Waterfall Bridge or left to head directly to a carriage road crossing.

0.9 Cross the carriage road and continue northeast on the trail.

1.1 Pass the junction with a trail that leads to Birch Spring, which comes in on the right (south).

1.6 Reach the junction with the Sargent South Ridge Trail. Turn left (north) to head up the ridge to Sargent Mountain.

1.8 Pass the junction with the upper end of the Maple Spring Trail, which you'll use to descend.

2.1 Summit Sargent, where the Grandgent, Sargent Northwest, and Sargent East Cliffs Trails also come in. Return down the Sargent South Ridge Trail toward the Maple Spring Trail.

2.4 Turn right (southwest) onto the Maple Spring Trail.

2.9 Reach the junction with the Grandgent Trail. Turn left (south) to continue on the Maple Spring Trail.

3.4 Reach the junction with the Giant Slide Trail, which comes in on the right (northwest). Stay on the Maple Spring Trail.

3.5 Cross a carriage road by the Hemlock Bridge.

3.8 Intersect the Hadlock Brook Trail and bear right (southwest) to head back to ME 198.

4.2 Arrive back at the trailhead.

51 Parkman Mountain and Bald Peak Loop via Hadlock Brook Trail

The 360-degree views from these 900-foot-plus peaks, plus the relatively easy access from ME 198, make these summits popular. You may encounter crowds and even hear the noise of traffic. But by looping up from this lesser-used trailhead near the Norumbega parking area, rather than from the more crowded Parkman Mountain parking lot, you may get more solitude.

Distance: 2.8-mile lollipop
Hiking time: About 2 to 3 hours
Difficulty: Moderate to strenuous
Trail surface: Forest floor, rock ledges
Best season: Spring through fall, particularly early morning or late afternoon in summer to avoid crowds

Other trail users: Hikers climbing Gilmore Peak and Sargent; bicyclists and walkers at carriage road crossings
Canine compatibility: Leashed dogs permitted
Map: USGS Acadia National Park and Vicinity
Special considerations: No facilities at the Norumbega parking area; chemical toilet at the nearby Parkman Mountain parking area. Bring insect repellent during mosquito season.

Finding the trailhead: From Bar Harbor head west on ME 233 for 4 miles. Turn left (south) onto ME 198 and travel nearly 3 miles, past the more crowded Parkman Mountain parking area, to the lesser-used Norumbega Mountain parking area on the right (west). The Hadlock Brook trailhead is on the left (east) side of ME 198, across from the Norumbega Mountain parking area. The Parkman Mountain trailhead is 0.1 mile in on the left. The closest Island Explorer stop is north on ME 198 at the Parkman Mountain parking area, along the Brown Mountain, but you can ask the bus driver to let you off at the Norumbega parking area if it is safe to do so. GPS at start: N44 19.33' / W68 17.28'

The Hike

Follow the Hadlock Brook Trail 0.1 mile to the less-frequented Parkman Mountain trailhead. You'll start the Parkman Mountain loop by crossing three carriage roads in quick succession within 0.3 mile.

The trail then parallels the carriage road for a bit, turns right at a huge rock, and soon takes a sharp left. At about tree line, a lone iron rung helps you up a rock face.

Next, in a series of switchbacks, the trail ascends the open ridge, with views west to Somes Sound and south to the Gulf of Maine. Watch for loose gravel on the path. As the trail takes you higher, you get glimpses of Upper and Lower Hadlock Ponds to the south. The trail levels off a bit and enters a short stretch of woods with huge birch trees, then begins a steep climb up dramatic pink granite ledges.

Bald Peak rises in the background.

At 1.4 miles the Bald Peak Trail heads to the right (east). You'll be looping down on this trail later.

Summit Parkman Mountain at 1.5 miles. The Grandgent Trail leads right (east) toward Gilmore Peak, and the Parkman Mountain Trail continues north to end at the Giant Slide Trail.

From 941-foot Parkman, you can see Bald Peak to the southeast, Sargent Mountain to the east, Somes Sound and Western and Norumbega Mountains to the west, and the Gulf of Maine to the south.

To loop back down, head south on the Parkman Mountain Trail. Turn left (east) at 1.6 miles to connect with the Bald Peak Trail. At this junction there's an interesting balanced rock of sorts—a huge boulder propped up on one end by a small rock, almost a pebble by comparison.

Attain 974-foot Bald Peak at 1.8 miles, with 360-degree views of Sargent and Gilmore Peak to the east, Parkman to the north, Norumbega and Western Mountains to the west, and the Cranberry Isles to the south. Bald and Parkman are so close to each other, you may even see some of the hikers you left behind on that slightly lower peak to the north.

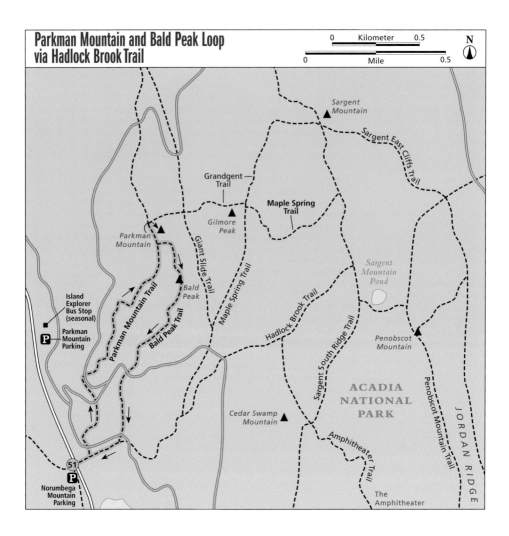

Head south on the Bald Peak Trail, going somewhat steeply down rocky ledges. Cross a carriage road at 2.3 miles. Cross another carriage road at 2.5 miles, and soon reach the junction with the Hadlock Brook Trail.

Turn right (west) onto the Hadlock Brook Trail to head back toward ME 198. Close the loop at 2.7 miles when you reach the Parkman Mountain trailhead, and return to the start at 2.8 miles.

Miles and Directions

0.0 Start at the Hadlock Brook trailhead, on the east side of ME 198, across from the Norumbega parking area.

0.1 Reach the Parkman Mountain trailhead, and turn left (north) onto the trail.

0.2 Cross a carriage road.

0.4 Cross two more carriage roads, one after another.

1.4 Pass the junction on the right (east) with the Bald Peak Trail, which you'll later be taking over Bald Peak and using to loop back down.

1.5 Summit Parkman Mountain. The Grandgent Trail heads right (east) toward Gilmore Peak, and the Parkman Mountain Trail continues north to end at the Giant Slide Trail. Retrace your steps to the junction with the Bald Peak Trail.

1.6 Turn left (east) onto the Bald Peak Trail and head toward that slightly higher peak.

1.8 Summit Bald Peak. Continue straight (south) on the Bald Peak Trail to loop back down.

2.3 Cross a carriage road.

2.5 Cross another carriage road. Soon reach the junction with the Hadlock Brook Trail. Turn right (west) onto the Hadlock Brook Trail to head back toward ME 198.

2.7 Close the loop at the Parkman Mountain trailhead, and stay straight on the Hadlock Brook Trail.

2.8 Arrive back at the Hadlock Brook trailhead.

52 Norumbega Mountain and Hadlock Ponds Loop

This loop, described counterclockwise, heads up the Goat Trail, since it's better to ascend this short but steep trail at the start than descend it at the end. Walk down along the mountain's ridge and loop back along the western shore of Lower Hadlock Pond. From 852-foot Norumbega Mountain you get views of Somes Sound close up and of Western Mountain in the distance.

Distance: 3.5-mile loop
Hiking time: About 2 to 3 hours
Difficulty: Moderate to strenuous
Trail surface: Wooden bridges, forest floor, rock ledges
Best season: Spring through fall
Other trail users: Local residents and anglers along Lower Hadlock Pond
Canine compatibility: Leashed dogs permitted but not recommended on the Goat Trail

Map: USGS Acadia National Park and Vicinity
Special considerations: No facilities at the Norumbega parking area; chemical toilet at the nearby Parkman Mountain parking area. Bring insect repellent during mosquito season. No swimming or dogs are allowed in Lower Hadlock Pond, which serves as a public water supply.

Finding the trailhead: From Bar Harbor, head west on ME 233 for 4 miles. Turn left (south) onto ME 198 and continue nearly 3 miles, past the Parkman Mountain parking area, to the Norumbega Mountain parking area on the right (west). The Goat trailhead is at the northern end of the parking area. The closest Island Explorer stop is north on ME 198 at the Parkman Mountain parking area, along the Brown Mountain line, but you can ask the bus driver to let you off at the Norumbega parking area if it is safe to do so. GPS: N44 19.33' / W68 17.28'

The Hike

Norumbega Mountain parallels the eastern edge of Somes Sound, providing fine views of the waterway and mountains to the west.

The toughest part of this hike is at the beginning on the Goat Trail, which definitely earns its name. First built around 1900, this trail brings you up 600 feet in elevation in 0.6 mile. It goes along boulders, open rock ledges, and some steep granite faces. Recent erosion control and rehabilitation by the Acadia trails crew on this stretch means you don't have to be as goat-like to successfully navigate this trail.

Near the top, turn sharply left, or south, and reach the 852-foot summit at 0.6 mile. The fine views here include the Cranberry Isles to the south, Parkman and Sargent Mountains to the east, and Somes Sound to the west.

The mountain offers some of the park's best views of the massive Somes Sound, the only fjord-like feature on the US Atlantic Coast. The entrance to the waterway is rather shallow at 30 feet, but the depth then plunges to as much as 150 feet.

These log stairs on the Goat Trail make the climb up Norumbega Mountain a little less strenuous.

Many people turn around here for a 1.2-mile round-trip, but it's a precipitous descent and cuts short the hiking pleasure.

Pick up the Norumbega Mountain Trail at the summit and follow it south down the open ridge, admiring the views west to Western Mountain and east to Sargent, as well as the unique Bates-style cairns.

At 1.4 miles, after a sharp climb down, reach the junction with the Golf Course Trail, a local trail that heads right (west) toward private land. Stay straight (south) on the Norumbega Mountain Trail, which eventually turns into a pleasant walk along a field of lichen and forest of pine.

At 2.0 miles reach the southwestern shore of Lower Hadlock Pond and turn sharply left (north) onto the Hadlock Ponds Trail, paralleling the western shore. You get a nice view to the northeast of Bald Peak here.

At 2.5 miles walk by beautiful cascades, cross a log bridge, and reach the junction with the Lower Hadlock Trail, which heads to the right (south) to circle around Lower Hadlock Pond. Stay straight (northeast) on the Hadlock Ponds Trail.

At 2.6 miles reach the junction with the Lower Norumbega Trail. The Hadlock Ponds Trail now turns right (northeast) to head toward Upper Hadlock Pond. Head left (northwest) on the Lower Norumbega Trail to loop back to the Goat trailhead.

At 3.5 miles return to the Goat trailhead and the Norumbega parking area.

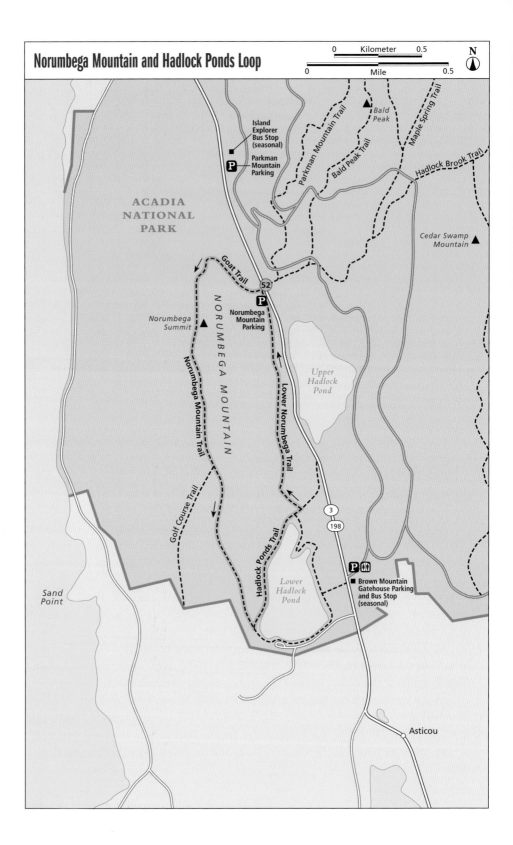

Norumbega Mountain and Hadlock Ponds Loop

0   Kilometer   0.5

0   Mile   0.5

N

ACADIA
NATIONAL
PARK

Island
Explorer
Bus Stop
(seasonal)

Parkman
Mountain
Parking

Parkman Mountain Trail

Bald Peak

Bald Peak Trail

Maple Spring Trail

Hadlock Brook Trail

Cedar Swamp
Mountain

Goat Trail

52

Norumbega
Mountain Parking

Norumbega
Summit

N O R U M B E G A   M O U N T A I N

Norumbega Mountain Trail

Lower Norumbega Trail

Upper
Hadlock
Pond

Golf Course Trail

Hadlock Ponds Trail

Lower
Hadlock
Pond

3

198

P

Brown Mountain
Gatehouse Parking
and Bus Stop
(seasonal)

Sand
Point

Asticou

Miles and Directions

0.0 Start at the Goat trailhead, at the north end of the Norumbega Mountain parking area.

0.6 Summit Norumbega Mountain and connect with the Norumbega Mountain Trail. Head straight (south) on the Norumbega Mountain Trail to loop down along the ridge.

1.4 Reach the junction with the Golf Course Trail, which heads right (west) toward private property. Stay straight (south) on the Norumbega Mountain Trail.

2.0 Reach the southwestern shore of Lower Hadlock Pond. Turn sharply left (north) onto the Hadlock Ponds Trail and follow the western shore of the pond.

2.5 Cross a log bridge and reach the junction with the Lower Hadlock Trail, which heads to the right (south) to circle around Lower Hadlock Pond. Stay straight (northeast) on the Hadlock Ponds Trail.

2.6 Reach the junction with the Lower Norumbega Trail, where the Hadlock Ponds Trail now turns right to head toward Upper Hadlock Pond. Turn left (northwest) onto the Lower Norumbega Trail to loop back to the Goat trailhead.

3.5 Arrive back at the Goat trailhead.

53 Lower Hadlock Pond Loop

This is a short loop that traverses counterclockwise around wooded and scenic Lower Hadlock Pond. The pond's southern shore, near the end of the loop and by a pump house, offers a great look back at Parkman Mountain, Bald Peak, Gilmore Peak, and Sargent Mountain.

Distance: 1.8-mile loop
Hiking time: About 45 minutes to 1.5 hours
Difficulty: Easy to moderate
Trail surface: Forest floor, with lots of exposed roots in spots
Best season: Spring through fall
Other trail users: Local residents and anglers accessing Lower Hadlock Pond; hikers climbing Norumbega Mountain

Canine compatibility: Leashed dogs permitted
Map: USGS Acadia National Park and Vicinity
Special considerations: Chemical toilet at the carriage road parking lot near the Brown Mountain Gatehouse. No swimming or dogs are allowed in Lower Hadlock Pond, which serves as a public water supply.

Finding the trailhead: From Bar Harbor head west on ME 233 for 4 miles. Turn left (south) on ME 198 and continue another 3.9 miles, past Upper Hadlock Pond on your left, to a carriage road parking lot on the left (east) side of ME 198 just before the Brown Mountain Gatehouse. From the parking area walk south along the east side of ME 198 until you reach the foot of the Brown Mountain Gatehouse driveway. Cross to a gravel path on the other side of ME 198, and walk southwest along the gravel path to the first junction, where you turn right (west) onto a spur. You'll see a blue blaze on a utility pole and you walk by a private residence on the left (south) as you head to the Lower Hadlock trailhead. Turn right (northwest) along Lower Hadlock Pond's eastern shore to start the trail. The Island Explorer's Brown Mountain line stops at the carriage road parking lot. GPS: N44 18.40' / W68 17.07'

The Hike

The picturesque views from the southern shore of Lower Hadlock Pond toward Parkman Mountain and Bald Peak are reminiscent of the Bubbles rising from Jordan Pond—but not quite. We call it a "poor man's Jordan Pond view."

From the gravel path directly across ME 198 from the Brown Mountain Gatehouse driveway, turn right (west) onto a spur at the first junction and walk past a private residence on your left (south). Reach Lower Hadlock Pond's eastern shore and the Lower Hadlock trailhead just beyond the private residence.

This section of trail on the pond's eastern shore probably dates back to at least 1914. When it was recently restored, it made it easier to complete a circuit of the pond.

Rustic wooden bridges bring you over what can be the rushing cascades of Hadlock Brook after the spring melt or heavy rains.

Head northwest along the pond with the woods to your right and the Norumbega ridge across the pond to your left (west). The trail rises over a swampy area and then goes through an eroded, rooty section.

The path turns to the right, passes a sandy beach, and then climbs along an inlet, taking you away from sight of the full length of Lower Hadlock.

At the farthest northern point of the pond, at 0.7 mile, reach the intersection with the Hadlock Ponds Trail. Turn left (southwest) onto the Hadlock Ponds Trail to head along Lower Hadlock's western shore. There's a new log bridge near the bubbling mouth of the pond and some nice cascades along here that were reduced to a trickle during a late-August visit.

The trail climbs along Lower Hadlock through a cedar forest and to some huge boulders, tossed there by the glaciers. Be prepared for some up-and-down boulder hiking here as the trail hugs Lower Hadlock to its southern shore.

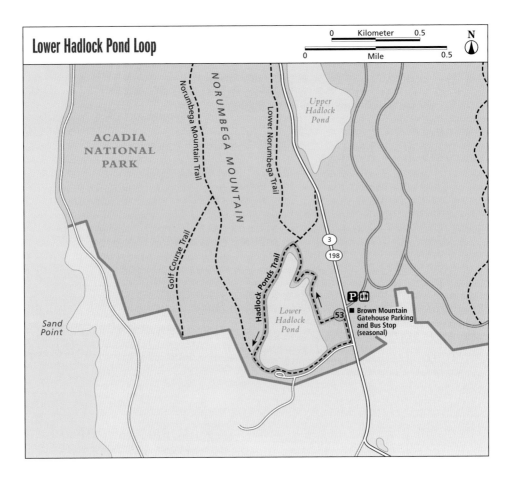

Reach the junction with the Norumbega Mountain Trail coming in on the right at 1.2 mile. We saw a loon diving for fish in Lower Hadlock Pond near here once (nearby Upper Hadlock Pond, across ME 198, is a loon nesting area). Continue circling around Lower Hadlock, past a pump house and over a dam via a modern footbridge.

This is where you get the "poor man's Jordan Pond view." You don't get the pink granite on the shore and the Bubbles, but, like Jordan, you do get unforgettable views across the water of mountains rising in the near distance.

To the left you can see the Norumbega ridge. Looking north you see four mountains: Parkman Mountain to the left, the turgid and distinctive Bald Peak, the partly wooded Gilmore Peak, and finally the big one—Sargent Mountain.

To finish the loop, continue circling around the southern shore. Pass some old Village Improvement Society signs at 1.3 miles and reach a T-shaped intersection at 1.4 miles. Turn left here onto a gravel road. Continue around the pond, past a gate, and past a private drive at 1.7 miles.

Just beyond the private drive, turn left (north) onto a gravel path to complete the circle back to ME 198 and the Brown Mountain Gatehouse at 1.8 miles.

Miles and Directions

0.0 Start at the gravel path across ME 198 from the Brown Mountain Gatehouse.

0.1 Turn right (west) at first junction onto a spur past a private residence. Reach the Lower Hadlock trailhead, on the eastern shore of Lower Hadlock Pond. Turn right (northwest) at the shore.

0.7 Reach the junction with the Hadlock Ponds Trail and the northern tip of Lower Hadlock Pond. Turn left (southeast) onto the Hadlock Ponds Trail to loop around the western shore of the pond.

1.2 Pass the junction with the Norumbega Mountain Trail, coming in from the right (northwest). Circle around the pond's southern shore, walking past the pump house and over the dam.

1.3 Pass the junction with old village trails and continue circling the pond.

1.4 At a T intersection with a gravel road, turn left (northeast) to continue around the pond.

1.7 Pass a gate and turn left (north) after a private drive onto a gravel road to circle back toward the Brown Mountain Gatehouse.

1.8 Cross ME 198 and return to the carriage road parking lot near the gatehouse.

Mount Desert Island
West of Somes Sound

T his is the quieter side of the island.

The major Acadia National Park trails here go up or around such land-marks as Acadia, St. Sauveur, and Flying Mountains; Beech Mountain; Beech Cliff; Long Pond; Echo Lake; and Bernard and Mansell Mountains, known collectively as Western Mountain.

The most popular routes in this section of the park are the Acadia and Flying Mountain trails, which offer close-up views of Somes Sound, the only fjord-like

Somes Sound, long described as the only fjord on the US East Coast, has been found by geologists to be too small and have too much water circulation to be called that. Rather, the glacially carved ocean inlet may be more properly called a fjard.

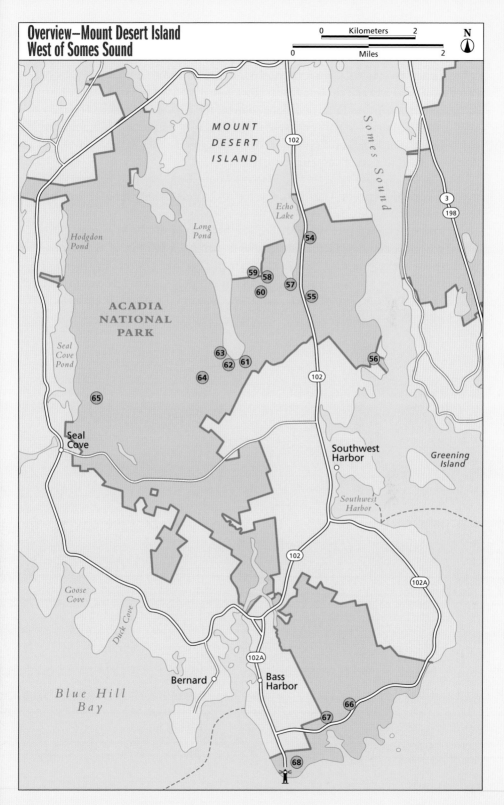

Kilometers 0 2

Miles 0 2

N

MOUNT
DESERT
ISLAND

Somes Sound

102

3
198

Echo
Lake

54

Hodgdon
Pond

Long
Pond

59 58 57
60 55

ACADIA
NATIONAL
PARK

Seal
Cove
Pond

63
62 61
64

56

102

65

Seal
Cove

Southwest
Harbor

Greening
Island

Southwest
Harbor

Goose
Cove

102

Duck Cove

102A

102A

Blue Hill
Bay

Bernard

Bass
Harbor

66
67

68

feature on the East Coast of the United States; the trail up Beech Mountain to its fire tower; and the loop to Beech Cliff, with its views down to Echo Lake.

The highest peak in this area is Bernard Mountain, at 1,071 feet. The summits of both Bernard and Mansell are wooded and therefore relatively less climbed, but there are views from nearby outlooks and along some of the trails' rocky ledges. The most popular starting point for trails up these mountains is at the Long Pond pumping station. Less-traveled trails up Bernard or Mansell begin off either the gravel Western Mountain Road or Long Pond Fire Road.

The popular and easy trails to Ship Harbor, Wonderland, and Bass Harbor Head Light are near Bass Harbor. They go along the rocky pink granite shore that makes Acadia stand out.

The Island Explorer's Southwest Harbor line has stops at Acadia Mountain, Echo Lake and Seawall and Bass Harbor campgrounds, making it possible to access some of these trails without needing to drive. The popular fare-free bus runs between late June and Columbus Day and can make special stops along the way upon request, if it's safe to do so. But be sure to buy a park pass to help cover the cost of the bus and other park services.

Acadia Mountain Area

54 Acadia Mountain Trail

The hike to 681-foot Acadia Mountain follows one of the older trails in the park and leads to a beautiful outlook of Somes Sound and toward nearby Norumbega and Beech Mountains. Another good option is a short side trip to Man o' War Brook, named for the French and British warships of the 1700s that came to get drinkable water where the brook cascades into Somes Sound.

Distance: 2.8-mile lollipop
Hiking time: About 1.5 to 2 hours
Difficulty: More challenging
Trail surface: Forest floor, rock ledges
Best season: Spring through fall, particularly early morning or late afternoon in summer to avoid the crowds

Other trail users: Horseback riders on the Man o' War Brook Trail section of the hike
Canine compatibility: Leashed dogs permitted but not recommended because of some steep sections
Map: USGS Acadia National Park and Vicinity
Special considerations: Chemical toilet at parking lot across from the trailhead

Finding the trailhead: From Somesville head south on ME 102 for about 3 miles, past Ikes Point, to the Acadia Mountain parking lot on the right (west) side of the highway. The trailhead is on the left (east) side of the road; be careful crossing the high-speed road. A new Island Explorer bus is on the east side of ME 102, diagonally across from the Acadia Mountain parking lot. GPS: N44 19.18' / W68 19.57'

The Hike

A popular trek on the west side of Somes Sound because of its great views, the Acadia Mountain Trail also offers a couple of unusual features: It goes along the sole mountain ridge on Mount Desert Island that goes east to west instead of north to south and takes you to a waterfall that tumbles into Somes Sound.

Benjamin F. DeCosta, who explored more remote parts of the island for his *Rambles in Mount Desert,* described this trail in 1871, around the time the island first became quite popular with hikers. Formerly called Robinson Mountain, Acadia is among many peaks in the park that were renamed under George B. Dorr's leadership as first park superintendent in the early 1900s, according to *Pathmakers,* by the National Park Service's Olmsted Center for Landscape Preservation.

The trail is easy at the start. From the trailhead across from the parking lot, turn immediately left (north) onto a new spur trail that parallels ME 102 and takes you to the Island Explorer bus stop at 0.1 mile. At the bus stop, head east into the woods

Man O' War Brook cascades into Somes Sound, at the base of Acadia Mountain.

and onto the gravel Man o' War Brook Trail, an old fire road. At 0.2 mile turn left (northeast) to pick up the Acadia Mountain Trail, across from the junction with the St. Sauveur Trail.

Watch your step on this hike. At one point you need to pull yourself up 20-foot rock crevices. The trail continues its steady rise through cedar and pine and then heads up a rocky section with switchbacks. Good views of the sound are right ahead, and you may hear the sounds of boats.

Echo Lake comes into view behind you to the west. The trail levels off a bit, and soon a couple of historic-style cairns tip you off to the peak, at 0.8 mile. Here you get expansive views of Somes Sound, the village of Somesville to the north, and the Gulf of Maine, Sutton Island, and the rest of the Cranberry Isles to the south.

Somes Sound had long been considered the East Coast's only fjord, a long, narrow, glacially carved ocean inlet, and is still listed as such on some of the park information. But in 1998, the Maine Geological Survey noted that it may be more properly described as a fjard, smaller than and not as limited in water circulation as a true fjord.

Atop Acadia you may find turkey vultures soaring overhead, unmistakable with their massive size and small red heads, or see and hear a peregrine falcon, as we have.

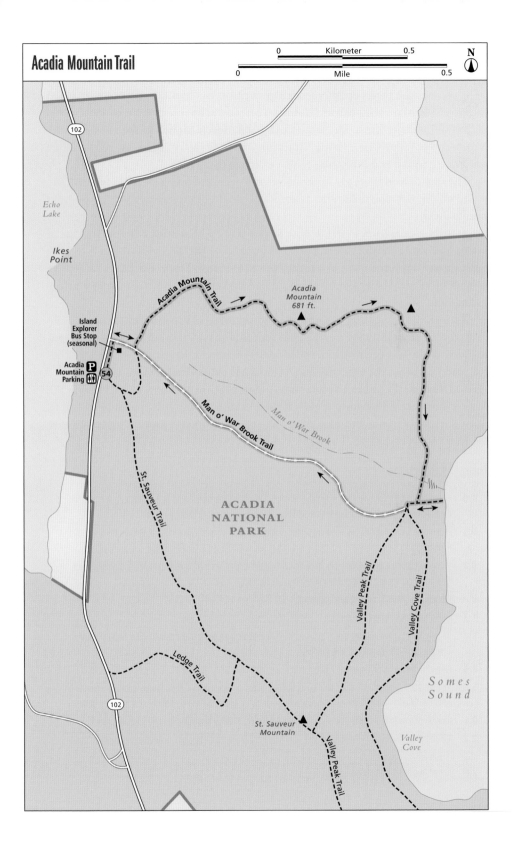

Acadia Mountain Trail

0   Kilometer   0.5

0   Mile   0.5

N

Echo Lake

Ikes Point

102

Acadia Mountain Trail

Acadia Mountain 681 ft.

Island Explorer Bus Stop (seasonal)

Acadia Mountain Parking

P

54

Man o' War Brook

Man o' War Brook Trail

St. Sauveur Trail

ACADIA NATIONAL PARK

Valley Peak Trail

Valley Cove Trail

Ledge Trail

Somes Sound

St. Sauveur Mountain

Valley Peak Trail

Valley Cove

102

Turn around here for an out-and-back hike of 1.6 miles, or continue on to complete the 2.8-mile loop.

If you choose to go on ahead, a tricky turn on the trail directs you over jagged rock to a second peak of sorts at 1.1 miles. This second open summit provides a splendid view—perhaps one of the best on the island. Beech Mountain with its fire tower is to the west; Valley Cove, Flying Mountain, and the Gulf of Maine are to the south; and Somes Sound and Norumbega Mountain are to the east.

The trail descends steeply from this second peak, providing close-up views of the sound on the way down. At times it's handy to hold onto trees and rocks as you head steeply down.

At 1.7 miles reach a junction with a spur trail to Man o' War Brook Trail and a side trail to Man o' War Brook. Turn left (east) onto the side trail, and at 1.8 miles follow stone steps to a nice spot at the base of a waterfall from the brook. When we were there in early June, the waterfall splashed along 20 to 30 feet of rock face before spilling into the sound.

Return to the junction with the spur to the Man o' War Brook Trail, an old fire road, and go straight (west) on the spur trail to a major trail intersection with signs pointing to the old fire road and other points of interest. Bear right and take the old fire road northwest back to where the Acadia Mountain Trail crosses at 2.6 miles.

To return to the Island Explorer bus stop or parking lot, continue straight on the Man o' War Brook Trail until it ends at the bus stop at ME 102 in another 0.1 mile. Turn left (south) onto the new spur trail to return to the parking lot in another 0.1 mile.

Miles and Directions

0.0 From the trailhead across from the parking lot, turn immediately left onto a new spur trail paralleling ME 102 that takes you to the Island Explorer bus stop.

0.1 From the bus stop head east into the woods on the gravel Man o' War Brook Trail, an old fire road.

0.2 Pick up the Acadia Mountain Trail on the left (north) side of the gravel Man o' War Brook Trail, across from the junction with the St. Sauveur Trail.

0.8 Reach the Acadia Mountain summit.

1.1 Reach a secondary summit.

1.7 At the junction with the spur to Man o' War Brook Trail and the spur trail to Man o' War Brook, turn left (east) to the brook.

1.8 Reach Man o' War Brook.

1.9 Return to the junction with the spur trail to Man o' War Brook Trail. Head straight (west) to another major trail junction, where you bear right (northwest) to follow the old fire road.

2.6 Reach the junction with the Acadia Mountain Trail. Stay straight on the old fire road.

2.7 Reach the Island Explorer bus stop on ME 102. Turn left (south) onto the spur trail paralleling ME 102.

2.8 Arrive back at the parking lot.

55 St. Sauveur Mountain and Valley Peak Loop

The actual peak of St. Sauveur is wooded, but some cliffs 0.1 mile from the summit offer great views of Somes Sound, Sargent and Penobscot Mountains, and the Cranberry Isles. This loop takes you from St. Sauveur along the cliffs to Valley Peak and back.

Distance: 2.5-mile lollipop
Hiking time: About 1.5 to 2.5 hours
Difficulty: Moderate
Trail surface: Wooden bridge, forest floor, rock ledges
Best season: Spring through fall

Other trail users: None
Canine compatibility: Leashed dogs permitted
Map: USGS Acadia National Park and Vicinity
Special considerations: No facilities; seasonal facilities a short drive away at Echo Lake

Finding the trailhead: From Somesville head south on ME 102 for 3.5 miles to a sign for St. Sauveur Mountain parking on the left (east) side of the road. The Ledge trailhead is at the south end of the parking area. The closest Island Explorer bus stop is at Echo Lake Beach on the Southwest Harbor line just south of the St. Sauveur Mountain parking; ask the bus driver to let you off if it is safe to do so. GPS: N44 18.42' / W68 19.56'

The Hike

The Ledge Trail is the shortest route to wooded, 679-foot St. Sauveur Mountain, not the official start of the St. Sauveur Trail over by the Acadia Mountain trailhead. This loop also provides an easier way to access the limited views on Valley Peak than does the official Valley Peak trailhead.

From the Ledge trailhead at the southern end of the St. Sauveur Mountain parking area, go left over a wooden bridge and then left along a rock face. Climb gradually up stone steps to a junction at 0.1 mile with a now-closed section of the Ledge Trail. Bear right (east) toward St. Sauveur Mountain. The trail climbs fairly steeply here up a wooded mountainside, with rocks and roots along the way. Follow the blue blazes along the rocky ledges for which the trail is named.

At 0.6 mile reach a junction with the St. Sauveur Trail. Turn right (southeast). Reach the wooded summit of St. Sauveur Mountain—once called Dog Mountain— at 0.8 mile.

Continuing straight (southeast) on the St. Sauveur Trail, reach a fork at 0.9 mile. Take the left (east) fork and reach the Valley Peak Trail and the cliffs overlooking Somes Sound at 1.0 mile. Turn right (south) along the cliffs, and enjoy the views down to Valley Cove and south and southeast to Southwest Harbor and the Cranberry Isles.

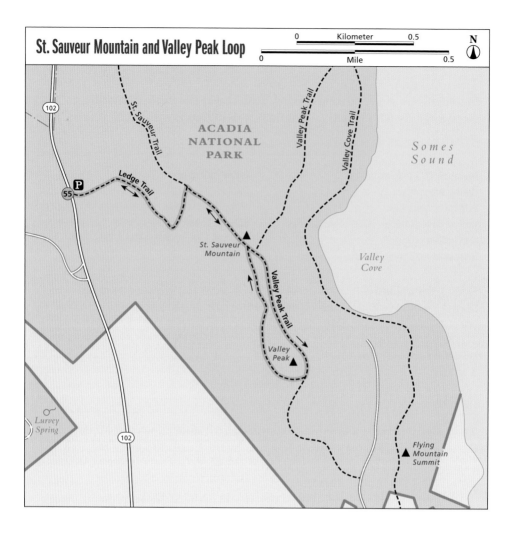

At 1.3 miles reach the 530-foot summit of Valley Peak. Over the course of a decade, we've seen trees grow and block much of the view from here, but you can still get glimpses to the south of the ocean and the Cranberry Isles.

Bear right (northwest) to circle back to St. Sauveur Mountain on the St. Sauveur Trail rather than continuing to follow the Valley Peak Trail on its steep descent to Valley Cove Trail, an old fire road.

Return to St. Sauveur's summit at 1.7 miles. Turn left (southwest) back onto the Ledge Trail at 1.9 miles, and arrive back at the parking area at 2.5 miles.

Greening Island and Southwest Harbor are visible from Valley Peak.

Miles and Directions

0.0 Start at the Ledge trailhead, on the south end of the St. Sauveur Mountain parking area.

0.1 Bear right (east) at an old junction with a now-closed section of the Ledge Trail.

0.6 Reach another junction; turn right (southeast) onto the St. Sauveur Trail.

0.8 Summit St. Sauveur Mountain. Continue straight (southeast) on the St. Sauveur Trail.

0.9 Reach a fork. Take the left (east) fork toward the Valley Peak Trail and cliffs overlooking Somes Sound.

1.0 Reach the Valley Peak Trail and turn right (south) along the cliffs.

1.3 Reach the summit of Valley Peak. Bear right (northwest) at the trail junction to loop back toward St. Sauveur Mountain on the St. Sauveur Trail.

1.7 Return to St. Sauveur Mountain.

1.9 Turn left (southwest) onto the Ledge Trail to return to the parking area.

2.5 Arrive back at the Ledge trailhead.

56 Flying Mountain, Valley Cove, and Valley Peak Loop

This hike takes you up Flying Mountain, by far the lowest of Acadia's twenty-six peaks, and down to the shoreline along a cove on Somes Sound. The peak may be low, but it boasts an exceptional panorama overlooking Somes Sound, Fernald Cove, and the Cranberry Isles, with views of Acadia and Norumbega Mountains.

Distance: 3.6-mile loop
Hiking time: About 2.5 to 3.5 hours
Difficulty: Moderate to strenuous
Trail surface: Wooden bridges, granite steps, forest floor, rock ledges, gravel road
Best season: Spring through fall for Flying Mountain and Valley Peak; late summer to fall for Valley Cove to avoid peregrine falcon nesting season

Other trail users: Boaters and kayakers who let themselves off in Valley Cove for a day hike; horseback riders on the section of the Valley Cove Trail that's an old fire road; hikers climbing St. Sauveur or Acadia Mountain
Canine compatibility: Leashed dogs permitted but not recommended
Map: USGS Acadia National Park and Vicinity
Special considerations: No facilities

Finding the trailhead: From Somesville head south on ME 102 for about 4.5 miles, past the St. Sauveur Mountain parking lot. Turn left (east) onto Fernald Point Road and travel about 1 mile to the small parking area at the foot of the gravel Valley Cove Trail, an old fire road. The Flying Mountain trailhead is on the right (east) side of the parking area. The Island Explorer does not stop here. GPS: N44 17.57' / W68 18.55'

The Hike

It's easy to see how Flying Mountain gets its name from the way the trail ascends swiftly to a bird's-eye view. In just 0.3 mile from the parking area, you reach the 284-foot summit and its dramatic vistas.

The trail, first described in the late 1800s, climbs through deep woods and then up rocky ledges. While in the shade of the woods, hikers should be pleased that the park service several years ago improved this old and well-trodden trail by adding log cribbing, or interlocked logs, to support the steep climb. We counted ninety-three newer log steps right at the start of the ascent. The work helps prevent erosion and makes it an easier climb for children and others. Soon granite ledges serve as stone steps, sometimes interspersed with cribbing.

Once above tree line and at the top of the rock face, you will get views to the southeast of Greening Island and the Cranberry Isles. To the northwest are the rocky cliffs of Valley Peak.

Dominating the view from the summit is the grassy peninsula known as Fernald Point. Across the Narrows at the mouth of Somes Sound is the town of Northeast Harbor; in the distance are Greening Island and the Cranberry Isles. From here you

The cliffs of Valley Cove have recently become home again to nesting peregrine falcons.

may look down on kayakers rounding Fernald Point or boaters entering and leaving Somes Sound. A ferry may blow its whistle in Northeast Harbor.

Some hikers turn around here, content with the views on Flying Mountain. But those who go on will be rewarded with scenes of Somes Sound; Valley Cove; and Norumbega, Acadia, Penobscot, and Sargent Mountains. Some may even be fortunate to see or hear peregrine falcons, which have returned to nesting in the cliffs above Valley Cove, one of Acadia's environmental success stories.

Just beyond the summit of Flying Mountain, at 0.4 mile, you get the first glimpse of the northern reaches of Somes Sound, as well as of Acadia Mountain to the north and Norumbega Mountain on the other side of the sound to the northeast. The ridge of Sargent and Penobscot Mountains is just beyond that of Norumbega.

There's a spur to an overlook to the right (east) before the trail begins its steep descent toward Valley Cove.

At the shore of the cove the trail turns left (west) and hugs the coastline, providing up-close views of Valley Cove and the cliffs rising above the shore.

At about 0.9 mile you reach the end of the Flying Mountain Trail and the junction with the Valley Cove Trail, a gravel section that used to be an old fire road that comes in on the left, and the portion that continues around the cove to the northwest. If the trail that continues around Valley Cove is closed for peregrine falcon nesting season, you can turn left (south) onto the old fire road and loop back to the parking area in another 0.5 mile. (In 2000, for the first time in decades, peregrine falcon chicks hatched along the cliffs here.)

If the 1.1-mile section of the trail that continues around Valley Cove is open and you're prepared for a long and rigorous loop, including a 500-foot elevation gain in about 0.5 mile along a section of the Valley Peak Trail on the return, continue northwest along the base of the cliffs, hugging the shore. (The Valley Cove Trail was once considered part of the Flying Mountain Trail, but it's back to its historic name under the park service's restoration efforts.)

You may see or hear peregrine falcons or ospreys along this section of the hike. One late summer day a short, chirping whistle echoed from the cliffs at Valley Cove. We looked up to see the flapping wings of an osprey, one of the largest birds of prey in North America.

The Valley Cove Trail soon crosses huge boulders and rock slabs. Pink granite steps take you over some of the biggest slabs. At one spot that's particularly treacherous when wet, you need to carefully make your way over a rock slab to reach the top of a series of stone steps. Remarkably, the steps are held against the side of a cliff only with iron rods.

Beyond the cove, another series of stone steps takes you up and over rocky cliffs. The trail then flattens out. A long series of log bridges takes you across a boggy area. You soon cross a cool brook meandering into Somes Sound and climb a rocky ledge that offers views of St. Sauveur Mountain and a last glimpse of the sound.

At 2.0 miles reach a major intersection where trails diverge to Acadia Mountain, Valley Peak, St. Sauveur Mountain, and Man o' War Brook Trail, an old fire road. The Valley Cove Trail officially ends here.

Turn left (southwest) onto the Valley Peak Trail to loop back over the cliffs and Valley Peak. You may see Indian pipe flowering in the rich woods before the trail takes you steeply up about 500 feet of elevation in 0.5 mile. Giant moosewood with its distinctive striped bark and large maple leaf, wild blueberry bushes, and low-lying juniper line the route as it rises from dark forest to exposed ledges.

As the trail levels off atop the cliffs, you reach the junction at 2.8 miles with a 0.1-mile spur to St. Sauveur Mountain. Stay straight (south) to continue on the Valley Peak Trail. Some of the best views are here—down to Valley Cove where you earlier skirted the shore; south to Southwest Harbor and the Cranberry Isles; and east across Somes Sound to Sargent, Penobscot, Parkman, Bald, and Norumbega Mountains. Although the vistas are grand, the trail is so low in elevation that it echoes with the sounds of motorboats and people talking below, especially during summer.

At 3.1 miles reach the 530-foot summit of Valley Peak with its limited views and a junction with the St. Sauveur Trail. Continue south on the Valley Peak Trail, descending steeply to the old fire road section of the Valley Cove Trail at 3.5 miles.

Turn right onto the old gravel road, which is closed to motor vehicles, and return to the parking area at 3.6 miles.

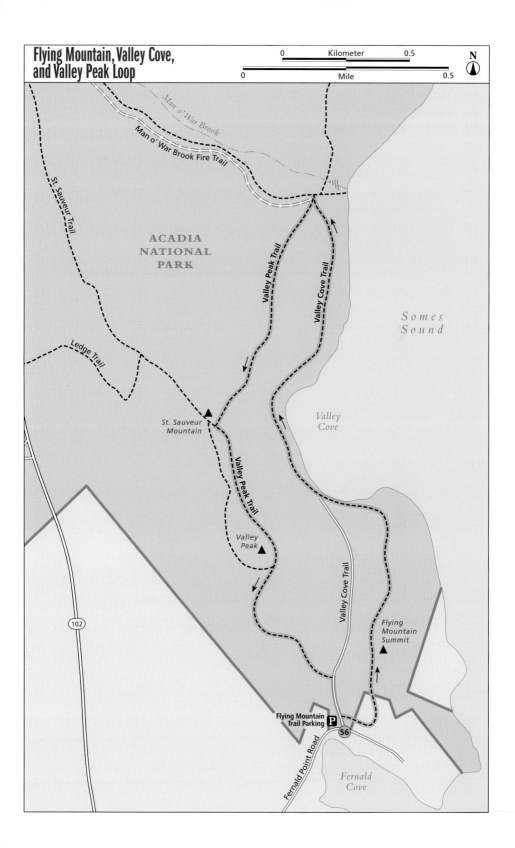

0   Kilometer   0.5

0   Mile   0.5

N

Man o' War Brook

Man o' War Brook Fire Trail

St. Sauveur Trail

ACADIA NATIONAL PARK

Valley Peak Trail

Valley Cove Trail

Somes Sound

Ledge Trail

St. Sauveur Mountain

Valley Cove

Valley Peak Trail

Valley Peak

Valley Cove Trail

Flying Mountain Summit

102

Flying Mountain Trail Parking **P**

56

Fernald Point Road

Fernald Cove

Miles and Directions

0.0 Start at the Flying Mountain trailhead, on the east side of the parking area at the foot of the gravel Valley Cove Trail, an old fire road.

0.3 Reach the summit of Flying Mountain.

0.9 Reach the junction with the Valley Cove Trail, the section that's an old gravel fire road coming in on the left, and the section that continues around the cove. Stay straight (northwest) to continue on the Valley Cove Trail along the cove.

2.0 Reach a major trail junction and the end of the Valley Cove Trail. Turn left (southwest) onto the Valley Peak Trail to loop back.

2.8 Reach the junction with a 0.1-mile spur to St. Sauveur Mountain. Stay straight (south) to continue on the Valley Peak Trail.

3.1 Reach the summit of Valley Peak and a junction with the St. Sauveur Mountain Trail. Continue south on the Valley Peak Trail to descend steeply to the gravel section of the Valley Cove Trail, an old fire road.

3.5 Turn right onto the old gravel road section of the Valley Cove Trail.

3.6 Arrive back at the parking area.

Beech Mountain Area

57 Beech Cliffs and Canada Cliff Trails (Beech Cliff Ladder Trail)

Featuring a nearly vertical climb up Beech Cliff along four long iron ladders, this hike takes you from Echo Lake Beach up to a clifftop loop and then back down a newly reopened historic section of the Canada Cliff Trail. Enjoy views of Echo Lake, Acadia and St. Sauveur Mountains, Somes Sound, the Gulf of Maine, and the fire tower on nearby Beech Mountain.

Distance: 2.1-mile figure eight
Hiking time: About 1.5 to 2 hours
Difficulty: Strenuous to expert only
Trail surface: Iron ladders, granite steps, forest floor, rock ledges, log bridge
Best season: Late summer through fall, to avoid peregrine falcon nesting season
Other trail users: Hikers on Beech Cliff Loop Trail

Canine compatibility: Dogs prohibited on Beech Cliffs Trail
Map: USGS Acadia National Park and Vicinity
Special considerations: Seasonal restrooms at Echo Lake Beach parking lot; portable toilets at Beech Mountain parking lot. Beech Cliffs Trail may be closed during peregrine falcon nesting season.

Finding the trailhead: From the flashing yellow light just south of Somesville, head south on ME 102 for 3.5 miles. Turn right at the Echo Lake Beach entrance. Go to the far end of the parking lot, walk down the stairs, and turn left along a walkway to the trailhead. The Island Explorer's Southwest Harbor line stops at the beach parking lot. GPS: N44 18.53' / W68 20.12'

The Hike

This tough hike climbs from Echo Lake straight up to the Canada and Beech Cliff ledges, offering excellent views of the lake and surrounding mountains. It features the restored section of the Canada Cliff Trail that has been so highly anticipated. We first learned of it months in advance of the 2011 reopening from an Acadia insider we met while hiking on Isle au Haut.

At the start of the Beech Cliffs Trail, a sign warns of exposed cliffs and fixed iron rungs. The first stretch of the trail is fairly level. But at a sign warning hikers to stay on the path to prevent erosion, the trail makes a left and begins to climb via switchbacks. Cross a rockslide at the base of the cliff, then watch for an overlook on the right, with views of Acadia and St. Sauveur Mountains east and Echo Lake below.

Continue climbing via switchbacks and stone stairs with a wooden handrail for protection. At one point you'll walk under a huge birch tree growing sideways out of

Stone steps and wooden handrail make the trip up Beech Cliffs from Echo Lake Beach a little easier.

the cliffside. Don't bump your head. Go up one more set of stone stairs with a wooden handrail.

Now begins the part of the trail that is so steep you need to climb up several iron ladders bolted into the rock face. The first ladder has ten rungs; the second has eighteen rungs and handholds made of steel poles and cable. Two more long ladders follow. After a final set of stone steps, you attain the ridge and the junction with the Canada Cliff Trail at 0.4 mile.

Turn right toward the Beech Cliff Loop Trail, then bear right on the half of the loop that brings you close to the edge of the cliff. Reach Beech Cliff and its dramatic cliff-top views at 0.5 mile. Circle inland and close the Beech Cliff Loop at 0.9 mile.

Head back on the Canada Cliff Trail, but instead of going left back down the ladder trail to Echo Lake, stay straight. You'll come to a junction in another 0.1 mile at 1.0 mile; bear left to continue on the Canada Cliff ridge to more views.

At 1.5 miles reach the junction with the newly reopened section of the Canada Cliff Trail. Turn left (south) onto the restored trail to loop down to the Echo Lake Beach parking lot, paralleling Lurvey Spring Road much of the way. (If you go straight at this junction instead of left toward Echo Lake, you'll connect to the Valley Trail. Some locals are using this section of the Canada Cliff Trail to access the Valley Trail and loop back on Lurvey Spring Road.) This restored section of the trail, which dates back to the early 1900s, before Acadia's creation, has been carefully reconstructed with more than one hundred granite steps and other extensive trail work. It takes you along a brook that flows into Echo Lake. Hiking this section, you can see why its reopening has been so highly anticipated. Close the loop by walking back to your car or the Island Explorer bus stop from the southern end of the Echo Lake Beach parking lot at 2.1 miles.

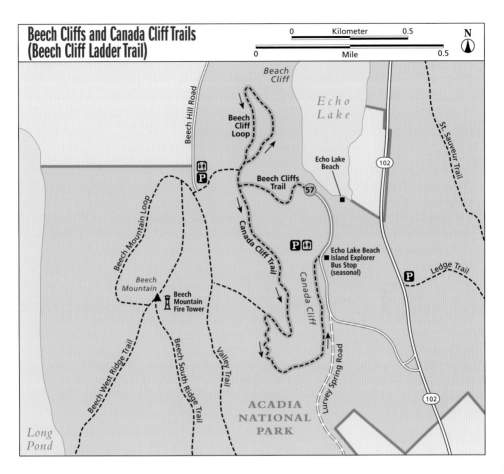

Beech Cliffs and Canada Cliff Trails (Beech Cliff Ladder Trail)

Miles and Directions

0.0 Start at the Beech Cliffs trailhead, at the far northern end of the Echo Lake Beach parking lot.

0.4 Reach the junction with the Canada Cliff Trail. Turn right (north); then bear right again at the Beech Cliff loop.

0.5 Reach Beech Cliff.

0.9 Circle back and close the Beech Cliff loop. Take the Canada Cliff Trail back, but instead of turning left to descend the ladder trail (Beech Cliffs Trail) to Echo Lake, stay straight (south).

1.0 Bear left (southeast) at junction with trail west to Beech Hill Road.

1.5 Reach the junction with the newly reopened section of the Canada Cliff Trail. Turn left (south) to loop west then north to the Echo Lake Beach parking lot, paralleling Lurvey Spring Road much of the way. (**Option:** Access the Valley Trail by going straight, northwest, at this junction.)

2.1 Close the loop at the southern end of the Echo Lake Beach parking lot.

58 Beech Cliff Loop Trail

Enjoy clifftop views of Echo Lake and beyond from this easy trail featuring a loop and out-and-back sections. You can see the fire tower on nearby Beech Mountain from a rocky knob. From spring to midsummer, peregrine falcons may be nesting in the cliffs below the trail.

Distance: 0.8-mile lollipop
Hiking time: About 30 minutes to 1 hour
Difficulty: Easy
Trail surface: Forest floor, graded gravel, rock ledges
Best season: Spring through fall, particularly early morning or late afternoon in summer to avoid the crowds

Other trail users: Hikers going to the Canada Cliff Trail or coming up a difficult ladder climb from Echo Lake
Canine compatibility: Leashed dogs permitted
Map: USGS Acadia National Park and Vicinity
Special considerations: Portable toilets at parking lot

Finding the trailhead: Head south from Somesville on ME 102, and turn right (west) at the flashing yellow light toward Pretty Marsh. Take the second left onto Beech Hill Road at a sign pointing to Beech Mountain and Beech Cliff. Follow Beech Hill Road south for 3.2 miles to the parking lot at its end. The Beech Cliff Loop trailhead is across from the parking lot, on the left (east) side of the road. The Island Explorer bus does not stop here, although the Southwest Harbor line lets riders off at Echo Lake, which is a strenuous ladder climb away. The ladder route is not recommended for the out of shape or faint of heart and dogs are not allowed. GPS: N44 18.55' / W68 20.36'

The Hike

This is the easier of two ways to access Beech Cliff and its views, because the trailhead is basically at the same elevation as the cliff. (The other way is a difficult ladder climb up Beech Cliff from Echo Lake.)

From the parking lot the trail rises gradually through the woods to a junction with the Canada Cliff Trail at 0.2 mile. Bear left (northeast) to the Beech Cliff Loop Trail, where you have a choice of taking the inland or the cliff side of the loop. Either way is relatively flat, with some granite steps to make the footing easier, but we prefer getting the views first: Bear right for the cliff side of the loop, reaching Beech Cliff at 0.3 mile. (If you bear left for the inland side of the loop first, it will be 0.5 mile from the trailhead before you get to the edge of the cliff.)

From Beech Cliff you can look down on Echo Lake Beach and the Appalachian Mountain Club (AMC) camp—but do not get too close to the edge.

Acadia and St. Sauveur Mountains are farther east. To the south are Somes Sound, the Gulf of Maine, and the Cranberry Isles; to the southwest is Beech Mountain, with its fire tower. You may also hear the traffic on ME 102, across the lake.

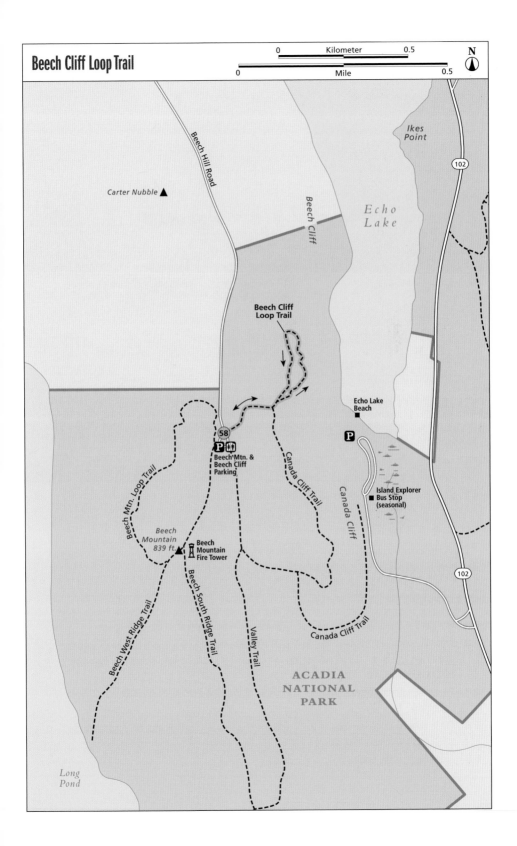

Beech Cliff Loop Trail

Carter Nubble ▲

Beech Hill Road

Beech Cliff

Echo Lake

Ikes Point

102

Beech Cliff Loop Trail

Echo Lake Beach ■

58 **P** 🚻
Beech Mtn. &
Beech Cliff
Parking

P

Island Explorer
■ Bus Stop
(seasonal)

Beech Mtn. Loop Trail

Canada Cliff Trail

Canada Cliff

Beech Mountain 839 ft. ▲ 🗼 Beech Mountain Fire Tower

Beech West Ridge Trail

Beech South Ridge Trail

Valley Trail

Canada Cliff Trail

102

ACADIA NATIONAL PARK

Long Pond

0 ———— Kilometer ———— 0.5

0 ———— Mile ———— 0.5

N

There's plenty of scenery to take in along the Beech Cliff Loop Trail.

The trail continues along the cliff then circles inland, closing the loop at 0.6 mile. Bear right (southwest) to return to the parking lot at 0.8 mile.

Miles and Directions

0.0   Start at the Beech Cliff Loop trailhead, across the road (east) from the parking lot.

0.2   At the junction with Canada Cliff Trail, bear left (northeast) to the Beech Cliff Loop Trail, where you can take the cliff side of the loop first (right) or the inland side (left). Turn right and head toward the cliff.

0.3   Reach Beech Cliff. (If you take the inland side of the loop first, you'll reach Beech Cliff at 0.5 mile.)

0.6   Circle back to close the loop at the junction with Canada Cliff Trail, and bear right (south-west) back to the parking lot.

0.8   Arrive back at the trailhead.

59 Beech Mountain Loop Trail

This hike offers great views of Long Pond and Somes Sound, along with a chance to climb to the first platform of the park's only fire tower—a steel structure, still in good condition, atop 839-foot Beech Mountain. The trail is also a good place to watch the migration of hawks; we saw four kestrels dive and soar above us during a hike one fall.

Distance: 1.1-mile loop
Hiking time: About 1 hour
Difficulty: Moderate
Trail surface: Forest floor, graded gravel path, rock ledges
Best season: Spring through fall

Other trail users: Hikers coming from the Beech South Ridge or Beech West Ridge Trails; birders
Canine compatibility: Leashed dogs permitted
Map: USGS Acadia National Park and Vicinity
Special considerations: Portable toilets at parking lot

Finding the trailhead: Head south from Somesville on ME 102, and turn right (west) at the flashing yellow light toward Pretty Marsh. Take the second left onto Beech Hill Road at a sign pointing to Beech Mountain and Beech Cliff. Follow Beech Hill Road south for 3.2 miles to the parking lot at its end. The trailhead is at the northwest end of the parking lot. The Island Explorer bus does not stop here, although the Southwest Harbor line lets riders off at Echo Lake, which is a strenuous ladder climb away. The ladder route is not recommended for the out of shape or faint of heart and dogs are not allowed. GPS: N44 18.55' / W68 20.36'

The Hike

Beech Mountain rises from a thin peninsula-like ridge of land sandwiched between Long Pond and Echo Lake, providing views all around. The trail begins off the parking lot and quickly leads to a loop at 0.1 mile.

The western half of this loop was carved in the 1960s as part of "Mission 66," an overhaul effort by the park service to celebrate its fiftieth anniversary in 1966. The trail's eastern section is much older, appearing on a 1906 map.

Bear right (northwest) at the fork to head along the easier Mission 66 way (counterclockwise) around the loop up to the summit. You will soon get spectacular views of Long Pond to the right (west) of the wide-open trail. At 0.6 mile reach the junction with the Beech West Ridge Trail. Bear left (east). A series of log stairs leads to the summit.

At 0.7 mile reach the steel fire tower atop Beech Mountain. From the first platform of the fire tower, you can enjoy nearly 360-degree views of the ocean and surrounding mountains. Echo Lake, Acadia Mountain, and St. Sauveur Mountain are to the east; Southwest Harbor, Northeast Harbor, and the Cranberry Isles are to the southeast; and Long Pond is to the west.

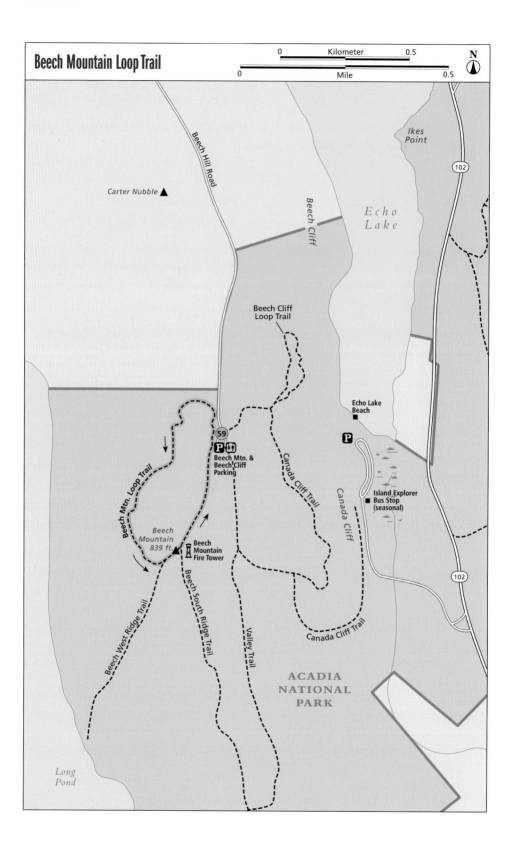

Beech Mountain Loop Trail

Kilometer
0   0.5

Mile
0   0.5

N

Carter Nubble ▲

Beech Hill Road

Beech Cliff

Ikes Point

Echo Lake

102

Beech Cliff Loop Trail

Echo Lake Beach

P

59

P

Beech Mtn. & Beech Cliff Parking

Beech Mtn. Loop Trail

Canada Cliff Trail

Canada Cliff

Island Explorer Bus Stop (seasonal)

Beech Mountain 839 ft.

Beech Mountain Fire Tower

Beech West Ridge Trail

Beech South Ridge Trail

Valley Trail

Canada Cliff Trail

102

ACADIA NATIONAL PARK

Long Pond

According to the park service, the fire tower was originally wooden, built around 1937 to 1941 by the Civilian Conservation Corps. It was replaced around 1960 to 1962 with a prefabricated steel tower flown in by helicopter and assembled on-site as part of the Mission 66 move to improve the parks.

The park service last staffed the tower in 1976. One or two weekends in October, depending on weather and staffing, the cabin is opened during part of a weekend day. It may also be open during ranger-led hikes during the summer. Call the park for current information at (207) 288-3338, or check the park calendar of events at www.nps.gov/acad/planyourvisit/index.htm.

From the summit bear north and loop back down quickly along the rough mountain terrain. Descend along switchbacks and rock ledges and through boulder fields. Go down a series of stone steps, then log steps. Bear right (southeast) at a fork at 1.0 mile, and reach the parking area at 1.1 miles.

Bear right to take the slightly longer, more gradual route up to Beech Mountain.

Miles and Directions

0.0   Start at the Beech Mountain Loop trailhead, at the northwest corner of the parking lot.

0.1   Bear right (northwest) at the fork, going around the loop counterclockwise.

0.6   At the junction with the Beech West Ridge Trail, bear left (east) to circle up Beech Mountain.

0.7   Reach the Beech Mountain summit with its fire tower. Bear north to circle back down the mountain.

1.0   Bear right (southeast) at the fork.

1.1   Arrive back at the trailhead.

60 Beech Mountain via Valley and Beech South Ridge Trails

Walk through a lush valley dotted with huge boulders, then climb a ridge with stunning views to the top of Beech Mountain. It's all in a day's loop hike.

Distance: 2.1-mile loop
Hiking time: About 2 to 3 hours
Difficulty: Moderate to strenuous
Trail surface: Granite steps, forest floor, rock ledges
Best season: Spring through fall

Other trail users: Hikers climbing the Beech Mountain Loop, Beech West Ridge, or Canada Cliff Trails; birders
Canine compatibility: Leashed dogs permitted
Map: USGS Acadia National Park and Vicinity
Special considerations: Portable toilets at parking lot

Finding the trailhead: Head south from Somesville on ME 102, and turn right (west) at the flashing yellow light toward Pretty Marsh. Take the second left onto Beech Hill Road at a sign pointing to Beech Mountain and Beech Cliff. Follow Beech Hill Road south for 3.2 miles to the parking lot at its end. The trailhead is at the southeastern edge of the parking lot. The Island Explorer bus does not stop here, although the Southwest Harbor line lets people off at Echo Lake, which is a strenuous ladder climb away. The ladder route is not recommended for the out of shape or faint of heart and dogs are not allowed. GPS: N44 18.54' / W68 20.37'

The Hike

The Valley Trail heads south from the parking lot, passing the Canada Cliff Trail at 0.2 mile coming in on the left. Go straight (south) to walk through the rich valley between Beech Mountain to the west and Canada Cliff to the east. On this portion of the hike, it feels as though you're walking through a hanging garden, with ferns draping over the top of house-size slabs of granite next to the trail.

At 0.8 mile, as the Valley Trail starts to circle west, reach the junction with the Beech South Ridge Trail coming in on the right (north). While the Valley Trail continues on to Long Pond, turn right onto the Beech South Ridge Trail to loop up and over Beech Mountain, with spectacular ridgetop views along the way.

Of the three ways up Beech Mountain, the Beech South Ridge Trail is the most architecturally fascinating. Heading north off the Valley Trail, Beech South Ridge starts with long stretches of carefully laid stone steps that take you up switchbacks. The steps make more manageable what would otherwise be an extremely difficult trail. The trail takes you up the open ridge and through wooded knobs, providing views south, east, and west. At 1.6 miles attain the 839-foot-high Beech Mountain with its fire tower.

The lush Valley Trail features ferns growing atop house-size boulders.

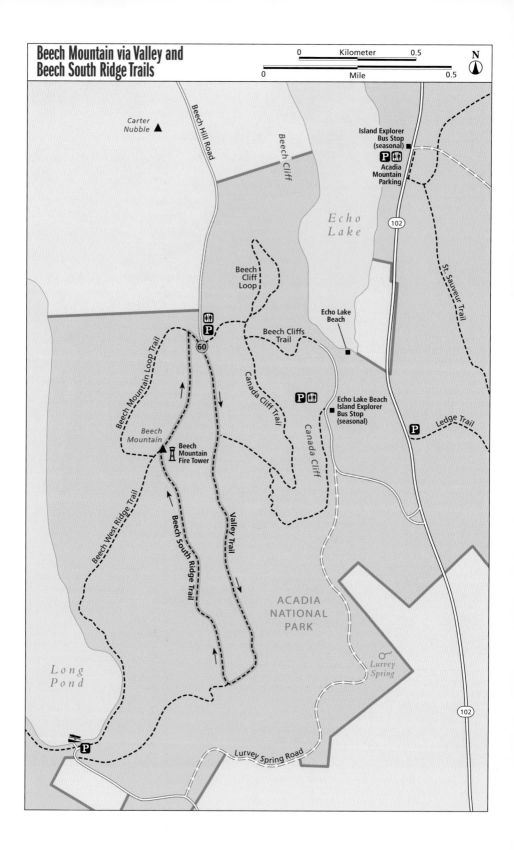

0   Kilometer   0.5

0   Mile   0.5

N

Carter Nubble ▲

Beech Hill Road

Beech Cliff

Island Explorer Bus Stop (seasonal)

Acadia Mountain Parking

Echo Lake

102

Beech Cliff Loop

St. Sauveur Trail

Beech Cliffs Trail

Echo Lake Beach

Beech Mountain Loop Trail

60

Canada Cliff Trail

Echo Lake Beach Island Explorer Bus Stop (seasonal)

Beech Mountain

Beech Mountain Fire Tower

Canada Cliff

Ledge Trail

Beech West Ridge Trail

Beech South Ridge Trail

Valley Trail

ACADIA NATIONAL PARK

Lurvey Spring

Long Pond

Lurvey Spring Road

102

Access to the deck of the US government–owned fire tower is usually blocked, although there are occasional special open houses during the summer or fall. You can always climb a dozen steps to the first platform and its almost 360-degree views of the ocean and surrounding mountains. Echo Lake, Acadia Mountain, and St. Sauveur Mountain are to the east; Southwest Harbor, Northeast Harbor, and the Cranberry Isles are to the southeast; and Long Pond is to the west.

Continue north down the other side of Beech on the Beech Mountain Loop Trail, and at 2.0 miles bear right (southeast) at a junction. Return to the parking lot at 2.1 miles.

Miles and Directions

0.0 Start at the Valley trailhead, off the southeastern edge of the parking lot.

0.2 Reach the junction with the Canada Cliff Trail coming in from the left (east). Stay straight (south) on the Valley Trail.

0.8 Reach the junction with the Beech South Ridge Trail. Turn right (north) to take the ridge trail to the top of Beech Mountain.

1.6 Summit Beech Mountain with its fire tower. Continue north and head down on the Beech Mountain Loop Trail.

2.0 Bear right (southeast) at the junction.

2.1 Arrive back at the parking lot.

61 Beech West Ridge Trail

This is the roughest way up Beech Mountain, climbing about 700 feet in less than a mile from the shore of Long Pond along the mountain's west face.

Distance: 2.0 miles out and back
Hiking time: About 2 to 3 hours
Difficulty: Moderate to strenuous
Trail surface: Wooden bridges, forest floor, rock ledges
Best season: Spring through fall

Other trail users: Hikers on the Beech Mountain Loop Trail
Canine compatibility: Leashed dogs permitted
Map: USGS Acadia National Park and Vicinity
Special considerations: No facilities. No swimming or dogs are allowed in Long Pond within 1,000 feet of the pumping station's intake.

Finding the trailhead: From Somesville head south on ME 102, continuing 1.5 miles beyond the Echo Lake Beach entrance. Turn right (west) at Seal Cove Road and travel 0.5 mile. Then go right (north) on Long Pond Road to the end at a pumping station on the shore of the pond. The trailhead is at the far end of the parking area to the east. The Island Explorer does not stop here. GPS: N44 18.01' / W68 21.00'

The Hike

The Beech West Ridge Trail starts easily enough, giving no hint of the rugged ascent ahead. The trail begins along Long Pond and heads through some tall cedars with views across the water of 949-foot Mansell Mountain.

At 0.3 mile, after passing a private home along the pond, the trail heads right (east) away from the pond and crosses the foot of a private footpath and skirts a gravel drive. Soon the trail begins its steep ascent over a smooth rock slab that can be extremely slick when wet. As the trail goes up the steep open west face, you get views down to the northern section of Long Pond and west to Mansell Mountain.

At 0.9 mile the Beech Mountain Loop Trail comes in from the left. Bear right, reaching 839-foot-high Beech Mountain and the summit fire tower at 1.0 mile.

Access to the deck of the US government–owned fire tower is usually blocked except during special open houses during the summer or fall. You can always climb a dozen steps to the first platform and its almost 360-degree views of the ocean and surrounding mountains. Echo Lake, Acadia Mountain, and St. Sauveur Mountain are to the east; Southwest Harbor, Northeast Harbor, and the Cranberry Isles are to the southeast; and Long Pond is to the west.

Return the way you came.

Long Pond glistens in the sun before Western Mountain casts its late-day shadow.

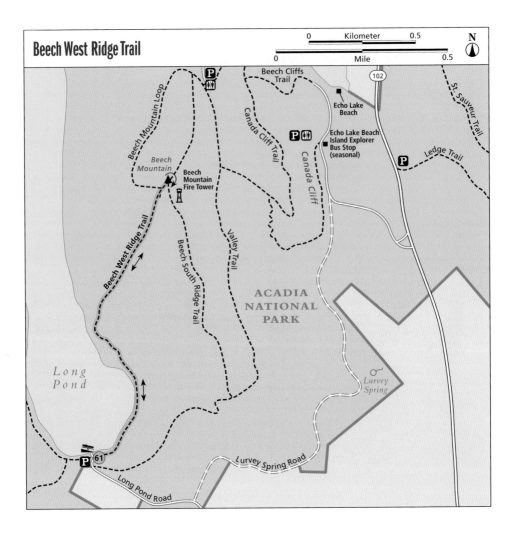

Miles and Directions

0.0 Start at the Beech West Ridge trailhead, at the far eastern end of the pump house parking area.

0.3 Head right (east) away from Long Pond. Cross the foot of a private footpath and skirt a gravel drive.

0.9 Reach the junction with the Beech Mountain Loop Trail; bear right (northeast) on that trail toward the summit.

1.0 Summit Beech Mountain.

2.0 Arrive back at the trailhead.

Bernard and Mansell Mountain Area

62 Long Pond and Great Notch Trails (Great Pond and Western Trails)

Hiker's choice: You can do just the first mile of the mostly flat walk along the southwestern shore of Long Pond, which the park service calls a moderate hike, or loop nearly 5 miles through Western Mountain's Great Notch. Either way you'll experience the quieter side of Acadia.

Distance: 2.0 miles out and back along Long Pond or 4.6-mile loop through the Great Notch
Hiking time: About 1.5 hours for Long Pond; 3.5 hours for Great Notch loop
Difficulty: Moderate
Trail surface: Wooden bridges, forest floor, rock ledges, graded gravel
Best season: Spring through fall

Other trail users: Hikers on the Cold Brook and Perpendicular Trails
Canine compatibility: Leashed dogs permitted
Map: USGS Acadia National Park and Vicinity
Special considerations: No facilities. No swimming or dogs are allowed in Long Pond within 1,000 feet of the pumping station's intake.

Finding the trailhead: From Somesville head south on ME 102, continuing 1.5 miles beyond the Echo Lake Beach entrance. Turn right (west) at Seal Cove Road and travel for 0.5 mile. Then go right (north) on Long Pond Road to the end at a pumping station on the shore of the pond. The trailhead is on the southwest shore of the pond on the west end of the parking area, behind the pump house. The Island Explorer does not stop here. GPS: N44 18.00' / W68 21.02'

The Hike

The Long Pond Trail (Great Pond Trail) is a pleasant walk offering the possibility of sunning on big, flat rocks along the shore. The trail can also serve as a jumping-off point for a challenging hike through the Great Notch of Western Mountain.

The Long Pond Trail, constructed by the Civilian Conservation Corps in the 1930s, heads left (west) from the pumping station. Cold Brook Trail goes inland, and the Long Pond Trail stays along the shore. At 0.2 mile the Perpendicular Trail heads steeply up toward the twin wooded summits—Mansell and Bernard—that make up Western Mountain. Continue straight on the Long Pond Trail, catching views of Beech Mountain with its fire tower.

Although the beginning of the trail is graded gravel, roots and rocks make the footing a bit more difficult farther in. You can decide to turn around after 1.0 mile along the pond, as suggested by the park service's "Paths into the Past: Acadia's Historic Trails" handout, for a moderate hike.

The Long Pond Trail was built by the Civilian Conservation Corps.

If you decide to continue on to the Great Notch for a long 4.7-mile loop over Western Mountain, continue following Long Pond as the trail hits its northernmost point at about 1.7 miles, then heads southwesterly and up the northern shoulder of Western Mountain, gaining about 400 feet elevation in approximately 1.0 mile.

At 2.7 miles the trail ends at the junction with the Great Notch Trail (Western Trail). Turn left (southeast) onto the Great Notch Trail (Western Trail) to loop over Western Mountain via the Great Notch. (The Great Notch Trail also heads northwest 1.1 miles to the gravel Long Pond Fire Road and one of the most remote Acadia trailheads on Mount Desert Island.)

At 3.1 miles reach the Great Notch at a four-way intersection at 640 feet, after an elevation gain of more than 100 feet in less than 0.5 mile. There are a couple of wooden benches conveniently placed here, but there are no mountaintop views unless you take one of the side trails to 949-foot Mansell Mountain (0.6 mile east, or left at the four-way intersection, via the Razorback and Mansell Mountain Trails) or visit 1,071-foot Bernard Mountain (0.7 mile southwest, or right at the intersection, via the Bernard Mountain Trail). Both summits are partly wooded, but there are nearby viewpoints.

Stay straight (south) on the Great Notch Trail to head toward an area known historically as Gilley Field. At 3.6 miles reach the junction with the Gilley and Sluiceway

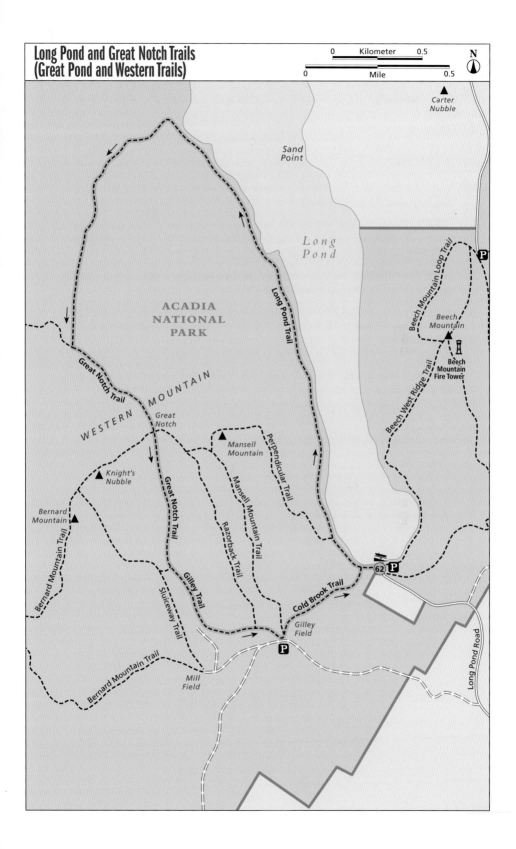

Long Pond and Great Notch Trails
(Great Pond and Western Trails)

0 Kilometer 0.5
0 Mile 0.5

N

Carter
Nubble

Sand
Point

Long
Pond

ACADIA
NATIONAL
PARK

Beech Mountain Loop Trail

Beech
Mountain

Beech
Mountain
Fire Tower

Beech West Ridge Trail

Long Pond Trail

Great Notch Trail

WESTERN MOUNTAIN

Great
Notch

Mansell
Mountain

Perpendicular Trail

Knight's
Nubble

Great Notch Trail

Mansell Mountain Trail

Bernard
Mountain

Razorback Trail

Bernard Mountain Trail

Gilley Trail

Sluiceway Trail

Cold Brook Trail

62

Gilley
Field

Bernard Mountain Trail

Mill
Field

Long Pond Road

Trails. Bear left (southeast) on the Gilley Trail to loop back to Long Pond, passing the southern ends of the Razorback and Mansell Mountain Trails along the way.

At 4.2 miles cross Gilley Field (now mostly grown in) to the Cold Brook Trail, and take that northeast back to Long Pond. Return to the pump house parking area at 4.6 miles.

Miles and Directions

0.0 Start at the Long Pond (Great Pond) trailhead, on the west end of the pump house parking area, near the Cold Brook trailhead.

0.2 Pass the junction with the Perpendicular Trail.

1.0 Reach your turnaround point for a moderate out-and-back hike.

1.7 Reach Long Pond Trail's northernmost point along the shore.

2.7 Reach the junction with the Great Notch Trail (Western Trail). Turn left (southeast) onto the Great Notch Trail to loop over Western Mountain.

3.1 Reach the Great Notch at the intersection with the Razorback and Bernard Mountain Trails, which head to Mansell and Bernard Mountains, respectively. Stay straight (south) on the Great Notch Trail.

3.6 Reach the junction with the Gilley and Sluiceway Trails. Bear left (southeast) on the Gilley Trail to loop back to Long Pond via the Gilley and Cold Brook Trails, passing the southern ends of the Razorback and Mansell Mountain Trails on the left along the way.

4.2 Cross a semi-open area known historically as Gilley Field to the Cold Brook Trail, and follow that trail northeast back to Long Pond.

4.6 Arrive back at the pump house parking area.

63 Perpendicular and Mansell Mountain Loop via Long Pond Trail

This loop takes you up almost vertically from the shore of Long Pond, along a series of spectacular stone steps on the Perpendicular Trail, and down the Mansell Mountain Trail. One of the two summits making up what's known collectively as Western Mountain, the 949-foot Mansell is wooded, but two overlooks on this hike provide good views.

Distance: 2.5-mile loop
Hiking time: About 2 to 3 hours
Difficulty: Strenuous to expert only
Trail surface: Iron ladder and rungs, wooden bridges, granite steps, forest floor, rock ledges
Best season: Spring through fall
Other trail users: Hikers on the Great Notch, Razorback, or Long Pond Trail

Canine compatibility: Dogs prohibited on the Perpendicular Trail
Map: USGS Acadia National Park and Vicinity
Special considerations: No facilities. No swimming or dogs are allowed in Long Pond within 1,000 feet of the pumping station's intake.

Finding the trailhead: From Somesville head south on ME 102, continuing 1.5 miles beyond the Echo Lake Beach entrance. Turn right (west) at Seal Cove Road and travel for 0.5 mile. Then go right (north) on Long Pond Road to the end at a pumping station on the shore of the pond. The Long Pond trailhead is off the west end of the parking area, behind the pump house. Take the Long Pond Trail 0.2 mile to the Perpendicular trailhead. The Island Explorer does not stop here. GPS at start: N44 18.00' / W68 21.01'

The Hike

Built by the Civilian Conservation Corps during the Great Depression, the Perpendicular Trail is an amazing architectural feat, constructed with about five hundred stone steps. The name of the trail is no exaggeration, although the 0.2 mile you first take along Long Pond gives no hint of the near-vertical grade to come.

From the Perpendicular trailhead, begin ascending steeply. You'll climb steps and an iron ladder and rungs, switchback across some of the steepest stuff, and clamber up a finely crafted, winding stone staircase. You'll get views down to Long Pond and northeast to Beech Mountain.

At 1.0 mile reach an overlook with the best views on the trail of Long Pond below and Beech Mountain and its fire tower to the northeast. You can also see the Cranberry Isles and the mouth of Somes Sound to the south.

At 1.1 miles the trail ends at the wooded summit of 949-foot Mansell Mountain. The Mansell Mountain Trail begins here. Head straight (south) on the Mansell Mountain Trail, first described as part of a pre–Revolutionary War road. At 1.3 miles

Some of the approximately five hundred stone steps of the Perpendicular Trail.

reach the junction with a spur to the Great Notch and Razorback Trails. Bear left (southeast) to head off the ridge on the Mansell Mountain Trail.

At 1.4 miles a sign points to an overlook. You'll get views here and farther along the trail of Southwest Harbor, Bass Harbor, and the Cranberry Isles to the south and southeast and Blue Hill Bay to the west.

At 2.1 miles reach a junction where you bear left (southeast) across a semi-grown-in area known historically as Gilley Field and pick up the Cold Brook Trail. Take the Cold Brook Trail northeast, and loop back to the pump house parking area at 2.5 miles.

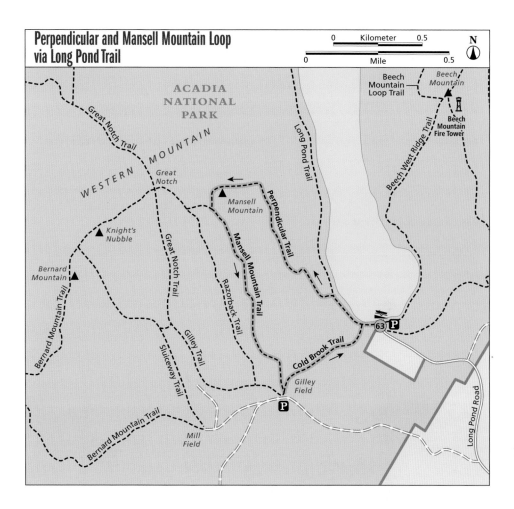

Perpendicular and Mansell Mountain Loop via Long Pond Trail

Miles and Directions

0.0 Start at the Long Pond (Great Pond) trailhead, on the west end of the pump house parking area, past the Cold Brook Trail junction.

0.2 Reach the Perpendicular trailhead and turn left (northwest) onto the trail.

1.0 Reach an overlook.

1.1 Summit wooded Mansell Mountain and head straight (south) on the Mansell Mountain Trail.

1.3 Reach a spur to the Great Notch and Razorback Trails. Bear left (southeast) to continue on the Mansell Mountain Trail.

1.4 Reach an overlook.

2.1 Bear left (southeast) across a semi-grown-in area known historically as Gilley Field, and take the Cold Brook Trail northeast.

2.5 Arrive back at the pump house parking area.

64 Razorback Trail via Gilley Trail

Climb up a rocky spine to wooded Mansell Mountain and an overlook down to Long Pond. You'll get views of the Cranberry Isles and the Gulf of Maine on the ascent.

Distance: 2.6 miles out and back
Hiking time: About 2.5 to 3 hours
Difficulty: Moderate
Trail surface: Granite steps, forest floor, rock ledges
Best season: Spring through fall

Other trail users: Hikers on Great Notch, Mansell Mountain, and Perpendicular Trails
Canine compatibility: Leashed dogs permitted
Map: USGS Acadia National Park and Vicinity
Special considerations: No facilities

Finding the trailhead: From Somesville head south on ME 102, continuing 1.5 miles beyond the Echo Lake Beach entrance. Turn right (west) at Seal Cove Road and follow the road for 2.9 miles as it turns from pavement to gravel. Turn right at a gravel road where a sign points to Seal Cove Pond and Western Mountain Road. Bear right at the next two junctions toward an area known historically as Gilley Field, where there's parking. Follow the Gilley Trail west from the Gilley Field parking area for 0.1 mile. The Razorback trailhead is the second right off the trail, after the Mansell Mountain Trail. GPS: N44 17.48' / W68 21.26'

Looking north toward the mainland from the Razorback Trail.

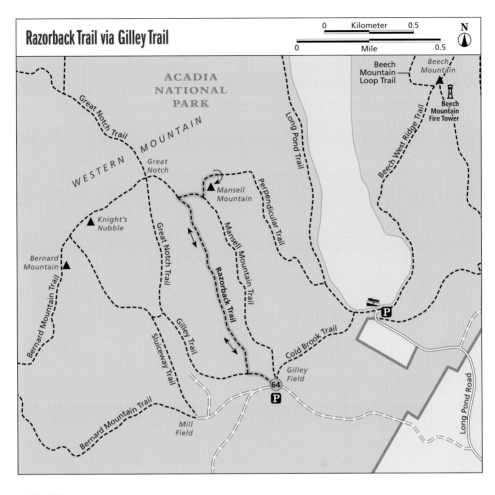

The Hike

The Razorback Trail, reached 0.1 mile west on the Gilley Trail, begins as a wide-open path carpeted with pine needles and then climbs a series of stone steps.

The trail next takes you along the narrow spine up Mansell Mountain, bringing you along cliffs and providing some wonderful open-ridge views. To the left (west) you can see the wooded hulk of Knight's Nubble and Bernard Mountain; to the south are the Gulf of Maine and the Cranberry Isles.

At 0.8 mile reach a junction at the top of the ridge and bear right. At 1.0 mile reach the junction with the Mansell Mountain Trail coming in on the right. Bear left (north) and reach the wooded Mansell Mountain summit, elevation 949 feet, and the junction with the Perpendicular Trail at 1.2 miles.

Continue on the Perpendicular Trail and reach an overlook at 1.3 miles that affords views down to Long Pond, northeast to Beech Mountain and its fire tower, and south to the Gulf of Maine.

Return the way you came.

Miles and Directions

0.0 Start at the trailhead for Gilley Trail, west from the semi-grown-in Gilley Field parking area.

0.1 Reach Razorback trailhead, the second right off Gilley Trail. Turn right onto Razorback Trail.

1.8 Reach a junction at the top of the ridge, and bear right (northeast) to Mansell Mountain.

1.0 Reach the junction with the Mansell Mountain Trail. Bear left (north).

1.2 Summit Mansell Mountain, and take the Perpendicular Trail east.

1.3 Arrive at an overlook.

2.6 Arrive back at the Gilley Field parking area.

65 Bernard Mountain Loop

The West Ledge Trail at the start and end of this hike is a great place to see the sun set over Seal Cove Pond and Blue Hill Bay. This route is also one of the most isolated in the park, taking you to a wooded summit via the Bernard Mountain Trail and down the Sluiceway Trail on the westernmost trail circuit on Mount Desert Island.

Distance: 4.8-mile lollipop
Hiking time: About 3 to 4 hours
Difficulty: Strenuous
Trail surface: Wooden bridges, forest floor, rock ledges
Best season: Spring through fall

Other trail users: Hikers climbing to Great Notch and Mansell Mountain
Canine compatibility: Leashed dogs permitted
Map: USGS Acadia National Park and Vicinity
Special considerations: No facilities

Finding the trailhead: Head south of Somesville on ME 102, and turn right at the flashing yellow light toward Pretty Marsh. Stay straight for 7.4 miles, traveling past Pretty Marsh and Seal Cove. Turn left onto the gravel Seal Cove Road and travel for 0.5 mile, and then turn left onto another gravel road. Reach a three-way intersection in another 0.3 mile, and turn right, following the sign to Western Mountain Road. Continue for 0.3 mile to the junction with Western Mountain Road, and turn left toward Seal Cove Pond. The West Ledge trailhead is on the right (north) in 0.4 mile. Park in a small pullout along the gravel Western Mountain Road on the left (south) beyond the trailhead. The Island Explorer does not stop here. GPS: N44 17.32' / W68 23.13'

The Hike

The hard-to-reach West Ledge Trail offers some of the best views up mostly wooded Bernard Mountain, the highest peak on Mount Desert Island west of Somes Sound.

Alternating between steep ascents through vintage Acadia forest and open rock ledges, the West Ledge Trail provides increasingly sweeping views the higher you go. At one point you get great vistas of the towns of Bernard and Bass Harbor and the Gulf of Maine to the south. Seal Cove Pond sits off to the west.

At 1.1 miles reach the junction with the Bernard Mountain Trail, the southern section of which used to be known as the South Face Trail. Bear left (northeast) toward Bernard Mountain, reaching the summit at 1.6 miles. The 1,071-foot peak is wooded, but there is an overlook that's less grown in; look for the sign.

Continue straight (north) on the Bernard Mountain Trail, reaching Little Notch, elevation 890 feet, and the junction with the Sluiceway Trail at 1.8 miles. Turn right (southeast) to loop off the ridge on the Sluiceway Trail, named for a fast-moving brook that it follows much of the way and featuring switchbacks, rough terrain, precipitous sections, and multiple brook crossings.

Bernard Mountain Loop

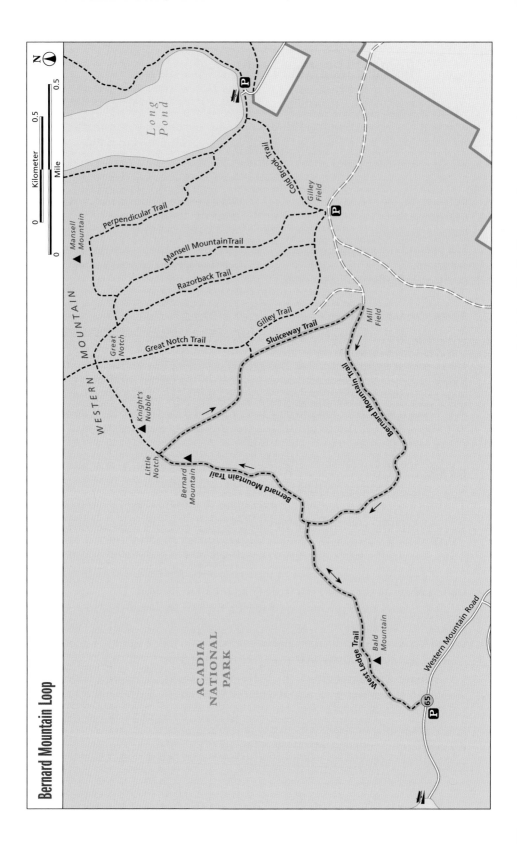

At 2.3 miles you'll reach the junction with a spur to the Gilley and Great Notch Trails. Continue straight ahead (southeast) and proceed down the Sluiceway, reaching Mill Field and the junction with the Bernard Mountain Trail at 2.7 miles.

Turn right (west) and loop back on the Bernard Mountain Trail on the section formerly known as the South Face Trail. This part of the hike takes you across wooden bridges over a gorge and cascades (in wet season), along a steep but wide rock-strewn path, and back up the Bernard Mountain ridge.

At 3.7 miles loop back to the junction with the West Ledge Trail. Turn left (west) to return to the trailhead at 4.8 miles.

Miles and Directions

0.0 Start at the West Ledge trailhead, on the right (north) side of gravel Western Mountain Road.

1.1 Reach the junction with Bernard Mountain Trail (South Face Trail). Bear left (northeast) toward Bernard Mountain.

1.6 Summit Bernard Mountain.

1.8 Reach the junction with the Sluiceway Trail at Little Notch. Turn right (southeast) to loop down on the Sluiceway Trail.

2.3 Reach the junction with a spur to the Gilley and Great Notch Trails. Stay straight (southeast) on the Sluiceway Trail toward Mill Field.

2.7 Reach Mill Field and the junction with the Bernard Mountain Trail. Turn right and take the Bernard Mountain Trail west.

3.7 Reach the junction with the West Ledge Trail. Turn left (west) onto the West Ledge Trail.

4.8 Arrive back at the trailhead.

There's solitude in these woods of Bernard Mountain, even during Acadia's busiest months.

Bass Harbor Area

66 Wonderland

This very easy trail along an old road brings you to pink granite outcrops along the shore and tide pools at low tide. You may see skunk cabbage along the way and wonder why there are broken mussel shells inland along the trail rather than on the coastline.

Distance: 1.4 miles out and back

Hiking time: About 1 hour

Difficulty: Easy

Trail surface: Graded gravel road

Best season: Spring through fall, particularly early morning or late afternoon in summer to avoid the crowds; low tide for tidal pool exploration

Other trail users: None

Canine compatibility: Leashed dogs permitted

Map: USGS Acadia National Park and Vicinity

Special considerations: Wheelchair accessible with assistance. Closest facilities are at the Seawall picnic area or Ship Harbor Trail.

Finding the trailhead: From Southwest Harbor head south about 1 mile on ME 102. Bear left (southeast) onto ME 102A, passing the town of Manset in about 1 mile and Seawall Campground and picnic area in about 3 miles. Reach the Wonderland trailhead in about 4 miles. Parking is on the left (southeast) side of the road. The trail heads southeast along an abandoned gravel road toward the shore. The Island Explorer's Southwest Harbor line stops at Seawall Campground, 1 mile away, and passes Wonderland on the way to Bass Harbor Campground. Ask if the bus driver will let you off at the Wonderland parking area. GPS: N44 14.01' / W68 19.12'

The Hike

Once you see the smooth pink granite along the shore, smell the salty sea, and explore the tide pools, you will know why they call this Wonderland. The very easy trail along an old gravel road starts by winding through dark woods, but a huge smooth pink granite rock on the left soon hints at the show to come.

At about 0.1 mile go up a slight hill and make your way carefully among some roots and rocks. This is the toughest part of an otherwise very easy, well-graded trail. Skunk cabbage is found along this section of the trail, with its purplish-red leaves and yellow flower in early spring and huge green foliage in summer. Through the trees you begin to see the ocean on the right (southeast). At 0.7 mile the trail brings you to the shore, where the pink granite dramatically meets the sea.

Low tide exposes kelp, snails and other wonders of the intertidal zone.

You can spend hours exploring here, especially when low tide exposes tide pools and their diverse marine life, from rockweed to barnacles to green crabs. Be careful of wet rocks, slick seaweed, and sudden waves.

You can also spend countless hours exploring inland along the trail, as our nieces Sharon and Michelle did when we hiked this together, wondering about the cracked-up seashells and seaweed they found far from shore.

We theorized that seagulls must have dropped the mussel shells from midair to open them for food. That was proven later in the trip when we hiked the Bar Island Trail at low tide and witnessed that very seagull feeding activity.

There are many things to wonder about along Wonderland.

Return the way you came.

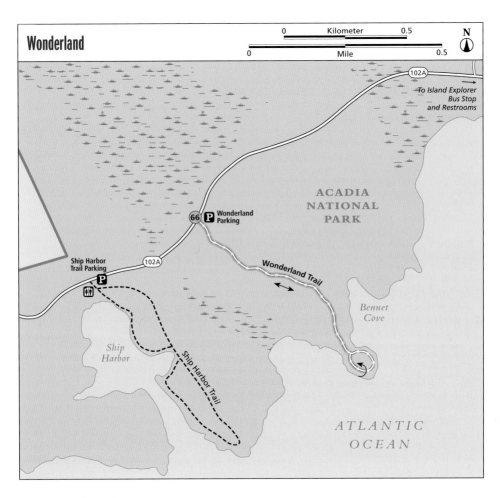

Wonderland

Kilometer
0   0.5

Mile
0   0.5

N

102A

To Island Explorer
Bus Stop
and Restrooms

ACADIA
NATIONAL
PARK

66 **P** Wonderland
Parking

Ship Harbor
Trail Parking
102A

Wonderland Trail

Bennet
Cove

Ship
Harbor

Ship Harbor Trail

ATLANTIC
OCEAN

Miles and Directions

0.0   Start at the Wonderland trailhead, on the southeast side of ME 102A at the edge of the parking area.

0.1   The trail heads slightly uphill.

0.7   Reach the shoreline, where you can add on a loop to explore the rocky outcroppings.

1.4   Arrive back at the trailhead.

67 Ship Harbor Trail

This trail features dramatic pink granite cliffs along the shoreline and the opportunity to explore tidal pools and mudflats at low tide. Although the hard-packed surface on the first 0.25 mile of the trail allows easy access to visitors with wheelchairs and baby strollers, subsequent sections can provide route-finding challenges, especially if you take shortcuts across mudflats, as we discovered one day.

Distance: 1.3-mile figure eight
Hiking time: About 1 hour
Difficulty: Easy
Trail surface: Graded gravel path, forest floor, rocky shore
Best season: Spring through fall, particularly early morning or late afternoon in summer to avoid the crowds; low tide to explore tidal pools

Other trail users: Visitors with wheelchairs or baby strollers
Canine compatibility: Leashed dogs permitted
Map: USGS Acadia National Park and Vicinity
Special considerations: Chemical toilet at trailhead. The first 0.25 mile of the trail is hard-packed surface, making it accessible to visitors with wheelchairs or baby strollers.

Finding the trailhead: From Southwest Harbor head south about 1 mile on ME 102. Bear left (southeast) onto ME 102A, passing the town of Manset in about 1 mile, Seawall Campground and picnic area in about 3 miles, and the Wonderland trail parking area in about 4 miles. The Ship Harbor trailhead is about 0.2 mile beyond Wonderland. The trailhead parking lot is on the left (south) side of ME 102A. The Island Explorer's Southwest Harbor line stops at Seawall Campground, more than 1 mile away, and passes Ship Harbor Trail on the way to Bass Harbor Campground. Ask if the bus driver will let you off at the Ship Harbor Trail parking area. GPS: N44 13.54' / W68 19.31'

The Hike

The drama of the sea crashing against the pink granite cliffs of Acadia is the greatest reward of this easy trail. But there are also other, smaller pleasures, such as seeing ocean ducks known as common eiders floating at the mouth of Ship Harbor, as we did on one hike, or leisurely exploring the coast at low tide on a late sunny afternoon, as we did on another hike with our nieces Sharon and Michelle.

The land around Ship Harbor became part of the park in 1937, but it was another twenty years before the trail was built as part of a decade-long Mission 66 program to celebrate the fiftieth anniversary of the National Park Service, according to Pathmakers, by the park service's Olmsted Center for Landscape Preservation. The trail begins with an open view toward the harbor in the distance and of apple trees from a farm that once stood here.

The trail is one of the easiest and most popular in the park, maybe because it offers so much—a thick forest, a tidal harbor, and intimate views of ocean, pink granite,

Pink granite contrasts with deep blue sea.

and islands. "It's an incredibly busy trail," said Gary Stellpflug, trails foreman at Acadia National Park. "It's immensely popular."

The first 0.25 mile of the trail is a hard-packed surface that leads to mudflats at low tide, making it accessible to people in wheelchairs or using walking canes and also to parents with young babies in strollers. But the rest of the trail is over rocky, uneven terrain, with some steep stretches.

At the first fork, at 0.1 mile at the base of the figure-eight loop, bear right (south), following the hard-packed surface to the edge of Ship Harbor channel and the mud-flats, which are viewable at low tide. The trail now begins to get rocky and uneven as it approaches an intersection at 0.3 mile, in the middle of the figure-eight loop. Bear right to continue along the edge of Ship Harbor channel.

In addition to the common eiders we've seen floating at the mouth of Ship Harbor, it's possible to catch glimpses along the trail of a bald eagle or osprey or even such uncommon birds as a palm warbler or an olive-sided flycatcher. (Birding information is available at www.nps.gov/acad.)

At 0.7 mile, at the mouth of Ship Harbor, you'll reach the rocky shore along the Atlantic. Here you can be awed by the dramatic pink cliffs or explore tidal pools at low tide, when barnacles, rockweed, snails, and other sea life are exposed by the receding waters.

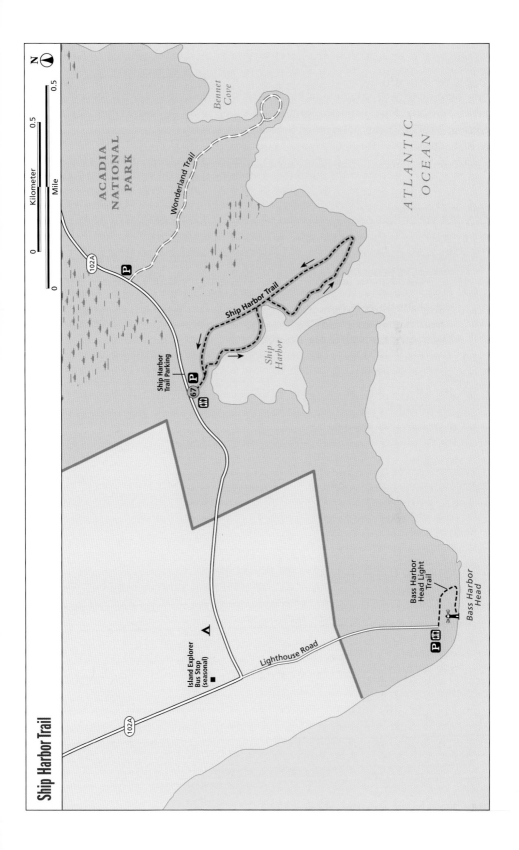

Ship Harbor Trail

Island Explorer Bus Stop (seasonal)

Lighthouse Road

Bass Harbor Head Light Trail

Bass Harbor Head

Ship Harbor Trail Parking

Ship Harbor Trail

Ship Harbor

Wonderland Trail

Bennet Cove

ACADIA NATIONAL PARK

ATLANTIC OCEAN

102A

67

N

Kilometer

Mile

0   0.5

0   0.5

Turn left to circle back along the hilly inland section of the figure-eight loop. When you reach an intersection at 1.0 mile, back at the center of the figure eight, bear right (northwest) to continue along the hilly inland section of the loop. If you prefer to return along the easier portion of the loop along the Ship Harbor channel, you can bear left at this intersection instead and follow the channel northwest back to the trailhead.

At a fork at the base of the figure-eight loop, bear northwest for 0.1 mile to return to the parking lot.

Miles and Directions

0.0 Start at the Ship Harbor trailhead, on the left (south) side of ME 102A.

0.1 Bear right (south) at the fork, at the base of the figure-eight loop, and head along the edge of Ship Harbor channel.

0.3 At the intersection in the middle of the figure eight, bear right again to continue along the edge of Ship Harbor channel.

0.7 Reach the rocky shoreline along the Atlantic; turn left (northwest) to circle back along the hilly inland section of the figure-eight loop.

1.0 At the intersection in the middle of the figure eight, bear right (northwest) to continue along the hilly inland section.

1.2 Reach the fork at the base of the figure-eight loop; bear right (northwest) to head back to the parking lot.

1.3 Arrive back at the trailhead.

68 Bass Harbor Head Light Trail

Get a close-up view of the only lighthouse on Mount Desert Island, which continues to guide boaters safely into Bass Harbor with its red beacon. Stairs bring you down the steep bluff to an overlook, providing views not only of Bass Harbor Head Light but also of Blue Hill Bay and Swan's Island.

Distance: 0.2 mile out and back
Hiking time: About 30 minutes
Difficulty: Moderate
Trail surface: Wooden deck and stairs, graded gravel path, rock ledges and steps
Best season: Spring through fall, particularly early morning or late afternoon in summer to avoid the crowds
Other trail users: None

Canine compatibility: Leashed dogs permitted
Map: USGS Acadia National Park and Vicinity
Special considerations: Chemical toilet. The automated lighthouse is not open to the public; neither is the former lighthouse keeper's house, which now serves as Coast Guard housing. Hike the trail only in safe conditions, that is, not when it's stormy or when surf is crashing against the cliffs.

Finding the trailhead: From Bass Harbor head south about 0.6 mile on ME 102A until you reach a sharp curve in the road as ME 102A heads left (east). Go straight ahead (south) on the 0.5-mile dead-end Lighthouse Road, which takes you to the Bass Harbor Head Light parking lot. The trail leads from the left (southeastern) edge of the parking lot. The Island Explorer bus does not stop here, although the Southwest Harbor line has a Bass Harbor Campground stop near the beginning of the dead-end road to the lighthouse. GPS: N44 13.21' / W68 20.13'

The Hike

Maine is synonymous with not only lobster but also lighthouses. More than sixty towering beacons still stand guard along the state's 3,500 miles of rocky coastline, with perhaps one of the most photogenic being Bass Harbor Head Light in Acadia National Park. Certainly the contrast of Acadia's distinctive pink granite against the lighthouse's white tower makes for a picture-postcard view, and many visitors come to create a picture of their own.

Built in 1858, the lighthouse even today guides boaters safely in and out of Bass Harbor and Blue Hill Bay with its now-automated red beacon.

The trail begins on the left (southeastern) edge of the parking lot. Head southeast along the trail through the woods to a wooden staircase. Go steeply down the wooden stairs, and loop back along the rocks toward the lighthouse to an overlook.

Bass Harbor Head Light, the only lighthouse in Acadia, is picture-postcard perfect.

The length of the trail, only 0.1 mile one way to the overlook, makes it seem easy, but its steepness, even if on wooden stairs, makes it moderately difficult. Take your time. Let the stunning views take your breath away, not overexertion.

From the overlook the view includes Bass Harbor Head Light, the ocean, and outlying islands, including Swan's Island, which has a year-round population serviced by a vehicle ferry from Bass Harbor.

If you clamber along the rocks to get different perspectives, as our nieces did on a trip here, be careful. The rocks can be slippery, especially when wet.

Return the way you came.

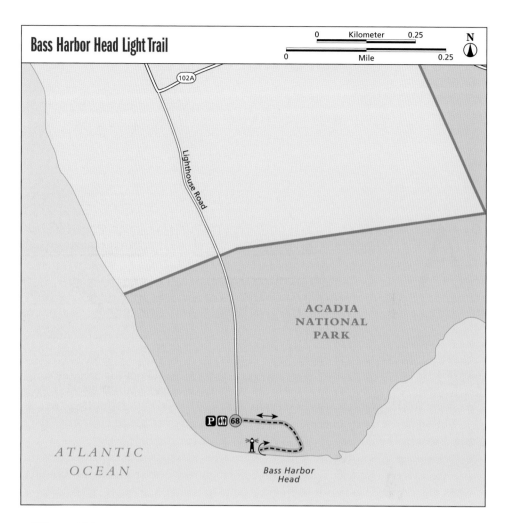

Miles and Directions

0.0 Start at the Bass Harbor Head Light trailhead, on the left (southeastern) edge of the parking lot.

0.1 Reach the overlook at the end of wooden stairs and rock path, with views of Bass Harbor Head Light, Blue Hill Bay, and outlying islands.

0.2 Arrive back at the trailhead.

Isle au Haut

A distant island of mountains and hills, Isle au Haut, pronounced locally as eye-la-ho, offers some of the wildest hiking in Acadia National Park. Its remote trails go through thick spruce and pine forests, along 100-foot-high cliffs, and next to giant coves with crashing surf and chasms.

On a sunny day the views are spectacular, with sweeping vistas across the sea to the mainland's Camden Hills and the island of Vinalhaven.

Five miles at sea, Isle au Haut is not easy to reach. But it's well worth the ninety-minute drive from Bar Harbor to catch the mail boat—not the ferry, as locals quickly point out.

There's a special quality to the passage of time here, the sense of humor of the residents, and the way the island stays with you.

The wildlife, diversity of plant life, and volcanic geology of Isle au Haut make the island special as well.

Park Ranger Alison Richardson sees bald eagles or ospreys almost daily. "That is an eagle, an immature eagle," she said, pointing to the sky as the raptor flew overhead when she welcomed visitors to the most remote section of Acadia.

Richardson said she's even seen river otters in Duck Harbor. "If people are looking for something different, out of the way, this is a great spot. We have 18 miles of trails. We're super beautiful. It's totally unique." More than seven hundred species of plants have been identified on the island, including orchids, sundews, pitch pine, and blueberries. And the geology stands out as well.

Henry Berry IV, physical geologist for the Maine Geological Survey, said Isle au Haut is special partly because of its well-preserved, spectacular volcanic rock along the western shore, including Duck Harbor to Western Head, and its 420-million-year-old granite on the eastern shore.

"It's a dynamic environment," Berry said after a geology tour of the island's shore-line. "It's all there to look at. It's better than a textbook."

Isle au Haut, French for "high island," was named by explorer Samuel Champlain in 1604. Some 6 miles long and 3 miles wide, the island was settled in 1792 by farmers, boat builders, and fishermen. Isle au Haut is still home to dozens of year-round residents and a few hundred summer residents.

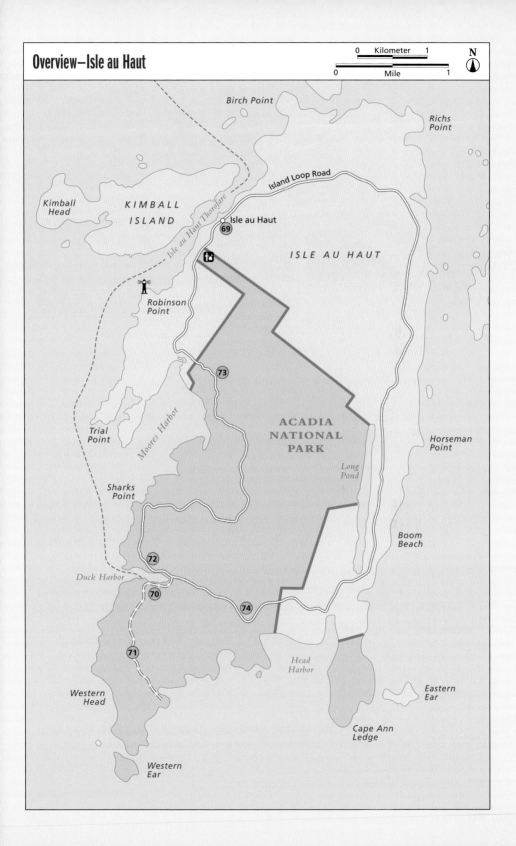

Overview–Isle au Haut

0 Kilometer 1

0 Mile 1

N

Birch Point

Richs Point

Island Loop Road

Kimball Head

KIMBALL ISLAND

Isle au Haut Thorofare

Isle au Haut

69

ISLE AU HAUT

Robinson Point

73

Trial Point

Moores Harbor

ACADIA NATIONAL PARK

Horseman Point

Sharks Point

Long Pond

Boom Beach

72

Duck Harbor

70

74

71

Head Harbor

Eastern Ear

Western Head

Cape Ann Ledge

Western Ear

A rustic cabin near Eli's Creek on the Duck Harbor Trail.

The southern end of the island was donated to the park service in 1943 by one of the Boston-area families that began summering here in the 1880s. The park property consists of 2,900 acres—about 50 percent of the island's total acres.

At the height of the tourist season, the mail boat makes a few trips daily from Stonington to the Isle au Haut town landing. The Duck Harbor Trail, the only park trail near the town landing, leads 3.8 miles south to where many of the other trails begin at Duck Harbor Landing.

Mid-June through mid-September, the boat also goes to Duck Harbor Landing, bringing people close to many of the island's other trailheads and Duck Harbor Campground. A 2014 updated park management plan slightly increased the daily visitor limit, from 120 to 128, to protect the island's resources.

It's best to come prepared with food and other essentials, such as water and insect repellent. The island's general store near town landing is open limited hours. There may also be a local cafe and food truck open seasonally near the town landing. And the most important aspect of planning a trip, as any Isle au Haut ranger will tell you, is to know when the last mail boat leaves for Stonington and from which landing.

To catch the mail boat to Isle au Haut, drive north on ME 3 from Bar Harbor to Ellsworth. Take ME 172 south to Blue Hill, then ME 15 south to Deer Isle and Stonington. Call the Isle au Haut Company at (207) 367-5193 for the boat schedule, or visit www.isleauhaut.com.

Advanced reservations for the campground, open May 15 through October 15, must be made using a special form, postmarked April 1 or later. Go to www.nps.gov/acad or call the park at (207) 288-3338 to get the form and information about the special use permit. No phone reservations are accepted.

69 Duck Harbor and Deep Cove Trails

The longest trail on Isle au Haut takes you through the woods and over rocky coast and passes a 0.2-mile spur trail to Deep Cove, where you can view some spectacular sunsets. Duck Harbor Trail is the only footpath that leaves from the year-round boat landing in town, and its 3.8-mile length must be backpacked by campers with off-peak reservations at Duck Harbor Campground.

Distance: 4.5 miles one way; option to take the mail boat back to town landing or Stonington in season

Hiking time: About 2.5 to 3 hours

Difficulty: Moderate

Trail surface: Wooden bridges, rocky coast, forest floor, rock ledges

Best season: Spring through fall, particularly mid-June through mid-September for a return on the mail boat

Other trail users: Area residents; hikers on Bowditch and Deep Cove Trails; mountain bikers on Island Loop Road

Canine compatibility: Leashed dogs permitted but not in the campground

Map: USGS Acadia National Park and Vicinity

Special considerations: Composting toilets at the ranger station near the town landing and at Duck Harbor Landing. Know when the last mail boat leaves for Stonington and from which landing; don't miss it.

Finding the trailhead: The hike starts from the Isle au Haut town landing. Turn right (southwest) on the paved road and walk for 0.3 mile. Turn left (southeast) at the ranger station to reach the trailhead. GPS at start: N44 04.22' / W68 38.20'

The Hike

From the ranger station, just 0.3 mile southwest of the town landing on the paved road, the blue-blazed trail immediately goes through a boggy area with plentiful skunk cabbage before entering an evergreen forest. At 1.7 miles, at the junction with the Bowditch Trail, bear right (south) and soon cross the road that circles the island. Day-trippers pressed to catch the mail boat back to the mainland can turn right on the road and loop back to the town landing in another 1.0 mile.

At 2.4 miles the Duck Harbor Trail begins to skirt the rocky shore of Goss Beach. The trail is tricky here, sometimes taking you along the beach over a bed of seaweed and mussel shells and other times swinging inland. Watch carefully for cairns on the beach to point the way.

Cross Eli's Creek on a wooden bridge at 2.7 miles. At 3.0 miles reach a junction with the Deep Cove Trail. Turn right (southwest) onto the short spur to explore Deep Cove at 3.2 miles.

Return to the Duck Harbor Trail at 3.4 miles and turn right (south), going through the woods and along some log bridges. Cross the Island Loop Road for a

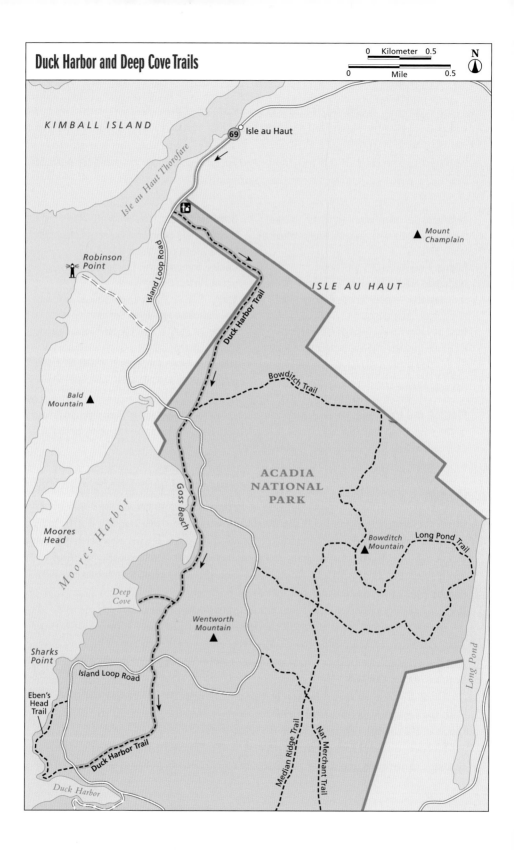

Duck Harbor and Deep Cove Trails

0 Kilometer 0.5

0 Mile 0.5

N

KIMBALL ISLAND

69 Isle au Haut

Isle au Haut Thorofare

Mount Champlain

Robinson Point

Island Loop Road

ISLE AU HAUT

Duck Harbor Trail

Bowditch Trail

Bald Mountain

Goss Beach

ACADIA NATIONAL PARK

Moores Head

Moores Harbor

Bowditch Mountain

Long Pond Trail

Deep Cove

Wentworth Mountain

Long Pond

Sharks Point

Island Loop Road

Eben's Head Trail

Duck Harbor Trail

Median Ridge Trail

Nat Merchant Trail

Duck Harbor

Whale bones on display at the Acadia National Park Ranger Station on Isle au Haut.

second time at 3.7 miles, and reach the trail's end at the third intersection with the loop road at 4.5 miles.

To add the 0.8-mile Eben's Head Trail, turn right (northwest) onto the loop road for 0.1 mile. To continue to the campground and boat landing in another 0.5 mile, turn left (southeast) onto the road, then bear right (south) at the next fork toward Duck Harbor Landing. The trail to the campground leads behind the composting toilet at the picnic area, just before the boat landing. You can catch the mail boat back to Stonington or town landing from here during the peak season.

Miles and Directions

0.0 Start at the Isle au Haut town landing, and turn right (southwest) onto the paved road.

0.3 Reach Duck Harbor trailhead, behind the ranger station.

1.7 Pass the junction with the Bowditch Trail.

1.8 Cross the Island Loop Road.

2.4 Walk along Goss Beach.

2.7 Cross Eli's Creek on wooden bridge.

3.0 Reach the junction with the Deep Cove Trail; turn right (west) onto the 0.2-mile spur.

3.2 Reach Deep Cove.

3.4 Return to the Duck Harbor Trail; turn right (south) to continue toward Duck Harbor.

3.7 Cross the island loop road.

4.5 Reach the end of the trail at the island loop road. The Eben's Head Trail is 0.1 mile to the right (northwest) along the road. Duck Harbor Landing is 0.5 mile to the left (southeast), then right (south) at the fork.

70 Duck Harbor Mountain and Goat Trails

The hike up Duck Harbor Mountain to its panoramic views is the most strenuous on Isle au Haut, with lots of ups and downs in less than 0.5 mile. Climb over steep rocky knobs known as the Puddings, and circle back along the rugged coast on the Goat Trail.

Distance: 2.8-mile loop, plus 0.1 mile on unpaved road to trailhead
Hiking time: About 2 to 3 hours
Difficulty: Moderate to strenuous
Trail surface: Rocky coast, unpaved road, forest floor, rock ledges
Best season: Mid-June through mid-September, when the mail boat goes to Duck Harbor Landing

Other trail users: Area residents; hikers on the Western Head and Cliff Trails; mountain bikers on Western Head Road
Canine compatibility: Leashed dogs permitted but not in the campground
Map: USGS Acadia National Park and Vicinity
Special considerations: Composting toilet at Duck Harbor Landing

Finding the trailhead: The hike starts from Duck Harbor Landing on Isle au Haut. From Duck Harbor Landing turn right (south) onto the unpaved Western Head Road. The Duck Harbor Mountain trailhead is on the left (east) in 0.1 mile. GPS at start: N44 01.41' / W68 39.11'

The Hike

The Duck Harbor Mountain Trail, reached 0.1 mile south of Duck Harbor Landing off the unpaved Western Head Road, begins steeply through the woods, alternating between switchbacks and brief flat sections on ridges. The sound of the surf is always in the background.

At 0.3 mile turn sharp right (south) onto an open ledge and see the vast forest to the east. Continue climbing up open ledges, reaching the 314-foot summit of Duck Harbor Mountain at 0.4 mile, marked by US Coast and Geodetic Survey metal disks. Here you can get great views to the west of Vinalhaven, the Camden Hills, and Saddleback Ledge Light.

Follow the trail through a flat wooded area. At 0.9 mile reach the Puddings, a series of challenging rocky knobs that require scrambling on all fours in some areas. There are no iron rungs here to help you along the smooth rock. To climb up you need to find nooks and crannies for handholds and footholds; to get down you may need to slide on your behind. Don't let the great views distract you from focusing on the nontechnical rock climbing you need to do here.

The trail takes you through a narrow rock chasm, and then descends a steep rock face. Reach Squeaker Cove and the Goat Trail at 1.3 miles, where the Duck Harbor Mountain Trail ends and the ocean knifes into a shoreline with spectacular

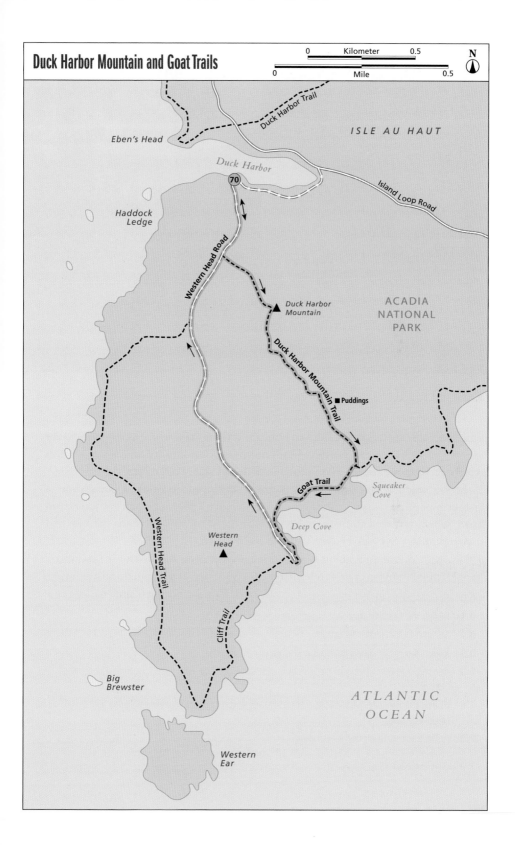

Duck Harbor Mountain and Goat Trails

0 Kilometer 0.5

0 Mile 0.5

N

ISLE AU HAUT

Duck Harbor Trail

Eben's Head

Duck Harbor

70

Island Loop Road

Haddock
Ledge

Western Head Road

Duck Harbor
Mountain

ACADIA
NATIONAL
PARK

Duck Harbor Mountain Trail

Puddings

Goat Trail

Squeaker
Cove

Deep Cove

Western
Head

Western Head Trail

Cliff Trail

Big
Brewster

ATLANTIC
OCEAN

Western
Ear

Isle au Haut is the most remote section of Acadia National Park, reachable only by boat.

spire-like cliffs. Turn right (southwest) onto the Goat Trail, which offers spectacular coastal scenery. (The Goat Trail also heads northeast for nearly 1.0 mile if you want to explore picturesque Barred Harbor or access the Median Ridge Trail.)

At 1.6 miles, as you near the Goat Trail's southwest end, skirt a cove where a 45-foot humpback whale washed ashore in February 1983 and reach Western Head Road, which is closed to motor vehicles. Turn right (northwest) onto the unpaved road, and return to Duck Harbor Landing at 2.9 miles.

Miles and Directions

0.0 Start at Duck Harbor Landing and turn right (south) onto the unpaved Western Head Road.

0.1 Reach the Duck Harbor Mountain trailhead on the left (southeast).

0.4 Summit Duck Harbor Mountain.

0.9 Reach the rocky knobs called the Puddings.

1.3 Reach Squeaker Cove and the junction with the Goat Trail. Turn right (southwest) onto the Goat Trail.

1.6 Reach the junction with Western Head Road, and turn right (northwest) onto the unpaved road.

2.9 Arrive back at Duck Harbor Landing.

71 Western Head and Cliff Trails

If you time the hike along this coastal loop right, you can walk across to a small isle known as Western Ear. If your timing's off, you still get spectacular, endless views along rocky shore and cliff.

Distance: 4.2-mile lollipop
Hiking time: About 2.5 to 3.5 hours
Difficulty: Moderate
Trail surface: Rocky coast, unpaved road, forest floor, rock ledges
Best season: Mid-June through mid-September, when the mail boat goes to Duck Harbor Landing

Other trail users: Area residents; hikers on the Duck Harbor Mountain and Goat Trails; mountain bikers on Western Head Road
Canine compatibility: Leashed dogs permitted but not in the campground
Map: USGS Acadia National Park and Vicinity
Special considerations: Composting toilet at Duck Harbor Landing

Finding the trailhead: The hike begins at Duck Harbor Landing on Isle au Haut. From Duck Harbor Landing turn right (south) onto the unpaved Western Head Road. The Western Head trailhead is on the right (west) in 0.7 mile. GPS at start: N44 01.41' / W68 39.11'

The Hike

The Western Head Trail, reached 0.7 mile south of Duck Harbor Landing on the unpaved Western Head Road, heads west over moss-covered roots to start, but you soon get views of the coast and offshore rocky outcroppings.

At 1.2 miles you quickly descend to the shore. The trail continues up and down along the craggy coast, passing a cove and a distinctive pink granite formation. It's easy to lose the trail, which gets tricky here, weaving inland at times through woods and coming back out to the rocky beach again. Just keep paralleling the shore until you pick up the path again.

At 1.7 miles the trail climbs steeply to cliffs and a tremendous rocky precipice, then continues through a rugged stretch of tall grass and woods, finally emerging at a cove of rounded boulders and flattened stone. Although the trail appears to follow the granite along the shore here, it actually heads inland a bit, ending at 2.0 miles at the junction with the Cliff Trail.

Turn right (southwest) onto the spur to the tip of Western Head, the jumping-off point for a low-tide walk across to Western Ear, arriving at 2.1 miles.

If you don't hit the tide right, do not attempt to cross to the island, since fast currents make this rocky ear inaccessible. If you do explore the rocky isle, remember not to get stranded by the incoming tide—or miss the last mail boat back to Stonington.

Return to the junction at 2.2 miles, and then go straight (northeast) onto the Cliff Trail to loop back.

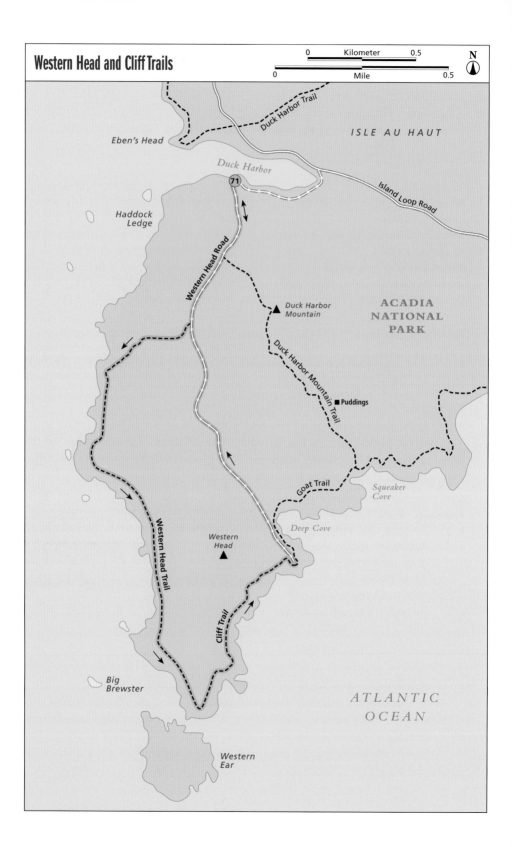

ISLE AU HAUT

Duck Harbor Trail

Eben's Head

Duck Harbor

71

Island Loop Road

Haddock
Ledge

Western Head Road

Duck Harbor
Mountain

ACADIA
NATIONAL
PARK

Duck Harbor Mountain Trail

Puddings

Goat Trail

Squeaker
Cove

Deep Cove

Western Head Trail

Western
Head

Cliff Trail

Big
Brewster

Western
Ear

ATLANTIC
OCEAN

Climbing up and down the craggy coast, the Cliff Trail takes you along clifftops and brings you by a deep chasm where the ocean spray spits through and the waves can boom, especially on a windy or stormy day.

Later, standing high on an open rocky face, enjoy awesome views of the cliffs and sea. The trail ends at the junction with Western Head Road at 2.8 miles.

Turn left (northwest) onto the unpaved road, which is closed to motor vehicles, and loop back to Duck Harbor Landing at 4.2 miles.

Miles and Directions

0.0 Start at Duck Harbor Landing and turn right onto the unpaved Western Head Road.

0.7 Reach Western Head trailhead.

1.2 Reach the shore.

1.7 Reach cliffs.

2.0 Reach the junction with the Cliff Trail; turn right (southwest) to head to Western Ear.

2.1 Arrive at the shore across from Western Ear, which is accessible at low tide. Retrace your steps to the intersection.

2.2 Arrive back at the intersection of the Western Head and Cliff Trails. Stay straight (northeast) on the Cliff Trail.

The Western Head Trail takes you by rugged cliffs.

2.8 Reach the junction with Western Head Road. Turn left (northwest) onto the unpaved road.

4.2 Arrive back at Duck Harbor Landing.

72 Eben's Head Trail

Rocky Eben's Head is an amazing place for watching the sunset if you are staying overnight on Isle au Haut. Standing high atop this wide-open knob, the views are south to Western Head, southeast to Duck Harbor Mountain, and west to the Camden Hills, Saddleback Ledge, and Vinalhaven.

Distance: 2.9-mile lollipop
Hiking time: About 2 to 2.5 hours
Difficulty: Easy to moderate
Trail surface: Rocky coast, unpaved road, forest floor, rock ledges
Best season: Mid-June through mid-September, when the mail boat goes to Duck Harbor Landing

Other trail users: Area residents; hikers on the Duck Harbor Trail; mountain bikers on the Western Head and Island Loop Roads
Canine compatibility: Leashed dogs permitted but not in the campground
Map: USGS Acadia National Park and Vicinity
Special considerations: Composting toilet at Duck Harbor Landing; picnic table near trailhead

Finding the trailhead: The hike starts at Duck Harbor Landing on Isle au Haut. From Duck Harbor Landing bear left (east) onto the unpaved Western Head Road and go around the harbor. At 0.3 mile turn left (northwest) onto the unpaved Island Loop Road. Reach the trailhead, on the left (southwest) side of the loop road, in another 0.5 mile. GPS at start: N44 01.41' / W68 39.11'

The Hike

The Eben's Head Trail is an easy to moderate hike for day-trippers and picnickers who arrive at nearby Duck Harbor Landing.

The trail, reached after a 0.8-mile walk from Duck Harbor Landing on unpaved roads, starts easily through the woods and then skirts the shore, with a view across Duck Harbor to the boat landing and possibly harbor seals. The trail curves right (northwest). At 1.1 miles a spur trail leads left (west) to a grassy area at the base of Eben's Head, a nice spot for a picnic, with views of the rocky coastline. The sights are even better if you climb to the top of the outcropping, which is about 75 feet high.

Once we saw nothing but fog at Eben's Head. Another time we got a spectacular sunset and had the rock formation all to ourselves.

The main trail then gets a little rougher, continuing northwest across a stretch of rocky beach toward a set of low rocky cliffs marked by blue blazes. Look behind you for a good view of Eben's Head.

From the top of Eben's Head, you can see the volcanic rock that makes up much of Isle au Haut's western shore.

Scramble up the low cliffs and follow the trail through the woods and among black crowberry. Keep hugging this astonishing rocky coast, sometimes walking over weathered yellow-and-orange granite or a cobble beach.

Return to the unpaved island road at 1.6 miles, and turn right (south) onto the road to loop back. Pass Eben's Head trailhead at 2.1 miles and Duck Harbor trailhead at 2.2 miles. Bear right at 2.6 miles onto the unpaved Western Head Road, which is closed to motor vehicles, and arrive back at Duck Harbor Landing at 2.9 miles.

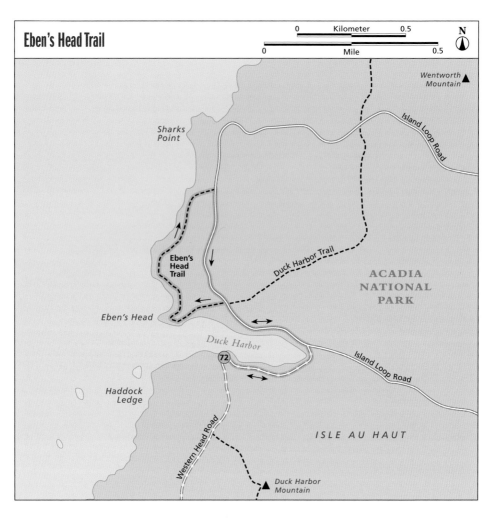

Eben's Head Trail

Miles and Directions

0.0 Start at Duck Harbor Landing and bear left (east) onto the unpaved Western Head Road.

0.3 Turn left (northwest) onto the unpaved Island Loop Road.

0.8 Reach Eben's Head trailhead, on the left (southwest) side of the loop road.

1.1 Reach the spur to Eben's Head.

1.6 Loop back to the unpaved Island Loop Road, and turn right (south) to return to Duck Harbor Landing.

2.1 Pass Eben's Head trailhead.

2.2 Pass the Duck Harbor trailhead.

2.6 Bear right (south) onto the unpaved Western Head Road.

2.9 Arrive back at Duck Harbor Landing.

73 Bowditch and Long Pond Trails via Duck Harbor Trail

A remote circuit, this hike provides plenty of solitude as you climb the wooded summit of Bowditch Mountain and skirt the western shore of 6,300-foot-long Long Pond, the only freshwater pond on the island.

Distance: 9.0-mile lollipop

Hiking time: About 5.5 to 6.5 hours

Difficulty: Moderate to strenuous

Trail surface: Wooden bridges, forest floor

Best season: Mid-June through mid-September

Other trail users: Area residents; hikers on the Duck Harbor and Median Ridge Trails; mountain bikers on the Island Loop Road

Canine compatibility: Leashed dogs permitted

Map: USGS Acadia National Park and Vicinity

Special considerations: Composting toilet at the ranger station near the town landing. Wear appropriate footwear, and bring insect repellent, especially during wet or buggy seasons.

Finding the trailhead: The hike starts from the Isle au Haut town landing. Turn right onto the paved road. Walk 0.3 mile to the ranger station. Turn left (southeast) at the ranger station to access the blue-blazed Duck Harbor Trail. Follow the trail for 1.4 miles to the Bowditch trailhead on the left (east). GPS at start: N44 04.22' / W68 38.20'

The Hike

There are no expansive views along wooded Bowditch Trail, but the path is fresh and not trampled. It's full of rich green moss and ferns and blooming with rhodora, sheep laurel, and tiny white star flowers in spring.

Reach the trailhead after a total 1.7-mile hike from town landing, first 0.3 mile on the paved road, and then 1.4 miles on the Duck Harbor Trail. From the junction with the Duck Harbor Trail, head east toward Bowditch Mountain and cross a long series of log bridges. The trail now begins a long, gradual ascent toward Isle au Haut's north-south ridge.

At 2.8 miles, after attaining the ridge, the trail makes a sharp right turn at a junction at the park boundary. Follow the sign that says "South." The trail, which can be overgrown, goes up and down the rocky ridge.

After you pass a field of ferns, you reach the wooded summit of Bowditch Mountain at 3.7 miles, at the junction with the Long Pond Trail. Turn left (east) onto the Long Pond Trail to head toward the pond views. (If you're rushing to catch the last boat to Stonington, you can turn right (west) onto the Long Pond Trail to get back to the unpaved island loop road more quickly, cutting the hike short by about 1.2 miles.)

The trail heads steeply down from the ridge to the pond, reaching the shore at 4.5 miles. Be sure to savor the views, because the path follows the pond for less than

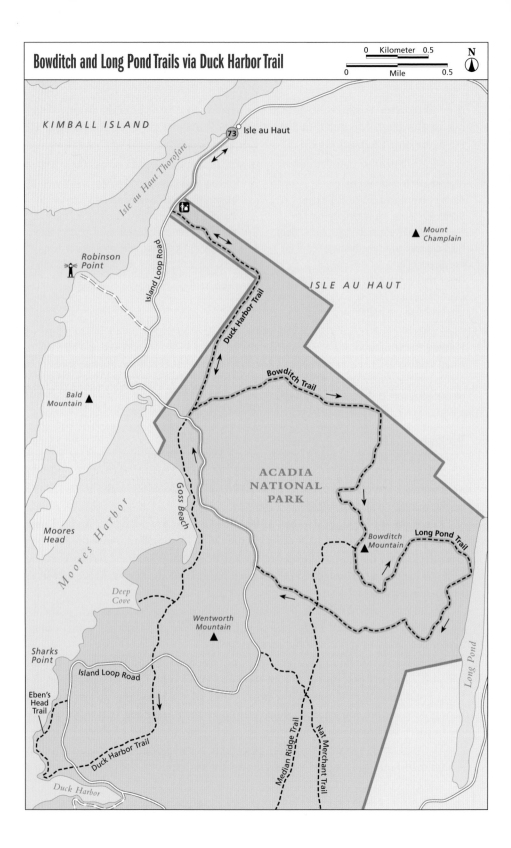

Bowditch and Long Pond Trails via Duck Harbor Trail

0   Kilometer   0.5

0   Mile   0.5

N

KIMBALL ISLAND

Isle au Haut Thorofare

73   Isle au Haut

Mount Champlain ▲

Robinson Point

Island Loop Road

ISLE AU HAUT

Duck Harbor Trail

Bowditch Trail

Bald Mountain ▲

Goss Beach

ACADIA NATIONAL PARK

Moores Head

Bowditch Mountain ▲

Long Pond Trail

Moores Harbor

Deep Cove

Wentworth Mountain ▲

Long Pond

Sharks Point

Island Loop Road

Eben's Head Trail

Duck Harbor Trail

Median Ridge Trail

Nat Merchant Trail

Duck Harbor

100 yards before heading back into the woods. The trail brings you back up the ridge, steeply at times, and at one point takes you by an old stone wall.

At 5.6 miles reach the junction with the Median Ridge Trail coming in on the left (south) and a spur of the Long Pond Trail coming in on the right (north). Stay straight (northwest) on the Long Pond Trail as it winds over log bridges through a bog and along a level stretch of woods.

At 6.0 miles reach the unpaved island loop road. Turn right onto the road, and arrive back at the town landing at 9.0 miles.

Miles and Directions

0.0 Start at the Isle au Haut town landing and turn right onto the paved road.

0.3 Turn left (southeast) at the ranger station to access the blue-blazed Duck Harbor Trail.

1.7 Turn left (east) onto the Bowditch Trail.

2.8 Take a sharp right (south).

3.7 Summit Bowditch Mountain and reach the junction with the Long Pond Trail. Turn left (east) to head to Long Pond. (**Option:** If you're pressed for time, turn right and take the Long Pond Trail south and then northwest back to the unpaved island loop road to cut short the hike by about 1.2 miles.)

4.5 Reach the shore of Long Pond.

5.6 Reach the junction with the Median Ridge Trail coming in on the left (south) and a spur of the Long Pond Trail coming in on the right (north). Stay straight (northwest) on the Long Pond Trail to get to the unpaved island loop road.

6.0 Reach the road. Turn right (north) to head back to the town landing on the road.

9.0 Arrive back at the town landing.

Beyond this field of ferns is the wooded summit of Bowditch Mountain.

74 Median Ridge and Nat Merchant Trails

This isolated inland loop takes you along the north-south ridge of Isle au Haut and a trail named for an early resident of Isle au Haut. There are no ocean views here unless you take the optional southern spur of the Median Ridge Trail, but there are towering old-growth trees, bogs with big skunk cabbages, and a rock garden.

Distance: 4.9-mile lollipop
Hiking time: About 2.5 to 3.5 hours
Difficulty: Easy to moderate
Trail surface: Wooden bridges, forest floor
Best season: Mid-June through mid-September, when the mail boat goes to Duck Harbor Landing
Other trail users: Area residents; mountain bikers on the island loop road

Canine compatibility: Leashed dogs permitted but not in the campground
Map: USGS Acadia National Park and Vicinity
Special considerations: Composting toilet at Duck Harbor Landing. Wear appropriate footwear, and bring insect repellent, especially during wet or buggy seasons.

Finding the trailhead: The hike starts from Duck Harbor Landing on Isle au Haut. From Duck Harbor Landing bear left (east) onto the unpaved Western Head Road and go around the harbor. At 0.3 mile turn right (southeast) onto the unpaved island loop road. Reach the trailhead for the northern section of the Median Ridge Trail on the left side of the loop road in another 1.0 mile. GPS at start: N44 01.41' / W68 39.11'

The Hike

Out of the way and with no coastal views, the north spur of the Median Ridge Trail is most useful for hikers with overnight accommodations as part of long day hikes traversing the island. The trail provides access to Isle au Haut's central ridge and other inland paths, including the Long Pond and Bowditch Trails.

Reached after a 1.3-mile hike from Duck Harbor Landing on unpaved roads, the north spur of the Median Ridge Trail quickly ascends the median ridge, crosses a brook, and goes through a rock garden. After a bit of up and down, the trail takes you by boggy areas with lots of skunk cabbage.

At 2.4 miles reach the intersection with the Nat Merchant Trail, named for a fisherman who owned 120 acres on Isle au Haut in the 1870s. Turn right (southeast) onto the Nat Merchant Trail to loop back. The trail descends slightly off rocky knobs until you reach boggy woods again. Head south through skunk cabbage that can grow so big that it pops up between cracks in long sections of log bridges here.

Reach the island loop road at 3.2 miles. Turn right (west) onto the unpaved road to loop back past the Median Ridge trailhead at 3.6 miles. Bear left onto Western Head Road at 4.6 miles, returning to Duck Harbor Landing at 4.9 miles.

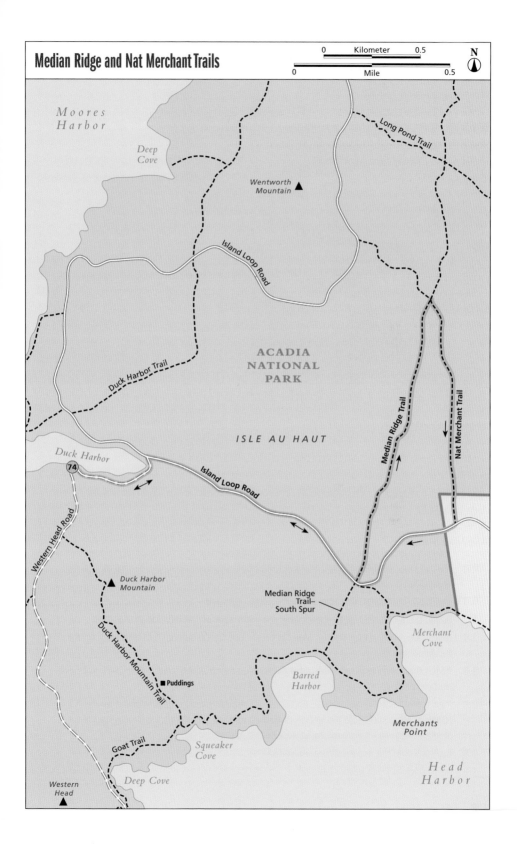

Median Ridge and Nat Merchant Trails

0   Kilometer   0.5

0   Mile   0.5

N

Moores Harbor

Deep Cove

Long Pond Trail

Wentworth Mountain ▲

Island Loop Road

Duck Harbor Trail

ACADIA NATIONAL PARK

ISLE AU HAUT

Median Ridge Trail

Nat Merchant Trail

Duck Harbor

74

Island Loop Road

Western Head Road

Duck Harbor Mountain ▲

Median Ridge Trail–South Spur

Merchant Cove

Duck Harbor Mountain Trail

■ Puddings

Barred Harbor

Merchants Point

Goat Trail

Squeaker Cove

Deep Cove

Head Harbor

Western Head ▲

No wonder park consulting botanist Jill Weber calls Isle au Haut "the skunk cabbage capital of the world."

If you have time on your return along the island loop road, turn left at the junction with the Median Ridge Trail's southern spur at 3.6 miles, and explore that 0.3-mile route to the coast. The spur ends at scenic Barred Harbor and the junction with the Goat Trail.

Miles and Directions

0.0 Start at Duck Harbor Landing, bear left (east) onto unpaved Western Head Road, and go around the harbor.

0.3 Turn right (southeast) onto the unpaved island loop road.

1.3 Reach the Median Ridge trailhead; take the north spur on the left side of the road.

2.4 Reach the junction with the Nat Merchant Trail. Turn right (southeast) to loop back on the Nat Merchant Trail.

3.2 Reach the island loop road. Turn right (west) onto the unpaved road to loop back to Duck Harbor Landing.

3.6 Pass the Median Ridge trailhead and continue straight (west) on the unpaved road. (***Option:*** For a short side trip to Barred Harbor, turn left [south] on a 0.3-mile spur of the Median Ridge Trail before returning west on the unpaved road.)

4.6 Bear left onto the unpaved Western Head Road.

4.9 Arrive back at Duck Harbor Landing.

Schoodic Peninsula

The only section of Acadia National Park on the mainland, the Schoodic Peninsula features hikes with dramatic views back to Mount Desert Island and some unforgettable rocky coast.

The peninsula is a 45-mile drive from Bar Harbor, but you don't have to get behind the wheel. A recent Bar Harbor–Winter Harbor ferry service, plus the fare-free Island Explorer bus during peak season, make it a snap to visit Schoodic without a car. You can even bring your bicycle on the ferry and the bus.

A former US Navy base near the tip of the peninsula has been converted to the Schoodic Education and Research Center. The former base also features the lovely Sundew Trail.

Traditionally a place away, the Schoodic Peninsula had been threatened by development of private open space adjacent to the park. But in late 2011, the Friends of Acadia and the Maine Coast Heritage Trust entered into an option agreement for a conservation easement with new owners of the land. In late summer 2015, part of the privately owned land was opened as a park-run campground, Schoodic Woods, featuring fifty car-side and nine hike-in camping sites, thirty-three RV sites and two group camping areas. A total of 4.7 miles of hiking trails and 8.3 miles of bike paths link the campground to the rest of the park. At the time this guide was going to press, there were on-going discussions to formally transfer ownership of Schoodic Woods to the park, as well as to expand ferry and Island Explorer service to accommodate increased visitation as a result of Schoodic Woods, and programs run by the non-profit Schoodic Institute at the Schoodic Education and Research Center.

The closest most visitors get to Schoodic is from atop Cadillac Mountain, when they look southeast from the summit parking lot and see the distinctive Schoodic Head in the distance across Frenchman Bay, but it's well worth the trip.

With its rocky coast jutting into the Atlantic, Schoodic is a magnificent place to see nature up close. Be careful during stormy weather. People have been swept away by waves violently crashing against the shore.

This section of the park includes prime examples of what geologists call dikes—prominent black bands of basalt in between the granite. Eons ago, magma intruded

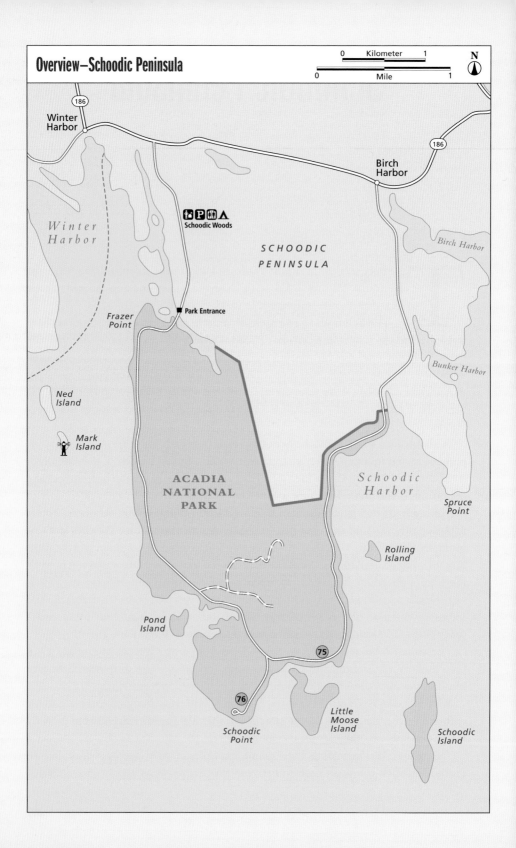

Overview–Schoodic Peninsula

0 Kilometer 1

0 Mile 1

N

186

Winter
Harbor

186

Birch
Harbor

*Winter
Harbor*

🚻 **P** 🏕️ ⛺
Schoodic Woods

SCHOODIC
PENINSULA

Birch Harbor

■ Park Entrance

Frazer
Point

Bunker Harbor

Ned
Island

Mark
Island

*Schoodic
Harbor*

**ACADIA
NATIONAL
PARK**

Spruce
Point

Rolling
Island

Pond
Island

75

76

Little
Moose
Island

Schoodic
Island

Schoodic
Point

St. John's wort along the Alder Trail in the Schoodic section of Acadia

into underground fractures in the granite under great pressure, then cooled and hardened into the black basaltic dikes.

You can find some uncommon plants here. During a tour on Schoodic Peninsula on a July day, Jill E. Weber, coauthor of *The Plants of Acadia National Park* and consulting biologist for the park, identified an unusual roseroot, the sub-shrub black crowberry, blooming blue flowers called harebells, mountain cranberry, common juniper, New York aster, and some of the sweetest iris ever seen. Weber pointed out plants flourishing in the ocean's spray zone—seaside goldenrod and seaside plantain.

A whole suite of plants reach their range limits at Acadia. For instance, jack pine grows no farther south and pitch pine no farther north, according to Weber. Arctic iris generally grows no farther west or south.

The waves of the Atlantic also weigh in. Bayberry often grows shoulder high, but it was diminutive along an exposed section of the Schoodic shore. Schoodic Peninsula is an hour away by car from Mount Desert Island, due east of Ellsworth on US 1, then south of West Gouldsboro off ME 186. The closest town to the Schoodic park entrance is a hamlet called Winter Harbor.

During the peak season, you can visit Schoodic car-free. Take the ferry that runs between Bar Harbor and Winter Harbor, then the Island Explorer's Schoodic line. Call

(207) 288-2984 for Bar Harbor–Winter Harbor ferry departure and fare information. Check the Island Explorer's Schoodic schedule online at www.exploreacadia.com.

There's only one way in and one way out of the Schoodic section of Acadia, along a one-way paved loop road that parallels the coast around the peninsula. The hiking trails described here can be accessed from the loop road or the Schoodic Education and Research Center.

To explore the new hiking trails that lead from the Schoodic Woods Ranger Station, turn left into the visitor parking lot before the park's one-way paved loop road. There's an Island Explorer bus stop here, as well as year-round restrooms. The 3.2-mile Buck Cove Mountain Trail, of moderate difficulty, leaves from the group camping area and heads over Buck Cove Mountain (elevation 224 feet) to Schoodic Head (elevation 442 feet), and connects with the Schoodic Head Trails (Hike 75). The easier 1.5-mile Lower Harbor Trail starts across the road from the entrance drive to the Schoodic Woods Ranger Station, and takes you along the coastline.

75 Schoodic Head Trails

A series of four short trails go up and around the distinctive Schoodic Head, allowing for a variety of loop or out-and-back hikes. The loop described here includes the Alder, Schoodic Head, and Anvil Trails, with options to loop down the East Trail or explore the new privately owned, park-run Schoodic Woods campground.

Distance: 2.3-mile loop
Hiking time: About 1.5 to 2 hours
Difficulty: Easy to moderate
Trail surface: Wooden ladder and bridges, forest floor, rock ledges
Best season: Spring through fall; late June through late August if you're taking the Bar Harbor–Winter Harbor ferry and the Island Explorer's Schoodic line

Other trail users: Hikers coming in from Schoodic Woods campground
Canine compatibility: Leashed dogs permitted
Map: USGS Acadia National Park and Vicinity
Special considerations: No facilities at the trailhead; restrooms and a picnic area near the start of the one-way Schoodic loop road; restrooms and ranger station at the day-use parking area of the new Schoodic Woods campground

Finding the trailhead: From the Schoodic park entrance off ME 186, head south on the one-way loop road. In 3.5 miles, at the turnoff for the Schoodic Education and Research Center and Schoodic Point, bear left to stay on the loop road. In another 0.5 mile reach the Blueberry Hill parking lot on the right. The Alder trailhead is diagonally across the parking area on the left (north) side of the road. The Island Explorer's Schoodic line does not have a stop here; ask the bus driver to let you off if it is safe to do so. GPS: N44 20.20' / W68 02.47'

The Hike

The loop starts easily on the grassy and lush Alder Trail and then goes to rugged Schoodic Head and the knob known as the Anvil.

At 0.6 mile the Alder Trail ends at a gravel road. Turn left (northwest) onto the road.

At 0.7 mile turn right (northeast) onto the Schoodic Head Trail, ascending steeply at times. At 1.1 miles reach an open ledge with dramatic vistas to the west to faraway Mount Desert Island and Cadillac Mountain, Frenchman Bay, the Porcupine Islands, and Egg Rock and its lighthouse. Closer by, to the northeast, are Ned and Turtle Islands. To the southeast is Pond Island.

Continue on the Schoodic Head Trail to the junction with the Anvil Trail at 1.2 miles. Coming in on the left (northwest) is a spur to a parking area at the top of Schoodic Head, where the 3.2-mile Buck Cove Mountain Trail from the park-run

The Alder Trail leads from the Schoodic coast to Schoodic Head.

Schoodic Woods campground intersects. Turn right (southeast) to head down toward the Anvil.

At 1.9 miles reach the 180-foot Anvil, with views of Mount Desert Island and Cadillac Mountain to the west and of Schoodic Head immediately to the northwest. Descend steadily.

At 2.2 miles reach the one-way Schoodic Loop Road. Turn right (southwest) and walk along the side of the road, returning to the Blueberry Hill parking lot at 2.3 miles.

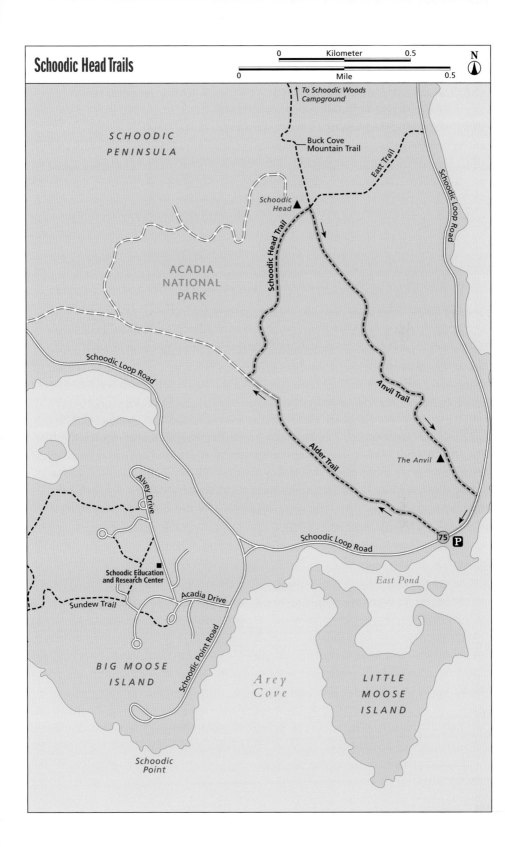

Schoodic Head Trails

0   Kilometer   0.5

0   Mile   0.5

N

To Schoodic Woods Campground

SCHOODIC PENINSULA

Buck Cove Mountain Trail

East Trail

Schoodic Loop Road

Schoodic Head

Schoodic Head Trail

ACADIA NATIONAL PARK

Schoodic Loop Road

Anvil Trail

Alder Trail

The Anvil

Alvey Drive

Schoodic Education and Research Center

Sundew Trail

Acadia Drive

Schoodic Loop Road

75

P

East Pond

Schoodic Point Road

BIG MOOSE ISLAND

Arey Cove

LITTLE MOOSE ISLAND

Schoodic Point

Miles and Directions

0.0 Start at the Alder trailhead, diagonally across the one-way Schoodic Loop Road from the Blueberry Hill parking lot, on the north side of the road.

0.6 Reach a gravel road; turn left (northwest) onto the road to head toward the Schoodic Head Trail.

0.7 Reach the junction with the Schoodic Head Trail; turn right (northeast) to head up Schoodic Head.

1.1 Take in the views.

1.2 Reach the junction with the Anvil Trail; turn right (southeast) to head down toward the Anvil.

1.9 Reach the Anvil.

2.2 Reach the Schoodic loop road. Turn right (southwest) and walk along the side of the road.

2.3 Arrive back at the Blueberry Hill parking lot.

Options

To officially summit the 440-foot Schoodic Head with its limited views, or hike down the shorter but steeper East Trail and walk back 1.0 mile on the loop road, or explore the Buck Cove Mountain Trail that connects to the new Schoodic Woods campground about 2.75 miles to the northwest, at the junction of the Schoodic Head and Anvil Trails, turn left (northwest) onto the Anvil Trail, rather than right (southeast). Cross the gravel Schoodic Head parking area and reach the junction with the East Trail atop Schoodic Head in another 0.1 mile. Go straight (north) if you want to hike 3.2 miles one-way to the campground, where you can take the Island Explorer bus in season, back to the Blueberry Hill parking lot. Or turn right (east) if you want to head down the East Trail to loop back to your car, reaching the one-way Schoodic Loop Road in 0.5 mile. Turn right onto the paved road and walk back to the Blueberry Hill parking lot in another 1.0 mile.

76 Sundew Trail

For a short hike, the Sundew Trail packs in a lot. There are three different spurs to some tremendous Schoodic shoreline, offering views of Cadillac Mountain across Frenchman Bay in the distance, huge granite gorges, and then a quiet cove.

Distance: 1.8 miles out and back, including three short spurs to the shore
Hiking time: About 1 to 2 hours
Difficulty: Easy
Trail surface: Wooden bridges, forest floor, rock ledges
Best season: Spring through fall; late June through late August if you're taking the Bar Harbor–Winter Harbor ferry and the Island Explorer's Schoodic line

Other trail users: Participants in Schoodic Education and Research Center programs; Acadia Artists-in-Residence
Canine compatibility: Leashed dogs permitted
Map: USGS Acadia National Park and Vicinity
Special considerations: No facilities at the trailhead; restrooms and a picnic area near the start of the one-way Schoodic Loop Road; restrooms and ranger station at the day-use parking area of the new Schoodic Woods campground

Finding the trailhead: From the Schoodic park entrance off ME 186, head south on the one-way loop road for 3.5 miles; bear right (southwest) onto the two-way road to Schoodic Point. Turn at your first right (west) onto Acadia Drive and into the Schoodic Education and Research Center campus. Drive straight past the entrance gatehouse and Rockefeller Hall and follow signs for campus parking, meeting halls and administration. Pass Jacobson Drive and bear right on Musetti Drive, following signs to campus parking and meeting halls. Go straight past Eliot Hall on the right, and park near a little pavilion at the edge of the parking lot, close to the trailhead. The Island Explorer's Schoodic line does not have a stop here; ask the bus driver to let you off at the entrance to the Schoodic Education and Research Center campus if it is safe to do so. GPS: N44 20.13' / W68 03.45'

The Hike

The Sundew Trail, named for the sticky, insect-eating plants of Acadia, starts over some log bridges and through a spruce forest.

At 0.2 mile, at the first of three junctions with short spurs to the shore, turn left (west) at a sign to ocean benches and start a mild descent over roots and some erosion-preventing logs. Listen for the sounds of waves hitting the shore.

In no time, reach the rocky coast of Schoodic and the Gulf of Maine, with a spectacular view of Cadillac, a good-size chasm, and rocky cliffs. There are two benches here—the first of three pairs spaced evenly along the trail.

That's Cadillac on the other side of Frenchman Bay, as seen from the Sundew Trail in the Schoodic section of Acadia.

This outpost on the gulf provides some stunning sights of the rocky shore, with some blooming goldenrod, the type of flower that attracts butterflies, in season among the granite crevices.

Hikers might also meet an artist-in-residence on the Sundew Trail, as we did one July afternoon.

Each year, the Acadia National Park Artist-in-Residence Program selects between twelve and twenty professional artists to serve two- to four-week residencies. Artists often paint or photograph the rocky shore of the Sundew Trail because their housing is nearby on the Schoodic campus.

It's a spectacular place to work. Cadillac Mountain and other Acadia peaks loom on the horizon across the ocean and the shoreline is dominated by huge granite.

"I come out to these rocks every day and spend six to eight hours," artist-in-residence Robert Dorlac, a professor of art at Southwest Minnesota State University, said while painting off the trail. "It's a great opportunity."

Back to the main trail, turn left, and then take the next spur left off the Sundew Trail to reach two more benches on this great Atlantic shoreline. A trail register here

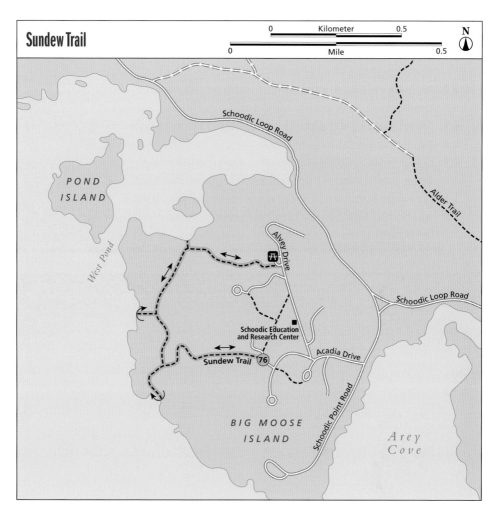

Sundew Trail

Kilometer 0 — 0.5
Mile 0 — 0.5

N

POND ISLAND

West Pond

Schoodic Loop Road

Alder Trail

Alvey Drive

Schoodic Education and Research Center

Schoodic Loop Road

Acadia Drive

Sundew Trail 76

Schoodic Point Road

BIG MOOSE ISLAND

Arey Cove

includes a check-off for people who explore the tidal zone. At low tide there is plenty of room to explore the zone.

Return to the main trail and take another spur to the left. This is the third and final side trail to the shore. Here the trail reaches the quiet and sprawling West Pond Cove, with two benches and views of wooded and marshy Pond Island. During a visit at low tide in July, seaweed covered the shore.

After leaving this cove and reaching the main trail again, turn left to hike to the northern end of the trail. This section of the trail has some log bridges, bogs, and forest. Return the way you came, skipping the shoreline spurs on the way back.

Miles and Directions

0.0 Start at the Sundew trailhead, the southern end of the trail, near a little pavilion at the edge of the parking lot, past Eliot Hall.

0.2 Reach the first junction with a spur to the shore. Turn left (southwest) onto the spur.

0.3 Return to the junction; turn left (north) to continue on the main Sundew Trail.

0.5 Turn left (west) at the next junction onto the second spur to the shore.

0.6 Return to the junction; turn left (northeast) to continue on the main Sundew Trail.

0.8 Turn left (north) at the third junction with a spur to the shore.

0.9 Return to the junction; turn left (east) to continue on the main Sundew Trail.

1.1 Arrive at the eastern end of the trail near a heliport and picnic pavilion.

1.8 Arrive back at the trailhead, skipping the shoreline spurs and staying on the main Sundew Trail.

Hike Index

About the Authors

Dolores Kong and Dan Ring have backpacked all of the more than 270 miles of the Appalachian Trail in Maine and have climbed virtually all the peaks that are 4,000 feet and higher in the Northeast. They are members of the White Mountains Four Thousand Footer, the New England Four Thousand Footer, the Adirondack 46Rs, the Northeast 111ers, and the New England Hundred Highest Clubs.

Dolores is a Certified Financial Planner™ professional and senior vice president with Winslow, Evans & Crocker, Inc. (member of FINRA/SIPC/NYSE Arca), in Boston. A Barnard College graduate, she is also a Pulitzer Prize finalist in public service from her previous career as a staff writer at the *Boston Globe*.

Dan is a writer and has been a statehouse bureau chief in Boston for a variety of newspapers. He graduated from Boston College with a bachelor's degree in English. Dan and Dolores are married and live outside Boston. They write a blog at acadiaonmymind.com.

Dan and Dolores along the Bowl Trail.

American Hiking Society

Because you **hike.**
We're with you every step of the way

As a national voice for hikers, **American Hiking Society** works every day:

- Building and maintaining hiking trails
- Educating and supporting hikers by providing information and resources
- Supporting hiking and trail organizations nationwide
- Speaking for hikers in the halls of Congress and with federal land managers

Whether you're a casual hiker or a seasoned backpacker, become a member of American Hiking Society and join the national hiking community! You'll enjoy great member benefits and help preserve the nation's hiking trails, so tomorrow's hike is even better than today's. We invite you to join us now!

American Hiking Society